CASE STUDIES FOR TEACHER PROBLEM SOLVING

CASE STUDIES FOR TEACHER PROBLEM SOLVING

RITA SILVERMAN
Professor of Teacher Education
School of Education
Pace University

WILLIAM M. WELTY
Professor of Management
Lubin Graduate School of Business
Pace University

SALLY LYON
Senior Research Assistant
School of Education
Pace University

McGraw-Hill, Inc.
New York   St. Louis   San Francisco   Auckland   Bogotá
Caracas   Lisbon   London   Madrid   Mexico   Milan
Montreal   New Delhi   Paris   San Juan   Singapore
Sydney   Tokyo   Toronto

This book was developed by Lane Akers, Inc.

Case Studies in Teacher Problem Solving

4 5 6 7 8 9 0 DOC DOC 9 0 9 8 7 6 5 4 3 2

ISBN 0-07-057567-3

This book was set in Times Roman by Monotype Composition Company.
The editors were Lane Akers and Laura D. Warner;
design was done by Caliber Design Planning, Inc.;
the production supervisor was Denise L. Puryear.
R. R. Donnelley & Sons Company was printer and binder.

Part-Opening Photo Credits

Page:
  1 Elizabeth Crews
 43 David S. Strickler / The Picture Cube
 87 Jerry Berndt / Stock, Boston
135 Schapiro / Gamma Liaison
165 Elizabeth Crews / Stock, Boston
191 Richard Hutchings / Photo Researchers

Library of Congress Cataloging-in-Publication Data

Silverman, Rita, (date).
   Case studies for teacher problem solving / by Rita Silverman, William M. Welty,
Sally Lyon.
       p.   cm.
    ISBN 0-07-057567-3 (Text). — ISBN 0-07-057568-1 (Instructors manual)
    1. Teaching—Case studies.   2. Problem solving—Case studies.   3. School
psychology—United States—Case studies.   4. Teachers—Training of—United States.
5. Case method.   I. Welty, William M., (date).   II. Lyon, Sally.   III. Title.
LB1025.3.S55   1992   91-7554
371.1'02—dc20

ABOUT THE AUTHORS

Rita Silverman is Professor of Education at Pace University and Co-Director (with William M. Welty) of the Pace University Center for Case Studies in Education. She came to Pace in 1984 as Chairperson of the Department of Teacher Education. Prior to that, she was on the faculty at Rutgers University. She now teaches courses in educational psychology, effective teaching methods, tests and measurement, and language arts methods. She is the author of several book chapters and journal articles, and she coauthored *Assessment for Instructional Planning in Special Education*. For the past six years, she has been the Co-Director of two federal grants funded by the Fund for the Improvement of Postsecondary Education (FIPSE). With William M. Welty, she has developed workshops for faculty in case method teaching.

William M. Welty is Professor of Management at Pace University's Lubin Graduate School of Business and Director of the Center for Faculty Development. He has been a member of the Pace faculty since 1964 and has also served as Director of Executive Programs and Associate Dean of the Graduate School. In the MBA program he teaches graduate courses in business policy, business and its environment, and public policy; and in the teacher education program he teaches educational psychology. For the past several years he has been working on an assignment to improve teaching at Pace, an activity now supported by grants from the Pforzheimer Foundation and the AT&T Foundation, and has developed a discussion method teaching course and a college teaching workshop for new faculty, both based on the case method.

Sally Lyon is completing graduate work in the Department of Teacher Education at Pace University, where as Senior Research Associate she has studied and taught educational psychology and related topics. Prior to pursuing her interest in education, she worked for twelve years in marketing and management positions for the IBM corporation, where she gained experience with the case method in a business context. She is a graduate of Northwestern University, where she was a member of Phi Beta Kappa, and the mother of two young children who give her experience as a consumer as well as a provider of educational services.

CONTENTS

PREFACE   xv

TO THE STUDENT   xix

PART ONE
CLASSROOM MANAGEMENT   1

Behavior learning theory / Classroom organization / Rules and procedures / Rewards and punishments / Social learning theory

Case 1—MARSHA WARREN
An experienced third-grade teacher is overwhelmed by the problems created by her heterogeneous class, which includes seven students who have unique home and personal situations that are affecting their schooling.   **3**

Case 2—KAREN LEE
A first-year Spanish teacher takes over a high school Spanish III class in midyear and faces an unruly group of students. One student in particular seems determined to make her miserable.   **9**

Case 3—MAGGIE LINDBERG
A first-year teacher is afraid to take her third-grade class on a nature walk because the children's behavior is so poor that she does not believe they can be controlled outside the classroom.   **15**

Case 4—GINA SHRADER
A student teacher learns about the complexities of a typical teaching day as she observes an effective second-grade teacher and her class go through their morning activities.   **21**

Case 5—BARBARA PARKER
An experienced high school teacher meets "the class from hell" and handles it by becoming extremely firm and autocratic. She comes to hate the class and is sure that the students hate her. **31**

PART TWO
LEARNING 43

Discovery learning / Information processing / Meaningful learning / Objectives

Case 6—THERESE CARMEN
A first-grade teacher in her second year of teaching is presented with a new districtwide science curriculum that she finds unteachable. **45**

Case 7—JOYCE DAVIDSON
A high school English teacher is not making much progress with a remedial English class and is particularly concerned about an extremely shy student. **49**

Case 8—SCOTT DONOVAN
A high school English teacher discovers that four of his students plagiarized parts of a lengthy writing assignment. **57**

Case 9—ALICE PETERSON
An experienced elementary school teacher is having problems with a prefirst-grade class in which every student brings unique (and difficult) problems into the classroom, leading her to wonder if she is reaching anyone. **63**

Case 10—ELIZABETH RHODES
A high school math teacher is frustrated by her advanced-placement (AP) calculus students, who want to work only for solutions to problems and do not want to apply higher-order reasoning skills. **79**

PART THREE
EFFECTIVE TEACHING 87

Grouping / Managing the teaching process / Motivation / Questioning / Promoting social awareness / Working with parents

Case 11—MARIE DUPONT
A college student observes a high school French class and learns how a good teacher handles all the events of a typical class.   **89**

Case 12—HELEN FRANKLIN
An experienced first-grade teacher who uses parent volunteers to help her run her unique class sees that one of the volunteers will work only with the white students and discovers that one of the black parents is aware of this.   **103**

Case 13—CHRIS KETTERING
A first-year high school social studies teacher finds to his dismay that his white, middle-class students are uninterested in becoming involved in social activism and suffer from narrow-mindedness.   **109**

Case 14—MARK SIEGEL
A fourth-grade teacher is irritated by a black parent who visits him regularly, demanding better teaching for her son. The teacher believes that he has tried everything and that the problem rests with the child and the demanding mother.   **117**

Case 15—DAN TYMKONOVICH
A social studies student teacher takes over a high school AP honors class whose students, he feels, are arrogant. His discussion plans go awry, and the class falls apart.   **121**

Case 16—KEN KELLY
A first-year social studies teacher having trouble encouraging discussion in his high school classes visits a fourth-grade philosophy class taught entirely through discussion.   **127**

PART FOUR
DIVERSITY   135

Cultural difference / Mainstreaming / Special education / Tracking / Within-class diversity

Case 17—MARY EWING
An experienced high school math teacher moves to the middle school and has problems with grouping in a remedial math class where each of the eleven students is working at a different level.   **137**

Case 18—ALLISON COHEN

A resource room teacher opens a resource room at an elementary school that has never had any special education classrooms. She believes the teachers are colluding to make the mainstreaming program fail.   **143**

Case 19—CAROL BROWN

A first-grade teacher, after socially integrating an extremely heterogeneous class, sees her efforts threatened when a child's pencil case disappears and is thought to have been stolen.   **149**

Case 20—JOAN MARTIN, MARILYN COE, WARREN GROVES

A classroom teacher, a special education teacher, and an elementary school principal hold different views about mainstreaming a boy with poor reading skills into a fourth-grade social studies class.   **155**

PART FIVE
EVALUATION   165

Formative/summative / Grading / Identification of differences / Role of standardized tests

Case 21—SARAH HANOVER

A first-year high school math teacher is confronted by angry parents when she gives their son, an outstanding math student, a lower grade than expected because he never turned in homework.   **167**

Case 22—DIANE NEWS

In a school district beginning a gifted and talented program, a first-year elementary school teacher must choose four students to recommend for the program, but she has five potential candidates.   **171**

Case 23—MELINDA GRANT

A first-year elementary school teacher with many innovative ideas is uncertain about her classroom activities because the teacher in the next classroom continually warns her that she will be held responsible for the students' end-of-year standardized test scores.   **177**

Case 24—LEIGH SCOTT
A high school social studies teacher gives a higher-than-earned report card grade to a mainstreamed student, on the basis of the boy's effort, and is confronted by another student with identical test grades who received a lower report card grade.   **183**

Case 25—JANE VINCENT
A high school math teacher is asked by her principal to consider giving a higher grade to a student whose numerical average for the marking period is just below the math department's cutoff score for that grade.   **187**

PART SIX
CONTEMPORARY TEACHING ISSUES   191

Maintaining a professional role / Teacher unions / Working with colleagues and administrators / Understanding the school as a system

Case 26—DAVID BURTON
A high school computer teacher whose principal brooks no challenges to his authority discovers that two students are being given unequal punishments by the principal for the same infraction.   **193**

Case 27—AMANDA JACKSON
A first-year elementary school art teacher wrestles with her response to a principal, whose drinking problem is well known but who has never been confronted about it or acknowledged it herself.   **197**

Case 28—ELLEN NORTON
A high school math teacher, whose concern for a shy, underachieving student has caused the student to become her "shadow," learns that another student is being abused at home, and the teacher does not know if she should become involved.   **203**

PREFACE

Case method is a relatively new phenomenon in teacher education. This book was prepared to provide case material in textbook form so that teacher educators can easily begin to use cases in their classes. Based on the business school model, most of the cases in this collection are problem-centered stories about teaching situations, developed from the actual experiences of elementary and secondary school teachers. Most end with a dilemma or a problem the teacher must resolve. The educational value of case method is in the analysis of the problem or problems, in the development and evaluation of possible solutions to these problems, and in the application of appropriate educational theory to the problem analysis, solution, and evaluation. Case studies are designed for use in a discussion class. The goal is to encourage student-generated analysis rather than teacher-manufactured solutions.

We are convinced that case method is an appropriate pedagogical technique for teacher education for the same reasons that it is appropriate for management education. Because it is an active learning process, because it requires that the learner understand and apply theory rather than receive it passively, case method prepares the teacher education student for the real world of teaching just as cases prepare business students for the real world of managing. Real world teaching requires problem analysis and decision making on a daily basis. Seldom is there time to consult textbook theory. Rarely is one problem exactly like another. Teachers must be prepared to assume responsibility for dealing with their problems rather than seek external causes beyond their control. They must learn to understand and analyze situations and to build and evaluate action plans. Teachers need to internalize theory, to understand its applications and adaptations. Teachers must learn how to be self-reflective and to think critically about their craft. They must learn how to adapt to change. Case method pedagogy is intended to encourage this.

This book is designed as a supplement to standard textbooks for courses in educational psychology, teaching methods, and introduction to teaching. Though the cases are independent and may be used in any order, we have imposed an organization that most closely matches an educational psychology approach. Part One includes a group of cases that center on classroom management issues; Part Two cases emphasize learning issues; Part Three, effective teaching; Part Four, diversity; Part Five, evaluation; and Part Six, contemporary teaching issues. The teacher's guide that accompanies this text suggests how the cases might be matched with the educational psychology and teaching methods texts most widely used.

A match to specific theory is suggested for each case, but keep in mind that these are all true stories, with names of teachers, students, and schools disguised to protect individual privacy. So, these are not single-issue situations that neatly illustrate textbook problems. Real teachers and students are complex characters, not all good or all bad. Problems are not obvious and unidimensional. No solution can be suggested that is without drawbacks. Indeed, like real life, cases are "messy" documents and are intended to be so. Without the messiness of reality, cases would not stimulate the kind of independent and critical thinking that teacher educators should encourage in their students.

It is important to understand, as well, that cases are written as pedagogical documents: they are written to be taught in a carefully organized discussion class. That class discussion is at the heart of the case method, for it is here that the power of building individual analyses into one class analysis becomes apparent. From this perspective, case method is a compelling way to encourage and develop effective group learning habits.

We think that case method is an exciting way to learn. We think it is a powerful way of preparing teacher education students for the classrooms of the twenty-first century. We hope you agree.

Acknowledgments

This book could not have been completed without the help of a grant from the Fund for the Improvement of Postsecondary Education (FIPSE) and the cooperating support of the School of Education and the Lubin Graduate School of Business at Pace University. We wish to acknowledge especially the roles of David Avdul, Dean of the School of Education, the late George M. Parks, Dean of the Lubin Schools of Business, and Joseph M. Pastore, Jr., Provost, for encouraging a research effort that required crossing disciplinary boundaries to an extent almost unheard of in higher education.

Four graduate assistants in the Department of Teacher Education— Phyllis Carr, Susan Gould, Keith Eddings, and Helen Egan—played vital roles in this project. They interviewed cooperating teachers, gathered information, wrote rough drafts of cases, and endured without complaint the difficulties of working on a project breaking new methodological ground.

We have profited from the thoughtful criticism and good ideas of a number of colleagues in the business education, teacher education, and higher education communities. The introduction of case method to teacher education owes a great debt to the work of C. Roland Christensen, Robert Walmsley University Professor, Harvard Business School. His seminars at

Harvard, his book, *Teaching and the Case Method,* and his personal encouragement and example have been an important impetus to this project. The President's Forum on Teaching as a Profession, sponsored by the Carnegie Foundation and based at the American Association of Higher Education (AAHE), was responsible for bringing together a number of teacher educators interested in case method for two conferences during the 1989–1990 academic year. These interchanges were very helpful in sharpening the focus of this book. We wish to thank Russell Edgerton, President of the AAHE, and Pat Hutchings, Director, Projects on Teaching, for encouraging that effort. And we want to acknowledge the colleagues brought together by those conferences who have so graciously shared their ideas with us, especially Helen Harrington, University of Michigan; Judith Kleinfeld, University of Alaska, Fairbanks; Katherine K. Merseth, University of California, Riverside; Anna Richert, Mills College; Judith H. Shulman, Far West Laboratory for Educational Research and Development; and Lee S. Shulman, Stanford University. In addition, for their interest, encouragement, and helpful criticism we are grateful to Linda Anderson, Michigan State University; Richard Arends, University of Maryland; Christopher Clark, Michigan State University; Sandra Flank, Pace University; Robert McNergney, University of Virginia; Ann Spindel, National Executive Service Corporation; Carol Weinstein, Rutgers University; and Mary Williams, Pace University.

Students in our graduate and undergraduate teacher education classes at Pace University have endured with good spirit and hard work the introduction of a new way of learning. Every one of the cases in this book has been "reality-tested" in a Pace University teacher education class. That experience helped improve the cases enormously.

Finally, we wish we could identify each of the classroom teachers whose stories form the reality base of the cases. But, for obvious reasons, their names and the physical locations have been disguised. They are the most important people behind the spirit that empowers this book—to improve the education of future classroom teachers in America—and for that reason we have dedicated this book to them.

RITA SILVERMAN
WILLIAM M. WELTY
SALLY LYON

TO THE STUDENT

For most of you this book will be a new experience in education. It is a collection of case studies centered on the experiences of elementary and secondary school teachers in the United States. Based on the concept of case study developed in schools of business, these cases present stories told by practicing teachers about their experiences. The stories introduce problems teachers have encountered and require that students preparing to be teachers use their analytic and critical thinking skills, their knowledge of educational theory and research, and their common sense and collective wisdom to identify and analyze problems and to evaluate possible solutions.

At first, case method may seem a strange way of learning. For one thing, this book is probably not like any other textbook you will encounter in your teacher education courses. It does not present educational theory in neatly organized chapters with carefully designed tables, charts, and explanations. Rather, it presents stories about real teachers in real schools and asks that *you* go to the theory and try to apply it to understand the stories and the problems they present. Part of the reason for using cases is to help you understand educational theory more completely by thinking about how it applies in actual situations. Case method requires that you interact with the theory; it requires that you decide how to use theory to analyze classroom situations in order to solve problems.

Deciding for yourself—that is really the heart of case-method pedagogy. It is based on the understanding that the most important learning, the most meaningful learning, the most long-lasting learning comes from the work the learner does on his or her own—active learning.

Problem-solving cases require that the learner be active in both the preparation for class and the participation in class. Your preparation for a case class will not be limited by the normal "I've got fifty pages to read tonight." Instead, it will be determined by how much work *you* want to put into the analysis, by the limitations you put on yourself. Usually the cases can be read in a relatively short time, since few are more than ten pages long. But for cases to have any lasting educational value, you must expend much more effort than simply reading them. Because these cases are problem-centered, there will be a more or less obvious "presenting problem." But there will be, as well, some more subtle problems, problems the teacher telling the case story may not have recognized. It will be up to you, in your preparation for class, to identify the problems, apply relevant theory, and develop solutions. There will never be one right solution; often there will be many possible solutions. For sure, there will be better or worse solutions, but better or worse will depend on the analysis you used to understand the problem. That analytic process is the heart of case method. This experience can be both frustrating and exhilarating, as it was for the student who describes her introduction to case method in the following excerpt:

> I entered the battle of the case method unarmed. The routines and tools that had allowed me to survive years of schooling no longer helped me; my old study habits were useless—counterproductive, in fact. For example, I had always been a diligent student, priding myself on completing the assignments I was given. If I was expected to read pages 220–256 of a book, I read them. As a student in a case class, though, my assignments were open-ended: prepare the case and develop recommendations. I was supposed to decide how to approach the material, but it was hard to know how much to do, hard to know where to stop. Was I supposed to consider two alternatives or six? Was I supposed to consult outside sources (textbooks, classnotes, the library)? I had always been an outliner, finding that outlining helped me see the structure of the material. But cases by their very nature could not be outlined. They were not books, logically organized by the author to facilitate my understanding. Just because a particular aspect of the case situation occupied the first three pages of the case booklet did not mean it was more important than an aspect mentioned in one small paragraph on page 17. Just because certain data was not provided did not mean it was not necessary.
>
> Like a "real" [teacher] in a "real" [teaching] situation, it was now my job to impose a meaningful framework on the unruliness of case facts. I had to search for the key nuggets of data, distinguishing central facts from peripheral ones. I had to sort out the conflicting explanations and alternatives presented to me, and arrive at a reasonable recommendation for action.
>
> I understand the importance of these skills in the real world. But that understanding didn't make the skills any easier to develop. . . . Every time I needed to make an assumption, . . . I hesitated and thought, How would I defend my assumption? How could I know what was reasonable? I rarely could walk into class secure in the knowledge that I had "cracked" the case. The uncertainty was frightening. [Robin Hacke, *The Case Method: A Student Perspective,* unpublished working paper, Harvard Business School, 1986, quoted in C. Roland Christensen, "Teaching with Cases at the Harvard Business School," in C. Roland Christensen and Abby Hansen, *Teaching and the Case Method,* Harvard Business School (Boston, 1987), pp. 29–30.]

Cases require active learning in the classroom, as well. Do not expect your instructor to prepare a neat lecture that summarizes the main points of the case, points out the relevant theory; provides a list of sources, and details the correct solution. Instead, the class will be a discussion. You will be asked questions designed to get you and your classmates to compare and build your individual analyses into a collective one. You will be challenged to defend your analysis and your solutions, to listen to and challenge others, and to take away from this collective process a deeper understanding of the case situation than you, your classmates, or your instructor could ever have done alone.

All of this is designed not only to make you an active participant in your own education but to prepare you for the *real* world of the elementary and secondary school teacher. That real world is one of constant action, of making decisions day in and day out. Seldom is there time to consult theory; seldom is one situation exactly like another. Real teachers, therefore, need to be prepared to analyze situations for themselves and to build and evaluate action plans on their own. They need to know how to go to colleagues and friends for help—again, not in seeking the single right answer but in seeking help in problem analysis. They need to learn to take responsibility for the problems encountered in teaching and, by taking responsibility, to develop a proactive attitude toward those problems. In short, they need to develop critical thinking skills for their profession. We believe that case method education provides a basis for developing these skills and for continuing to use them during one's professional teaching career.

How do I prepare a case?

For the teacher education student encountering cases for the first time, the following are some concrete, step-by-step suggestions for case preparation:

1. *Understand the assignment in context.* Your instructor will probably assign one case at a time and include in the assignment some study questions or issues to think about while you are preparing it. As well, each case will most likely be accompanied or preceded by traditional textbook assignments. These may alert you to theoretical concepts related to the case. So before you begin to read the case, be sure that you understand the overall framework within which the case is being used and the points your instructor may want to emphasize.

2. *Read the case for an overview.* Try reading the case first rather quickly, to get a general idea of what it is about: what happened, who the main characters are, what the problems are, and how the issues in the case relate to the overall assignment.

3. *Analyze the case.* Go back and read the case again, this time much more carefully. Begin to try to make sense of the study questions assigned by your instructor. Make notes of main characters and their relationships with each other. Try to understand the problems, both obvious and hidden. Try to understand the point of view of the case; that is, determine who is providing the information. Identify what impact this perspective may have on the information in the case. Make a list of questions you

have about the material, and identify any other information you would like to have. At the end of this stage you should have a list of problems and an understanding of the causes of these problems.

4. *Seek outside information.* At this point you might want to turn to outside sources for help in understanding the problems you have identified and to develop solutions. Go to the textbook, especially the chapter assigned to accompany the case. Anything that helps you understand the case better at this point is fair game to use.

5. *Develop solutions.* Ultimately, cases call for solutions to problems, not to determine the one right answer but to focus analysis and to prepare you for a real world of teacher action and decision making. Relate your solutions to your analysis of the problems. Since there are no perfect decisions, be sure you understand both the weaknesses and the strengths of your solutions. Every good solution has a downside; it may not negate the solution, but you should at least always understand the negatives as well as the positives of what you are proposing. Prepare to argue for your ideas in class. Come armed with the relevant theory that supports your position. Be ready to take risks. The case class is a teaching laboratory. The case is the lab experiment, and you are the social scientist seeking to test your ideas.

How do I participate in class discussion?

Thoughtful participation in case discussion has two components: you should state your own informed ideas and analysis, and you should listen actively to the contributions of your classmates. The case class is a learning community; collectively you and your classmates are proceeding toward a more complete understanding of the case situation and possible solutions. No one person can do it all. Your instructor will guide the class toward this collective understanding, but your active participation and active listening are necessary to further this process. You must listen actively in order to understand where the discussion is going and where the group is in the process of the case analysis so that your contributions are relevant to the discussion of the moment.

After the discussion is over, go back over your analysis of the case and think about how the discussion changed or added to it. Try to summarize in a few thoughts the main points of the whole case exercise, from original assignment to summary statement at the end of class. Be sure you understand how and where the case related to theory. Think about the questions you still have relating to the case or the general assignment and about the ways you might begin to answer them.

Case method is an exciting new venture in teacher education. Our experiences using case method teaching have demonstrated that new teachers go into their own classrooms more ready to deal with the myriad of problems they must face if as students they have prepared seriously for case discussions by taking the time to analyze the cases and to develop solutions based on the educational theory and have taken part in case discussions with both thoughtful contributions and active listening.

The setting for the cases

The cases in this book are the true stories of practicing teachers. Each tries to capture an event or experience that was particularly significant or memorable in the teacher's life. As you read the cases and then analyze them, you will need some information about the settings in which they occur. Knowing the socioeconomic, ethnic, and racial makeup of the communities and having information about class size and availability of ancillary services will help you make decisions about the cases. On the other hand, since the cases are true stories, for privacy reasons we have changed the names of all individuals, both teachers and students, and of all actual places.

Most of the cases in this collection are set in a school district we have named "Littleton," a suburb of a large northeastern city. It is big enough to be classified by the state as a small city district, and made up of neighborhoods with a wide range of incomes. While many homes in the area are valued at $350,000 or more, the city is also plagued with the problems faced by most urban centers: poverty, decaying public housing, crime, and a recent increase in the homeless population.

Once primarily a bedroom community of its core-city metropolitan area, Littleton has recently become a business and local government center. Some residents still commute to the city, but many others work in local corporate and government offices. Several companies have moved into the Littleton area, taking advantage of the more affordable space and small-town amenities. In addition, over the past ten years Littleton has become a major shopping hub, and this has created new jobs in the retail and service industries.

There is wide ethnic representation in the district, and that diversity is reflected in the school population: approximately 50 percent of the students are white, 30 percent are black, nearly 20 percent are Hispanic, and about 2 percent are Asian.

The district serves approximately 8000 children in six K–6 elementary schools, one middle school (serving grades 7 and 8), and one high school. The average class size is twenty-two students. There are 500 teachers, 60 school administrators, and more than 300 ancillary (nonteaching) staff members. Teachers average fifteen years of experience. Salaries in Littleton are well above the national average.

The Littleton school budget is more than $75 million. The district spends well above the state average per student per year. As a result of its operating budget, the district is able to offer some unique features. Class sizes are smaller than average. Teacher aides are available in the buildings to work with teachers and small groups of children. There are a variety of services for children classified as eligible for special education, for English-as-a-second-language (ESL) students, and for high school students who function best in a smaller, less structured environment.

The high school tracks the students into four levels: honors, above average, average, and remedial. Students typically enter one of the tracks in ninth grade and usually remain at the same level throughout their four years of high school.

Gifted students are served in a pullout program of enrichment activities for two half-days a week. Teachers of the gifted students also work with teachers in regular classrooms, offering enrichment options for all students.

There is a great deal of cooperation between the school system and the education-oriented local government. Joint programs such as after-school play groups and summer day camps have been successfully established and now operate in the community.

The district also maintains close ties with the local universities. Teachers in all the schools accept student teachers each semester; some of the Littleton teachers and administrators teach as adjunct professors at the local colleges; and professors are involved in the gifted program and action research efforts, and they bring classes to the schools for field experiences.

The cases in the book that do not take place in Littleton are clearly identified, and background information for each setting is provided within the case itself.

CASE STUDIES FOR TEACHER PROBLEM SOLVING

PART ONE

CLASSROOM
MANAGEMENT

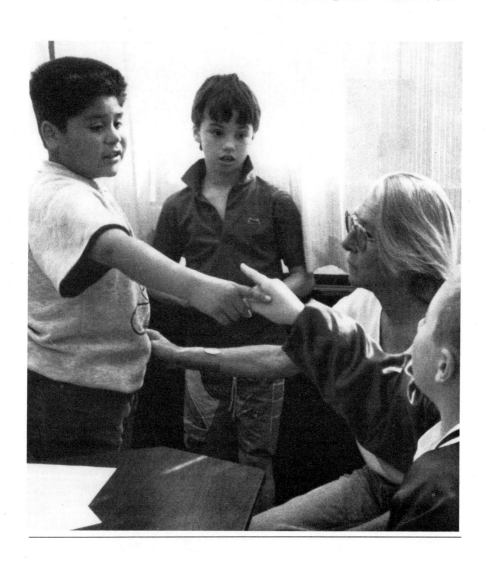

MARSHA WARREN

*An experienced third-grade teacher is overwhelmed by the
problems created by her heterogeneous class, which includes seven
students who have unique home and personal situations that are
affecting their schooling.*

José glared at Tyrone. "Quit looking at me, you jerk!"

"I wasn't lookin' at nothin', creepy," replied Tyrone vehemently.

Marsha Warren looked up sharply at the two boys and made a cutting
gesture through the air. "That's enough from both of you. You should both
be looking at your books, not each other."

"I *was* lookin' at my book!" protested Tyrone.

"Just stop!" repeated Marsha. "Please continue reading, Angela."

Angela rolled her eyes at no one in particular and resumed reading aloud
in a bored, expressionless tone. Her progress was slow and halting.

Marsha Warren was a third-grade teacher at the Roosevelt Elementary
School in Littleton. She was trying to conduct a reading group with the
eight slowest readers in her class of twenty-two while the other children
worked in workbooks at their seats. But each time an argument erupted
among the children in the reading group, most of the children at their desks
snapped to attention to watch the sparks fly.

"You can stop there, Angela," interrupted Marsha as Angela came to
the end of a paragraph. "Bettie Ann, will you read next?" As she spoke,
Marsha also put a hand out to touch another child, Katie, on the shoulder
in an attempt to stop her from bouncing in her chair.

Bettie Ann didn't respond. She was gazing out the window at the leafless
November landscape, sucking her thumb and twirling her hair with her other
hand. "Bettie Ann, I'm talking to you," repeated Marsha.

"Your turn," yelled José as he poked Bettie Ann's shoulder.

"Shut up, José," interjected Sarah. Sarah often tried to mediate between
the members of the group, but her argumentative streak pulled her into the
fray as often as not.

"Quiet!" insisted Marsha in a hushed, but emphatic, tone. As she spoke, she turned her head to glance over her shoulder at the rest of the class. The hum of conversation was growing in the room. Tension crept into her voice as she addressed the reading group. "We're distracting the other children. Do we need to discuss rule 3 again? Everyone pull out the class rules from your notebook, now."

The chemistry in the reading group—and in the class in general—had been so explosive since September that Marsha had gone beyond her normal first-of-the-year review of rules and procedures. All the children in the class had copied the four class rules into their notebooks, and she had led long discussions of what they meant. Rule 3 was "Be considerate of other people."

Loud groans from the reading group greeted Marsha's mention of rules. Simultaneously, a loud BANG sounded in the back of the room. Marsha turned and saw a student reaching to the floor for a book as his neighbor snickered. She also noticed three girls in the far-left row leaning into a conversation over a drawing, and she saw most of the students quickly turn back to their work, as if they were not enjoying the entertainment of the reading group once again.

"That's it!" Marsha exclaimed. She slammed her hand down on the reading-circle table and stood to face the entire class. "Put your heads on your desks, and don't say another word—everyone!" By the time she finished the sentence, Marsha realized she had been shouting, but she didn't care. Her class gazed at her in stunned disbelief. Mrs. Warren had always been so gentle! "Now!"

Marsha quickly turned and walked from the room, not bothering to look back to see if her command had been obeyed. She closed the door to her classroom, managing not to slam it, and tried to control her temper and collect her thoughts. "What in God's name am I going to do with this class?" she asked herself. "I've got to calm down. Here I am in the hallway with twenty-two kids inside who have driven me out—they've absolutely won." Marsha suddenly felt paralyzed.

Marsha tried to remember if there was ever a time in her eleven years of teaching when discipline and control were such a challenge. "It's not as though I were a rookie. I ought to know what to do!" she agonized. But Marsha had tried everything she had ever learned or done before to interest and control this group, and the class as a whole, yet there she was, standing in the hall.

Marsha's third-grade class was indeed a difficult group of children. There were a few students who liked school and really tried to learn, but overall it was a class full of children who were just not focused on learning. It was impossible to relax with them. If Marsha let down her guard and tried to engage them on a more friendly or casual level, the class would disintegrate. Marsha's natural inclination in teaching was to maintain a friendly, relaxed manner; she usually enjoyed her students and her enjoyment showed. But with this class she constantly had to be firm and vigilant ("witchlike," she thought) in order to keep the students under control.

Academically the class was fairly average, but Marsha did have two instructional challenges: There were three really bright students, whom Marsha tried to encourage with extra instruction and higher expectations, and there were three students (besides the Hispanic children in her slow-reading group) who spoke little or no English. The most remarkable characteristic of the students, though, was their overall immaturity. Each child seemed to feed off the antics of the others, and every issue was taken to its extreme. For example, whenever one child laughed, the entire class would begin to giggle uncontrollably. The students' behavior was simply inappropriate for their age and grade.

The core of Marsha's problem was the lowest-level reading group. This group provided the spark that set off fireworks in the entire class, day after day. The slow readers were rude and disruptive as a group, and they were instigators on their own.

When Marsha thought of each child in the lowest reading group individually, she was usually able to summon some sympathy and understanding. Each of the eight had an emotional or academic problem that probably accounted, at least in part, for his or her behavior.

José, for instance, topped her list of troublemakers. He was a loud, egocentric child. His mother, Marsha thought, probably had surrendered long ago, and his father did not live with them. José had little respect for or recognition of authority; he was boisterous and argumentative; and he was unable to take turns under any condition. When something didn't go his way, he would explode. This low flash point, Marsha felt, was just one of many signs of his immaturity, even though José was repeating the third grade and was actually older than his classmates.

José had a slight learning disability in the area of organizational skills, but Marsha didn't think this justified his behavior. His mother spoke only Spanish, and—although José was fluent in both Spanish and English—when Marsha sent notes home, she would first have to find someone to translate for her. Conferring with José's mother on the telephone was out of the question.

Angela was also repeating the third grade, and Marsha thought the child's anger over this contributed to her terrible attitude in class. The child just refused to learn. She could be a low-average achiever if she would apply herself, but it was clear that Angela's agenda was not school. She was concerned with her hair, her looks, her clothes—preoccupations that Marsha found inappropriate for a third-grader. Angela came from a middle-class black family, and her parents were also angry that she had been held back; consultations with them were not usually fruitful. Angela seemed truly upset if Marsha asked her to do any work, and Marsha was sure her frustration with the child was occasionally apparent.

Tyrone, on the other hand, was a very low average learner, but he, at least, worked to his capabilities. He even tried to mediate arguments among the members of the group. But Tyrone had a very stubborn streak, which was typical, Marsha thought, of slow learners. If he was on the wrong track, he just would not get off of it. She frequently asked him to redo work and helped him with his errors, but when he presented it to her the next day as though it were different, it would contain the same mistakes.

Sarah, too, knew right from wrong and generally wanted to do her work, but she was easily pulled into the fray. Sarah had appointed herself protector of Bettie Ann, an overweight, emotionally insecure child who had difficulty focusing on the topic at hand. Bettie Ann was the baby of her family, with several near-adult siblings at home. Marsha wondered if Bettie Ann's position in the family was the reason she assumed no responsibility for her own actions and no control over her own fate. Bettie Ann seemed hungry for Marsha's attention, but she exhibited no independence or initiative at all.

Katie was one of the brighter students in the reading group, but her hyperactivity caused her to be easily distracted and argumentative. She could neither sit still physically nor pay attention mentally. Katie had a rich home background, full of books and middle-class aspirations, but Marsha thought she also encountered pressure at home to perform, perhaps to levels beyond her capability.

Rhea, another child with at least average intelligence, was one of the more heartrending cases. Her mother was an alcoholic who neglected her, and Rhea had to do the housework and care for her older brother, who was in a special education class. She had no time for homework, and there were no books or even conversations at home. Rhea had been held back in the second grade, and while she tried to do her work, the language deficit at home was so severe that she kept falling further behind.

Finally, there was Maria, a petite, immature native of El Salvador. She had average intelligence and a cooperative spirit, but Spanish was spoken in her home and her limited English vocabulary severely limited her progress.

Marsha tried to analyze what it was among these children that fostered such animosity. Not a day passed that they didn't argue, fight, or insult one another. The reading group was not the only arena for these combatants; they fought in the playground, in line, on the bus, and in the cafeteria. They were troublemakers in previous grades, and some of the teachers at Roosevelt called them the "Infidels."

They tended to be at their worst as a group, and so Marsha had tried separating them, but with little improvement. Three weeks before, in early October, she rearranged and reorganized all three reading groups, distributing the students in the lowest section among three new groups. But she found that the inappropriate behavior did not stop; it only spread. Now all three of her reading groups, rather than one, were disrupted, and mixing her slow and her average readers dramatically reduced the pace of both groups.

Finding this arrangement unfair to her other students, she reorganized back to her original group assignments last week.

Marsha also tried other remedies. She introduced popular reading material for the reading groups and tried innovations such as having the children act out the stories they read. She wrote a contingency contract with the groups when she reconstituted them last week, promising that they could use the school's audiovisual equipment to make filmstrips illustrating their current book if they behaved, but so far that wasn't working either.

Marsha did not think she was generally too lax. She had procedures for incomplete work (the students had to come to her room during lunch hour or after school to finish); she had rules for appropriate behavior in school; and she never hesitated to involve parents. She praised the children for completing work, and she sent positive notes home when they did so. She also sent home disciplinary cards (much more frequently, unfortunately), which parents were supposed to sign, and she telephoned parents when she thought it would help.

Marsha also tried punishment. She sent individual troublemakers to the office, and she held detention during lunch. She isolated children for misbehavior by separating their desks from the rest of the class, and she used denial of privileges (the children really liked using the class computer, so she withdrew that privilege frequently). Marsha even tried talking honestly with the children, giving them pep talks about the value of education and their need to read and write and think in order to participate in life. But nothing was fundamentally altering the course of the class's behavior.

Besides having the desire to teach the "Infidels," Marsha knew that the progress of the rest of the class was being slowed because of the time she was forced to spend on policing. Her patience, her ideas, and her fortitude were fast evaporating, and she knew she had to solve the problem even though she felt like giving up.

Marsha stood on tiptoe to look through the window of the classroom door. The children were sitting in their places looking at each other uneasily and at the door, clearly wondering what would happen next. With a sigh, Marsha turned the knob.

KAREN LEE

A first-year Spanish teacher takes over a high school Spanish III
class in midyear and faces an unruly group of students. One
student in particular seems determined to make her miserable.

"Three strikes, you're out," Karen thought as she walked briskly to Jeff's desk in the back of the room. Standing beside him, she tore a piece of paper from his hand and ordered him out of the class. It was the third time in three weeks that she had found Jeff—an A student who was easily capable of doing the work—cheating on a test.

"I wasn't cheating! Read what it says!" Jeff said as he willingly surrendered the paper. Karen felt the rest of the class looking on almost conspiratorially, gleeful that another confrontation was developing between the two.

"Out! Out! Now!" Karen shouted, incredulous that Jeff could plead his innocence even as she held prima facie evidence of his cheating in her hand. "Get down to the guidance office. I'll see you there after class."

"I wasn't cheating! Read it!"

"Out!"

"I wasn't cheating, you bitch!"

"What?"

"You want me to say it again? I wasn't cheating, you bitch!" Shoving his books from his desk and flinging his test paper in Karen's direction, Jeff stormed from the room, slamming the door behind him.

Karen, just four months into her first teaching job, fought to contain her rage and hold back her tears as she returned to her desk. As she gazed at her grinning students, she wondered who they thought had won this latest struggle for control of the class.

"Back to work," she said. While the students spent the remaining twenty minutes finishing their tests, Karen sat at her desk wondering why this class had gone so wrong.

Although it was only December and the school year was just fourteen weeks old, Karen Lee was the fifth teacher for this tenth-grade, above-average-track Spanish III class. Three substitutes had been hired after the regular teacher went on a leave to receive treatment for cancer just before classes started in September. The teacher returned to school in mid-November, but she left again after only a few days when she found the treatments had left her too weak to resume her work.

The principal was reluctant to return Spanish III, a language and culture class, to another string of substitutes. Karen had been teaching part-time and eagerly accepted the class when she was asked to take it, even though her entire schedule had to be shuffled to accommodate it. Nevertheless, the new assignment brought Karen up to a full class load at Littleton High School, and although it wasn't a permanent appointment, Karen was pleased that she now would be working full-time as a teacher after being out of college only a few months. Both of her parents were teachers, and she had held the hope all through high school and college that she would be a teacher also. At just 24, Karen felt she had reached her career goal.

Spanish was a passion for Karen. She began studying the language in ninth grade at a public high school not far from Littleton. She spent her senior year as an exchange student at La Escuela Superior de Cardinal Cushing, a private school for Catholic girls in Bolivia. After a year in Bolivia, Karen returned home and enrolled at a college near Littleton, where she received a bachelor's degree with a major in Spanish and a minor in education. After graduation, she rewarded herself with a summer of traveling in Mexico. In the fall, she returned to the United States to accept the part-time position at Littleton High School.

Karen started with three classes in September and picked up a fourth when another teacher was named an assistant principal and had to give up his classes. She added the Spanish III class to her schedule the Monday after Thanksgiving.

There had been no warning that the new class might be a problem. The principal told her only that it was an above-average-track class of twenty college-bound students, all sophomores. Her other classes were going well, and Karen had no reason to suspect that this one would be any different. She expected that she would simply open the text to chapter 4, where the state curriculum indicated the class should be, and pick up where the other teachers had left off.

But Karen discovered on the first day that the substitutes had made little progress. The students were far behind the course outline and would have to do nine months' work in six months' time if they were to complete the Spanish III curriculum and be ready for Spanish IV in the fall.

Karen's second discovery was that the different-teacher-every-three-weeks syndrome had left the class in near anarchy, with little respect for the teachers and with no expectation that any real learning would take place.

The sense of lawlessness was heightened by the fact that there seemed to be no real cohesion among the twenty students. Although there were two distinct groups of students in the class—Karen had categorized them in her mind as "greasers" (those who wore leather motorcycle jackets and boots and seemed indifferent to school) and "jocks" (the clean-cut students dressed in the latest fashion)—there was little unity even within those groups. It was difficult to get any of the students to work together. The only thing that united them, Karen thought, was their ability to sabotage her lessons and frustrate her teaching efforts. They would rally around that and nothing else.

The class had only one leader: Jeff Cole, a 16-year-old fullback on Littleton's football team, who was one of the brightest students in the class as well as the most disruptive. He seemed to have a constant need to retain his role as leader, or at least as chief instigator. Jeff never missed an opportunity to disrupt the class or to obstruct any momentum Karen tried to build. Most of the others would follow Jeff's lead without much hesitation.

To try to contain their disruptiveness, Karen organized the students into five neat rows of four, with as much space between rows as possible. Her strategy was to divide and conquer and to try to keep the students focused on her as she introduced new nouns, verbs, and sentence constructions from the front of the room. The students needed a great deal of drill work to bring them up to date, so Karen emphasized repetitive grammar exercises. Most days, she reviewed the material, had the students repeat it, and then assigned related written exercises in their books.

From the outset, however, Karen felt that they regarded her as only another substitute, and she constantly struggled for control. At first, the problems seemed relatively minor: side-bar conversations, off-task activities, minor disruptions. But gradually the students' inattention increased, and whenever she demanded their focus, they would chatter about a football or basketball game or about the upcoming ski season or anything else that was unrelated to the material.

Gradually the problems escalated. During the first day of her second week, Karen was caught in a crossfire of coins being flung around the room behind her as she tried to conjugate a verb on the chalkboard.

"This is craziness, absolute craziness," Karen thought as she listened to the ping of coins bouncing off the walls. She held the brief hope that the disruption would subside on its own if she ignored it. She continued writing on the board, reciting the verb as she conjugated it and pushing dutifully ahead with the lesson plan. "Comi, comiste, comio," she said. "I ate, you ate, he-she-it ate."

A sudden loud CRACK! shattered Karen's concentration and her sense of safety. Instinctively, she jumped back from the board and swerved to face the class. A Kennedy half-dollar, which had ricocheted off the chalkboard only a few inches from her ear, fell to the floor and rolled to the back of the room, accompanied by a chorus of chuckles from her students.

That was the last time Karen turned her back on the students. From then on, she used the overhead projector rather than the chalkboard whenever she needed to illustrate something to the whole class.

After the coin-tossing incident, Karen tried a variety of the assertive discipline techniques she had learned in her college education courses, but few seemed to have any effect. For example, each time a student acted up, she placed a check next to his or her name on the chalkboard. If a student received five checks, he or she was assigned an hour of detention. But it became a game before long as students competed for the checks and ignored the detention assignments.

That illustrated another problem. The school's policy concerning after-school detention undercut her efforts to run the class. At Littleton High School, only an administrator could authorize after-school detention, and school officials would not back up Karen's detention assignments. They said that the district's inflexible bus schedule made it awkward to detain students who lived far from the school.

Another school policy, one which allowed students to have class schedules without a lunch period, gave Jeff and six or seven others a daily opportunity to disrupt the class. According to the policy, students who did not have a regularly scheduled lunch period could take five minutes from their sixth-period class and ten minutes from their seventh-period class to eat. Jeff and several others had no scheduled lunch. Invariably, they would arrive fifteen minutes late for the forty-minute class and would require another five minutes to settle down. Once seated, with their notebooks open, they would complain that the lesson was difficult to follow, forcing Karen to start over again.

Karen worried that the abbreviated classes might be an insurmountable handicap to a class that already was several months behind. She offered the students a compromise: Come to class on time, and you may eat at your desks. Jeff and the others seemed to appreciate the compromise at first, and they regularly brought their lunches to class. But within a week, they slipped back to their routine of showing up ten to fifteen minutes late, and they brought their lunches to class as well.

For Jeff, the potential for disruption was doubled by his luncheon selections: carrots, potato chips, hot peppers, sardine and onion sandwiches, carbonated sodas—anything that made a loud crunch or sprayed into the air or that was exotic enough to provoke some reaction from the others. After the first few days of Jeff's in-class luncheons, the students would sit each day in breathless anticipation of what Jeff would have in his lunch bag. Almost always, it drew a reaction, which only encouraged Jeff to be even more outrageous the next day. Karen felt that the lunch fiasco was typical of the way Jeff turned her peace gestures against her.

The cheating incidents also were typical. Karen could tell from Jeff's transcripts and test scores and from the brief moments when he did participate in her class that he didn't need to cheat to get good grades. Instead, Karen believed, Jeff's cheating was only an attempt to entertain himself and to prove to the other students that he could outwit her.

Jeff cheated on the first two tests, and both times she caught him. Because Jeff was a leader and an instigator for the rest of the class, Karen feared that his cheating would spread unless she made an example of him. She responded harshly; each time, she gave him a zero on the test, plus two days' detention, and she sent notes to the guidance office and to his parents.

But now, sitting at her desk after ordering Jeff from the class for his third cheating episode, Karen thought that this incident was different from the earlier two. In the other two, Jeff clearly wanted to get away with it and was embarrassed at being discovered. This time, his cheating was blatant. He had nearly waved his crib sheet in the air. Karen felt sure that he wanted to get caught.

The period ended, and the other students turned in their tests and shuffled from the room. Karen's mind turned back to the paper she had taken from Jeff before sending him to the guidance office. When the last student left the room, Karen took the paper from Jeff's test, where she had stapled it. She unfolded it to see what he had written.

In bold red letters, it read: "¡No estoy haciendo trampa, Tonta!"

Karen mentally translated—"I'm not cheating, you idiot"—and sank into her chair, thinking that Jeff had won again.

MAGGIE LINDBERG

A first-year teacher is afraid to take her third-grade class on a nature walk because the children's behavior is so poor that she does not believe they can be controlled outside the classroom.

It was already the third week of October, and Maggie Lindberg knew she couldn't put off taking her students on a nature walk much longer. All the other third-grade classes had ventured out and returned with the materials they would study as part of a science lesson. Her students were asking when they were going, and Maggie knew she was running out of time; in another two weeks there would be no more brightly colored leaves to study.

Walking past a bulletin-board display entitled "The Splendor of the Changing Seasons," the result of a nature walk taken by the third-grade class next to hers, Maggie couldn't help smiling to herself. "I guess it would be irresponsible of me to just ignore this annual phenomenon of nature," she thought. But she wished that she could.

This was Maggie's first year as a full-time teacher. She had graduated from college midyear and then substituted in several nearby school districts for the rest of the school year. Littleton had offered her a full-time position starting in September, and she was assigned a third-grade class of twenty-six students. Maggie had been excited by the prospect of teaching her own class. She spent much of the summer defining her objectives for the year and planning activities and curriculum materials to achieve them. Maggie had wanted to be a teacher for as long as she could remember, and now her goal was a reality.

Maggie's experiences as a substitute teacher had shaped her opinions about teaching almost as much as had student teaching. Maggie knew that substitute teaching was often just an exercise in crowd control, and she had "baby-sat" many classrooms full of unruly children with grace and patience. But she vowed to herself that her own classroom would be orderly and her students better behaved. Unfortunately, that goal was proving elusive.

Maggie also had a specific experience while she was substitute teaching that really frightened her. The incident involved a fourth-grade class scheduled to take a field trip to a local fire station. She vividly recalled the feeling of panic that overtook her when one of the students bolted from the group and ran off the school grounds into a nearby wooded area. Maggie had the parent volunteer who was accompanying the class on the field trip take the rest of the students back to their classroom. Maggie then went after the runaway student, eventually located her, and brought her back to the classroom. When she returned, she found the principal with her class. While the principal did not rebuke her, the memory was a constant reminder of what could happen when the students were not in the teacher's control.

At the moment, Maggie was headed for the art room to pick up her class. As she stood in the doorway, she couldn't believe how intent her students seemed to be on their projects. "These kids must love art," she thought. "They never act like this in my class."

Maggie reflected on the reading lessons she had taught earlier that morning. Because the students had art on Tuesdays, Maggie felt real pressure to have the reading groups stay on schedule so that she could meet with all three groups between 9:15 and 10:30, when art was scheduled. But the students seemed to be even less cooperative when Maggie most needed them to stay on task.

She had begun the lesson by reminding the students of the morning schedule. "Since today is Tuesday, we really need to get everything done on time so that we can go to the art room with all our reading work finished."

Some of the children began to clap. Several commented to each other about going to art. Maggie ignored the interruptions and continued, "Look up at the board, and you'll see the assignments for each group. I want the Chocolate Chips with me first today. Twinkies should be reading the story that starts on page 49 of your reading books and then doing the workbook pages on the board. Oreos have to complete the workbook pages left from yesterday and then start a new story, beginning on page 141 of your reading books." Maggie pointed to each group's assignment, which she had written on the chalkboard.

As Maggie was giving the students their directions, many of them were occupied with other activities. Several were walking around the room—some to the pencil sharpener, others to the cubbies to retrieve books or supplies—and a few were gathered at the reading center in the back of the room.

Maggie spoke sharply. "You're not listening to me! I want the Chocolate Chips at the reading table *now*. Everyone else, in your seat and doing the work that's on the board."

The children began moving toward their places. Four children gathered at the reading table, while others went for their books and then headed to the table. Two children, sitting at their desks, had their hands up. Maggie noticed and said, "Yes, Melody, what is it?"

"Why do we have to do yesterday's pages? I'm tired of them."
Other children immediately joined in.
"Yeah, don't make us do the old stuff."
"I already did that stuff."
"All we do is the same stuff all the time."
Maggie again raised her voice to be heard over the din. "That 'stuff,' as you all refer to it, is our work. And you will do it, *now*. I don't want to hear any more complaints, and I want to see everyone hard at work or the whole class will stay in and do the work during recess. Chocolate Chips, you should all be at the reading table. Let's move it."
Maggie's frustration was evident in her voice and the set of her shoulders. Ten minutes of an already shortened reading period had been lost getting the children to settle down to their tasks. She sat down with the Chocolate Chips and, trying to lighten her tone, said, "Okay, Chippers, we're reading on page 76. Emanual, why don't you begin."
Emanual was quiet. John said, "He don't got his book."
"Where's your book, Emanual?" Maggie tried to keep the impatience from her voice.
"In my cubby."
"What good will it do you in your cubby? What have you been doing all this time? Emanual, you know that one of our class rules is 'Be prepared,' but you're not, are you?" Maggie's voice again began to reflect her tension. She turned to the rest of the Chocolate Chips. "Does everyone else have a book?"
Of the nine children in the group, three had come to the reading table without their books. Maggie sent them to get their books and tried to keep the other children quiet while they waited to get started. It was taking all her control to remain calm. She was tempted to banish the three children who had not brought their books, to make a point about being prepared, but she knew that they needed the reading time too much. However, as a result of all the confusion and interruptions, all the reading groups spent far less time reading on Tuesday than they should have. That was one of the things that bothered Maggie the most.
Of the twenty-six children in her class, more than half had come into third grade below grade level in reading. Maggie wanted them to leave her class reading far better than they did when they came in, and she needed maximum reading time to accomplish her goal. She also knew that third grade was a crucial time for these children. In order to succeed in the upper grades, where there was more emphasis on reading content than on reading skills, they would have to "break the code" and learn to be efficient readers this year. Maggie wanted to be the teacher who enabled them to meet that goal. But, so far, she had not been very successful.
Maggie's reverie about the morning was interrupted when the art teacher noticed her in the doorway. She called to Maggie and waved her

into the room. The art teacher directed the children to put away their work. As Maggie watched the children clean up the art room, she was fascinated by what she observed. When the art teacher was satisfied with the cleanup, she had the children line up at the door. Maggie found it hard to believe these were the same children who, forty minutes earlier, had been causing her such consternation. However, as soon as the class stepped into the hall, Maggie remembered why the children frustrated her. She walked down the hall trying to keep order.

"Tommy, don't run ahead of the class. You know the rules."

"Maria, please try to keep up. Don't dawdle."

"Matt, come walk next to me. I've told you not to bother the girls. Could we all please keep the noise down?"

Maggie looked at the children straggling into the classroom and thought, "What's the matter with these kids? Why don't they listen to me? Is it because I'm so young?"

Eventually Maggie was able to herd the last of the students into the classroom. She looked at the clock and saw that it was 11:25; her social studies lesson was beginning late.

"Okay, everyone in your seat now and take out your social studies book."

The students continued talking to each other as they made their way to their desks.

"Please quiet down. I want to see all of you in your seats, because we have a lot of work to do."

Looking out over her class, Maggie saw that most of the students were ignoring her. Two students were in the library corner; a group of boys had their heads together over a comic book; and one little girl, looking for a pencil, had emptied the contents of her desk onto the floor.

Maggie went over to the boys, took the comic book, and told them to take their seats. The boys complied but continued to talk above the noise of the rest of the class.

As Maggie walked toward the girls in the library corner, she heard a loud crash from the front of the room.

"Miss Lindberg, it wasn't my fault. Tony was pulling it down too hard."

Maggie saw the world map crumpled in a heap on the floor in front of the chalkboard.

"Well, why were you pulling the map down? Please sit down, and I will take care of the map."

The sound of the map crashing to the floor had captured everyone's attention, and the students listened to hear what would happen next. Maggie was angry enough to raise her voice.

"I mean it. I want all of you in your seats *now*. Let's get out those social studies notebooks, and if I hear one more word from anyone, there will be no free time this afternoon."

As Maggie walked briskly to the front of the classroom, she looked at the clock. It was 11:35. She would barely have time to introduce the social studies lesson before the lunch bell at 11:45.

The classroom was filled with the sound of rustling papers as the children searched for their notebooks. As Maggie watched them, she tried through sheer force of will to repress her dismay and replace it with the excitement and anticipation she had felt on the first day of class. Maggie did not want to let herself become discouraged; she wanted to teach these children something! But too often they wouldn't even listen to her, and the idea of organizing the group for a field trip seemed like a nightmare.

Looking out the window, she again noticed how brilliant the leaves had become. She knew she had to take the students on a nature walk, and she had to do it soon. She was sure that they would enjoy some time outside and that a science lesson based on materials they had gathered themselves would be a good learning experience for them. "But," she thought, "I can't even control them in here!"

GINA SHRADER

A student teacher learns about the complexities of a typical teaching day as she observes an effective second-grade teacher and her class go through their morning activities.

Jennifer Mallory watched Gina Shrader again this morning with a mixture of admiration and trepidation. Jennie was student teaching this semester in Gina's second-grade class at Roosevelt Elementary, and in the three weeks she had been watching Gina, Jennie had been increasingly impressed. She was also becoming a bit intimidated, as she wondered how to duplicate Gina's style.

Gina Shrader, a tall, slim woman, was in her fourth year of teaching and had recently been granted tenure. The mother of four children ranging in age from 9 to 14, Gina had spent ten years getting her undergraduate degree and in a few months she would receive her master's. Gina now sat at a student's desk and spoke quietly with several children. Jennie thought again about how soft-spoken Gina was and how bright her face became as she interacted with the children. Jennie applauded Gina's general teaching methods, which included the use of a whole-language approach in addition to the required basal readers, and she felt fortunate to be student teaching with such a professional.

The students in this class had been working on writing their autobiographies for almost a month and were now finishing the project. By 9:15 on this sunny March day, sixteen of the twenty-two children were working busily. The other six students were out of the room, attending a reading lab.

Gina's classroom was large and cheerful. The desks were arranged in three groups of eight, forming three rectangles in the middle of the room. In addition to the groups of desks there were two round tables near the back and sides of the room and a long brown leather couch next to a reading corner.

Jennie had come into the room a few minutes late after completing some administrative chores for Gina at the office, and she checked the schedule for the day, which was always printed on the chalkboard. She remembered that the class would be painting during art, following lunch, and so she unobtrusively went to the supply cabinets in the back of the room to mix paint and prepare supplies. Jennie knew that Gina appreciated her help, and she liked to be productive while she observed.

She noted as she worked that every student appeared to have a task. Seven children were sitting at their desks, working independently or quietly together. They shared crayons and colored paper, and some of the students were checking each other's work. Six students sat at a round table at the back of the room, talking to each other as they began to glue the pages of their books to colored paper.

"How many pages is yours?" Sally asked Susan.

"Mine is ten pages and ten chapters," Susan replied proudly.

Kenny leaned toward the girls. "I have some pictures on one page. Should I include them in my table of contents?"

Susan answered authoritatively. "Yes, just write the word *Pictures* at the top of that page."

Gina approached and sat down with the children at the table. "Are you all ready to glue here? Sally?"

Sally shook her head. "No."

Gina smiled. "Then you have to skedaddle until your work is ready to be glued." After Sally departed, Gina looked around the table and addressed the group. "OK, let's check your chapters and tables of contents so that you only have to glue the pages once." She took a moment to look at the pile of papers in front of Jay. "Jay, do you want 'My Family' to be the second chapter?" Jay looked through his papers, thought for a moment, and nodded. Gina watched as he put the sheet in the proper order, and then she turned to Nicholas. "Nicholas, let's check your table of contents before you glue: 'When I Was Born' will be page 2; 'My Parents' will be page 3. . . ." Gina paused. "Nick, what a nice picture of your family."

Nicholas smiled broadly. "Yes, I really like it." He passed the picture around the table to the other children, who smiled and nodded appreciatively. Gina finished reading Nicholas's chapter titles. " 'I Love Drawing'—is that chapter going to be on page 9? It doesn't look like it's on page 9."

Nicholas looked at his materials. "Yes it is."

"But it's not written where the other page numbers are written," Gina said, and she leafed through each page, reading out the titles: " 'My Favorite Place,' 'Future Job,' 'Where I Am Now.' . . ." She stopped at one sheet and turned to Nicholas. "Wasn't *friends* one of our spelling words?"

He thought for a moment. "Yes, I think so."

"Then check your rough copy carefully. There's no excuse for that word being misspelled." Gina handed the pages back to Nicholas. "OK, you can go to Writing Workshop now that you are finished, and I don't want to see you roaming around." Gina spoke in a firm but quiet voice, and Jennie marveled at the authority she managed to convey with such a gentle manner.

Gina then rose and walked around the room. She looked over the shoulder of a girl who was writing the title of her book on an unlined piece of paper. "Darlene, I didn't check your rough copy. Do you know how I know? I would have said, 'Draw straight lines with a ruler first for the words on your cover.' "

Darlene looked up at her teacher and then back down at her crooked lettering. "It is slanty, isn't it?" she asked with a sheepish smile. Without further instruction, Darlene got up to get a fresh piece of paper and a ruler and then returned to her desk.

Gina continued walking around the room, stopping to look at each student's papers, sometimes making a comment or suggestion and other times just looking over the work. Bobby walked up to her with a stack of papers. "I don't know where my good copy of my table of contents is."

Gina looked through the stack. "You're right. It's not here. You'll have to copy it over, I guess. OK?" Bobby shrugged, took back the papers, and returned to his desk to work. Gina resumed her tour of the room, commenting on page numbers and spelling or helping a student solve a problem so that he or she wouldn't have to recopy an entire page. She soon returned to the six students in the back of the room and settled in to work with each in turn. Occasionally a student from elsewhere in the room would approach to speak with her, and Gina patiently answered questions and sent each child back to work.

There was an atmosphere of quiet intensity throughout the room, Jennie thought, and each child seemed to be on task even though the children were all at different stages of the project. Two students were quietly writing side by side at their desks, and five students were checking the order of chapters and the page numbers of each other's work. They were all talking out loud but the tone remained low.

Gina rose again and moved from one group to another, politely excusing herself and returning to students as necessary. As she stood talking with Betsy, Gina looked around the room for a moment and called to another student who was sitting at her desk staring off into space. "Janet, you look like you're lost." Janet looked startled, smiled, and then began to write again. When Gina finished her conversation with Betsy, she walked over to Janet's side.

"Janet, are you still writing more chapters?" Janet nodded. "Have you written your introduction yet?"

"No."

"Why not?"

"Ummm . . ."

"The first thing you have to do is write your introduction today. Let's look through your copies and make sure everything else is here.'' As she scanned Janet's work, Gina glanced around the room. She spotted a student wandering around. ''Kyle,'' she called, ''get yourself back on track.''

As she was speaking to Kyle, two additional students returned to the classroom, went to their desks, and took out their folders. Gina handed Janet's work back to her and walked toward the newcomers. ''Ernie, Laura, do you know what we're doing?''

''Yes. Autobiographies,'' replied Ernie for both of them.

Jennie had completed the preparations for art and was now simply observing from a seat at the side of the room. She saw that two students remained at the back table, glueing their books; the others who had been working there had returned to their desks. Students were moving freely around the room as they wrote or helped one another organize their projects. As other students returned to the classroom from the reading lab, they headed for their desks and took out work without being told to do so.

Jennie realized that the noise level had picked up because there were now twenty students in the room, but there was still no loud talking. Kyle and Allison stopped writing and began talking about a TV show. Gina looked up immediately and announced to the class at large, ''OK, guys, we're going to be stopping in about five minutes.'' She then addressed another student directly. ''George, put that other work away. We are still working on our autobiographies.''

Gina continued circling the room for another five minutes, and at 10:10 she addressed the entire class. ''Listen up, please. Miss Mallory, would you turn out the lights for me?'' Jennie got up, turned off the room lights, and then returned to her seat. ''The lights are out now. Place your autobiographies in your folders and put them away.'' Gina waited a moment while the children put away their work. When they were looking up at her, she continued, ''If your table of contents is not done, please raise your hand.'' Three hands went up, and Gina made eye contact with their owners. ''OK, you can work with me at lunch.'' She then turned the lights back on and walked from the light switch to an easel that held an oversize pad of paper. ''The lights are back on, but listen for a minute. Let's go over the title page for the autobiographies. This is the last step before we laminate our books.'' Gina paused because this statement generated excitement throughout the room, and a number of children began to chatter. Gina started over. ''I'm ready.'' She looked around the room. ''I see eight of you are ready . . . nine . . . ten. . . .'' The class gradually settled down and became attentive, and Gina continued.

''For a lot of you, all you have left is the title page. Does anyone know what goes on a title page?'' She waited, and twelve hands went up. ''Oh, you must have a good teacher.'' The children giggled but then quickly quieted, and individual students began to postulate various ideas about what should be on a title page. Gina listened attentively, nodding encouragingly as she solicited their thoughts. She then summed up their contributions:

"The title page includes everything that is on the front cover, as well as the date the book is published, the name of the company, and the city. You don't have to call it 'The Title Page,' even though our other pages all have titles."

Using a classroom book for illustration, Gina began a specific list of information the children should include, annotating their decisions on the easel pad. An energetic conversation ensued when the children debated whether the words *author* and *illustrator* were necessary if the same person had both written and illustrated the book. Then Gina artfully steered the discussion forward: "All right, I think you've agreed on several possible ways to handle that. Choose the one that you think would be OK for your book. Now, what information should follow the title and the author of the book?"

Nicholas answered tentatively. "Who published it?"

"Yes, and we should agree as a class on what we will call ourselves." Gina called on another student. "Janelle? What do you think?"

"Let's write 'R.E.S.' as the publishing place."

Jay had a suggestion. "We could put 'Published in Mrs. Shrader's Class.' "

Nicholas raised his hand. "We could put 'Published at R.E.S. in Mrs. Shrader's Class.' "

Gina crossed to the chalkboard and said, "Let's take the three choices and vote." She wrote the three suggestions for the name of the publisher on the board and called for a vote. Sixteen children chose "Published at R.E.S. in Mrs. Shrader's Class." Three voted for the other two choices. Not everyone voted for a selection, prompting Gina to observe, "Some of you didn't vote. That means the others chose for you."

Gina addressed Nicholas as she walked back to the easel. "Congratulations on your idea." Nicholas smiled proudly. Positioned again at the easel, Gina looked across the group and waited for everyone to settle down. She noticed one student fiddling with a pencil. "Ernie, are you with us?"

Ernie looked up and grinned. "Yes. Sorry."

Jennie was amazed that the class as a whole stayed so alert to the discussion and that there was so little fidgeting or side conversation. Gina really commanded the students' attention with the next announcement. "We are really getting close now, class. Each of you must be finished so that all books are ready for lamination by the end of next week." An excited murmur filled the room. "I also want to tell you about a decision I have made. I have changed my mind about something."

Gina had initially told the class that only those books that were ten or more chapters in length would be laminated. "I have decided that everyone's book will be finished in the same way, no matter how long it is. I said otherwise at the beginning of the project because in some classes the students have needed an extra push. But not in this class. You have all worked hard enough. In past years, some children did not get busy enough; but all of you were dying to work, and you always came in and took your folders right out. You all worked hard enough, so we will laminate all your books. Does that make some of you happy?'' There was a happy chorus of agreement.

"Good. Me, too. Now I want to talk about how important it is for you to put your pages together carefully before you glue them to construction paper. You can check with me or with one of your classmates who is finished. Let's see. . . . Nicholas and Mary and Mark are finished.'' Gina noticed Betsy waving her hand.

"Betsy?''

"What if some people continue to write?''

"I'm glad you like to write, but we have to finish the book. When the laminating machine is put away next week, you won't have a book published if you are still writing.''

"But I have three more chapters!''

"Betsy, we have had this conversation before.''

Now Allison interrupted. "I have lots more chapters to write too!''

Gina shook her head. "Sorry, girls. Do them at home this weekend. You've had plenty of time—more than a month.'' She glanced at the clock—Jennie saw that it was 10:30—and announced, "Time to get ready for reading.''

The class, Jennie knew, was quite familiar with this routine. Twelve students quickly rose and left to go to the classroom next door, and eight children came in from that class to join the ten left in the room. The second-graders at Roosevelt were grouped homogeneously for reading, and Gina taught the children at the middle reading level, which meant that they were reading at grade level.

Gina had one hour with the reading group today. The time varied from thirty to ninety minutes, depending on the school schedule, assemblies, or other special events. Jennie knew that Gina was about to introduce a new book to the group. Gina had told her student teacher that she planned to teach it through a whole-language approach, and since there were no prewritten workbooks or worksheets available, Jennie had helped Gina prepare her own material.

Gina told Jennie that this preparation was both the joy and the difficulty of the method. "You discover things about the material and about the class as you develop your own curriculum, and you can build on and improve presentations from year to year, but creating your own materials is very time-consuming.''

Jennie was glad to have been of assistance to Gina on this lesson, and she was anxious to see it taught.

Gina had several worksheets for the first lesson. One sheet had a one-sentence description of the book and a single question: "In what ways do you think an 8-year-old's life was different 300 years ago?'' The second sheet listed Gina's choice of vocabulary words from the first chapter and six questions that she would use at the end of that chapter.

Gina did not hand out either sheet as she introduced the lesson. The children knew that they were going to begin a new book, and Gina first reviewed the title with them. The class remembered that the book was about a girl who lived in Connecticut, and Gina's plan was to start with a discussion of the location and the distance between Connecticut and other places the students knew in the area. To illustrate her comments, Gina pulled down a large, simple map of the United States and incorporated a brief geography lesson into the discussion. Jennie observed that Gina was also interested in the group's concept of distance. "You remember I said that this story is about a girl who moved from Massachusetts to Connecticut." She pointed to the states as she spoke. "It's a quick trip for us today. Do you know why?"

Several students raised their hands. "George?"

"Well, we can drive."

"Yes, that's right. Kyle, what is your thought?"

"We can take a bus!"

"OK, now imagine a time when you couldn't drive a car or take a bus or train because they weren't invented yet. How long would the trip take then?"

"Two hours," called Laura.

"No, more like twenty!" added Janelle.

"Maybe two days?" wondered Sally. "Maybe even longer!"

"Yes, maybe," acknowledged Gina. "This story happened a long time ago, in 1707. What does that tell you?"

Janet answered seriously, "That she's dead."

Jennie, sitting at the circular table in the back of the room, repressed a smile, but Gina did not even flinch. Instead, she nodded a simple acknowledgment and asked, "What else?"

Bobby raised his hand. "It means two centuries and ninety years."

"What's a century?"

Bobby replied, "Two hundred and ninety years."

"That's a long, long time." Gina paused because most of the students began to talk all at once. "I can't hear when there are eighteen voices all at once." She waited until the class settled down. "Before I pass out the book, I want you to read this." As she spoke, she handed out the worksheet with Jennie's single question about life for an 8-year-old 300 years ago. She asked Darlene to read the question out loud, and then she repeated it. "Now write about how you think life was different."

Students raised their hands. "Can we draw?"

"Write what you think."

"Were there schools?"

"Write it."

"There was child abuse."

"Write it. There is no right or wrong answer." Gina winked conspiratorily at Jennie and waited for several minutes while the children were writing or staring off thoughtfully into space. "Would any of you like to share your ideas?"

Jennie was gratified to witness the lively conversation that ensued as students spoke about their responses. They shared their ideas about life long ago: Medicines were not very good, so "lots of people got sick and died." They wondered if people wore rags, and then they decided that children did not have as many choices about clothes as they do today. "Maybe they only had about two pairs of shoes and two dresses that they wore over and over."

"Where did the clothes come from?" Jennie loved the way Gina used her single question to direct the children's thoughts in so many directions. This query took the children to the recognition that there was no electricity.

"There was no Nintendo!" cried Stephen.

"Why?"

Allison responded, "Because there were no movies, no TV. . . ."

"Why not?"

The children suddenly realized that these things need electricity, and they excitedly began a list of modern conveniences that could not have existed 300 years ago. Janet then volunteered, with amazement in her voice, "There were no cars!" In a sense, Jennie thought, the discussion had now come full circle, as Gina once again asked the class how people moved from place to place. Some of the children began to visualize people walking or riding in wagons, but other students were still thinking of more things that must have been different. They asked about stores, toilets, dishes, water in houses. Jennie was amazed at the curiosity and interest such a simple question had sparked.

Gina's final comment was designed to keep them thinking even though the class conversation was at an end. "Life was so different that it's hard for you to imagine it." The class again began to talk all at once, and Gina paused. "I'm waiting." The class quieted, and she resumed. "I'm passing out folders for your work. We will decorate the folders and bookmarks now. While you are working on that, I will hand out your books too." Jennie rose without being asked and quickly helped several children distribute supplies. "In ten minutes I will read the beginning of the book to you." The class quieted as children concentrated on the drawing task.

Without raising her voice, Gina interrupted the work after ten minutes, and the children put down their crayons and pencils. Gina stood in front of the chalkboard and began an explanation of the vocabulary that the children would encounter in the first chapter. "Lots of times I'm not going to tell you what you are reading. I want you to figure out the words from the sentence, the paragraph—what's around the word. Betsy, Tyler, put your pencils down and listen to me. You can say to yourself, 'I'll figure it out from what's around, or I'll look it up.' The words I think some of you might not know for chapter 1 are . . .'' Gina wrote five words on the board: *quilt, cloak, journey, wilderness,* and *musket.* Even as she was writing the fourth and fifth words, she held up her left hand to stifle the immediate attempt by several children to provide definitions. "Don't tell me if you know them." Gina turned and smiled. "I want people to figure them out as we read. You may have heard them, but you may not know what they mean. Tyler, I need you to stop writing so that you can listen. If you know all of them, terrific. How many aren't sure of a couple?" Several hands went up. "OK, we'll figure them out as we read."

Gina sat down on a tall stool and paused. "I'm ready. Read along with me. No talking." She read a brief author's note, which indicated that the book was based on real events, and then stopped again. "I want to talk about the title of the book first. There are lots of meanings for *courage.* What do you think about courage?"

Hands shot up. "Brave."

"To stand up for yourself."

"To have a lot of guts."

"Using your brain a lot."

"Believing in yourself."

Gina nodded approval. "Those are all good definitions of courage." Looking down again at the page, she began to read the first chapter without further introduction, and the students followed in their own copies. Gina led them through the vocabulary words on the board as they were encountered, rereading a sentence or asking for additional examples when necessary. She had to interrupt the discussion only once, to again reprimand Tyler, who was still fiddling with his pencil. "I'll see you at lunch today," she said quietly; then she continued reading.

After the students had clarified their understanding of all the words on the board, Gina added one more. "What is a *settlement?* I should have put that word up too." The students were not sure of the meaning, and Gina patiently led them to a definition. At one point, a student put her head down on her desk. "Janet." At the sound of her name, Janet sat up straight, and Gina continued her comments without further interruption.

At the conclusion of the chapter, Gina looked up from her book. "Reading is over for today. We will reread chapter 1 on Monday silently and answer some more questions."

The students stood and returned to their rooms quietly. When Gina's other students returned from reading, they joined their classmates in line at the doorway for lunch. A few approached Gina with questions about their projects or afternoon activities—they had seen Jennie mixing paint—and Gina answered them in her calm, patient manner.

As the students filed out of the room for lunch, Gina turned to Jennie. "I thought the question you designed for that lesson went well, didn't you?"

"Yes, well, you are so open with the students when you lead a conversation—they'll talk a lot." Jennie hoped she didn't sound ingratiating, but she really was impressed.

"Well, I think it's time for you to take a spin. On Monday, I want you to lead the reading group, OK?"

Jennie was thrilled to finally have a chance to work directly with the children, but she was also apprehensive. How would she duplicate Gina's easy, relaxed manner with the class and still not let the students wander and digress? Jennie suddenly knew that her weekend would be punctuated with nervous moments of anticipation whenever she thought of Monday.

To Gina, though, Jennie simply said, "Sure, Mrs. Shrader. That's great. Thanks." Jennie followed Gina out the door and switched off the lights, not knowing what else to say. She had a tough act to follow.

BARBARA PARKER

*An experienced high school teacher meets "the class from hell"
and handles it by becoming extremely firm and autocratic. She
comes to hate the class and is sure that the students hate her.*

Barbara Parker walked toward the room assigned for her seventh-period
social studies class feeling the rush of adrenalin that always greeted the first
day of school. In spite of the fact that she was beginning her fifth year of
teaching, Barbara felt excitement and anticipation at meeting each new class
of students and getting the year under way.

Barbara's morning classes went well, and she enjoyed visiting with some
of her former students during lunch. Her next class was an average-level
ninth-grade class in Afro-Asian studies. While the title of the course implied
a focus on cultures not normally studied in suburban high schools, the
course essentially covered typical world history content, except for European
history, which comprised the sophomore social studies curriculum. Even
with that major omission, Barbara found the breadth of content a challenge;
the course covered the Middle East, Africa, India, China, and Japan,
spanning history from the dawn of civilization to present-day culture and
politics. But the planning and review that Barbara began over the summer
renewed her interest in the subject and the possibilities she could explore
to teach it. In the morning she had taught this same course to honors classes,
and she was encouraged by their reaction to her introduction.

Barbara entered room 303 a few minutes before the bell and walked to
the front to check that textbooks had been delivered to the room. As she
pulled the class roster and her introductory notes from her book bag,
students began to drift in from lunch.

"Hey, watch it!" snarled a girl standing in the classroom doorway as she
turned and confronted the student behind her.

"Well, move your feet, girl!" replied the perpetrator, a pretty girl with
long dark hair. She sauntered past the girl she had pushed and came into
the room. Calling over the heads of several students, the dark-haired girl

addressed her friend in the back of the room: "Hey, Angela, how was math? Was Alan there?" Angela's reply was lost in the general din, which escalated as more students spilled into the room.

Barbara stood up at the sound of the bell—a harsh, discordant note guaranteed to command attention—and walked toward the classroom door. She expected a certain amount of dawdling right after lunch and was prepared to usher the few students who remained in the hallway into the room and to their seats. But there were fifteen or more students milling around in the hall, and Barbara wasn't sure which ones belonged in her class.

"Would those of you enrolled in ninth-grade social studies please come in?" Barbara asked the throng in the hall.

"Yo, Miss. Name's Jackson," replied a skinny, wiry black student who slid past Barbara into the room. "Hey, Marcus, how's my man?" Jackson spied a compatriot standing at the back of the room and made his way into the classroom.

"Excuse me, class has begun," repeated Barbara to the students in the hall. It was apparent that she was not capturing anyone's attention, so she backed into the room and began to close the door.

"Hey, what are ya doin'!" A few students bolted toward the closing door and muscled their way past their teacher.

"Class begins with the bell, and I expect you to be in your seats," Barbara said to their retreating backs. Not one of them seemed to hear her, and no one made a move to sit down. Barbara closed the door the rest of the way and walked to the front of the classroom to address her class.

"Please take your seats," she called, thinking to herself that the typical first-day excitement was extreme with these kids. "This is Afro-Asian studies, and anyone who doesn't belong . . ." Barbara let her voice trail off as she realized that no one was listening to her. Students were grouped in pairs and threes, mostly standing, but some had turned their desks to face each other and converse more comfortably. The door opened and two girls entered, deep in conversation. After surveying the commotion in the room, the girls resumed their discussion and walked toward the windows on the other side of the room.

Barbara had always found ninth-graders to be somewhat shy and intimidated on their first day of high school. The possibility that opening day would be a disciplinary challenge hadn't occurred to her. She raised her voice slightly. "Would you please choose a desk so that I can take attendance and distribute your texts?" Barbara felt as though there was an invisible partition between herself and the students, so totally did they ignore her request. With exasperation she reached for the pointer lying in the chalkboard tray and banged it on her desk. "Take your seats!"

"Oooohhh . . ." The sound floated tauntingly toward Barbara as most of the students turned to look at her appraisingly. A few groups arranged themselves at desks near where they had been standing, but at least ten of the thirty or so students in the room assumed "make me" postures and continued to speak to each other. The conversation in the room subsided but did not disappear.

Barbara immediately regretted her act but at least tried to seize the opportunity to be heard. "This is ninth-grade Afro-Asian studies. In this class you can study some interesting and exciting things. I want to get to know you and tell you about the class. Would the rest of you please sit down so that I can call your names?" By the end of her speech, Barbara realized that the noise in the room was increasing rather than diminishing in response to her message; unbelievably, two students who had sat down when she banged the pointer now left their desks to call to someone out the open window. None of those standing made any move to sit.

Barbara looked at the unruly group for a moment and then picked up her roster and walked to the nearest boy. "Who are you?" she tapped him on the shoulder to interrupt his conversation with the boy at the desk behind him.

"Mason Dixon," replied the boy with a respectful smile. Barbara instinctively looked down her roster to the D's, prompting uproarious laughter from the student who had spoken and three others within earshot. As she searched in vain for "Dixon" on her printout, Barbara thought about his reply and realized she had been had. She couldn't resist a smile, though, as she reflected that at least this boy had learned something from eighth-grade American history.

"Very funny, Mason. What else do they call you?" Barbara's easy response was natural; she could usually take and even enjoy a little teasing from her students. She had found that this approach tended to minimize the us-her attitude that could fester in classrooms. But the quartet's reaction to Barbara's friendly response was anything but appreciative. Her failure to be punitive or angry was apparently taken as license to act out. The boy sitting behind "Mason" pushed him roughly, and the two boys sitting across the aisle laughed so hard—or pretended to—that they rolled out of their seats and into the aisle. Once away from their desks, they simply stood up and moved off in search of more interesting pursuits out of Barbara's range.

Barbara couldn't believe what had just happened, and when she looked up, she saw that the brief tempering effect achieved with the pointer had evaporated while she focused on Mason Dixon. She turned to him angrily. "What is your *name?*"

"Lincoln Maxwell," replied Mason Dixon. His tone was now matter-of-fact, and a small smile played at the corner of his mouth. His expression was so soft that Barbara almost read pity in his eyes.

"Thank you." She glanced down the roster, found his name, and checked it off. She consulted the seating chart she had tucked under the roster on her clipboard. "You will sit at the second desk in the third row." Glancing at the thirty other students milling around the room, Barbara turned to the boy behind Lincoln with a growing sense of futility. "What is your name?"

"George," replied the tall student who lounged easily at the tiny tablet desk.

"George what?" asked Barbara as patiently as possible.

"George Washington, nice to meet you. What's your name?"

Barbara looked at the student's irritating grin and turned away without reply. She marched to the front of the room and over to the metal filing cabinet that abutted the teacher's desk. Retrieving the pointer, Barbara called as loudly as she could without yelling, "Class, enough. *Take a seat!*" With that, she slammed the pointer into the side of the metal cabinet and felt the impact travel through her wrist and up her arm.

The crack commanded the students' attention, at least, and Barbara moved swiftly to seize what might be her only chance. "You, in the back. Sit down. Here, take a seat." As she spoke, Barbara moved toward the windows and the few students who remained standing. As they sat in nearby desks, she quickly filled the silence. "I will read your names. When your name is called, come to the front and sign out a book. Then go sit at the desk I assign."

"What, assigned seats?" The long-haired girl who had pushed her way into the room complained loudly from the rear.

"What is this, middle school again?" Angela took up her friend's cause.

"I don' wanna move!" Another student joined the fray.

Barbara ignored them and walked to the front desk in the row by the windows. "Andersen, Christine." Barbara scanned the faces now watching her sullenly. "Is Christine here?"

A tall blonde who looked at least 16 rose gracefully—and provocatively, Barbara thought. "Ooohh . . ." A soft sound of appreciation arose from the back of the room, but the rest of the class remained mercifully quiet.

"Hello, Christine. Please sign this card, take a book, and sit at this desk. Baxter, Manuel? Is Manuel here?"

"What—I gotta sit in the front just because my name starts with *B?* Forget it!"

"Manuel, I am assigning seats alphabetically, and yours is here behind Christine. We will change seating periodically throughout the year. Now go get a book."

Barbara proceeded as quickly as she could down her roster, tolerating the soft conversation that recurred among those students not getting a book or moving to a new seat. She had twelve of them seated when she got to Jared Jackson.

"Jackson, Jared? Come on, Marsha, hurry now." As she looked for a response to her call for Jared, she encouraged a girl in the book line to move along. Barbara glanced at her watch and realized she had ten minutes left in the period in which to finish assigning seats and signing out texts, explain class rules, introduce the course, and make tomorrow's assignment. She tried not to let impatience show in her voice.

"Is Jared here?" Suddenly the small boy who had introduced himself as he entered the classroom a half hour ago popped up from a seat at the back of the room. He glanced at the desk Barbara now stood beside.

"Call me Jackson. I don' wanna sit there."

"I'm assigning seats alphabetically for now, Jackson. Please get your book and then sit here."

"No. I don' wanna sit there." Jackson glanced furtively at two boys Barbara had already placed at desks nearby.

"Well, little man, come sit by us!" Sasha Campeau grinned innocently.

"Yea, wassa matter? Hey, lady, he's in the wrong class anyway. Jackson, din' you know ya gotta be as tall as this line to go on this ride? Get back to grade school." Joe Denton held out his hand about 4 feet above the floor and looked around the room for a response to his witticism. As Sasha complied with loud and affected laughter, Barbara felt her irritation rise again.

"Sasha and Joe, quiet down. Jackson, you sit up there, in the first seat of the next row." Jackson swaggered past Barbara and his enemies, and Barbara glanced again at her watch. She realized that she was never going to get everyone rearranged before the bell rang.

As she looked up from her watch, Barbara spotted Lincoln, the student who had relented by giving her his real name twenty minutes ago. Sitting at a desk she had not yet reassigned, he was speaking softly to "George Washington," whose real identity she still did not know. "Lincoln, will you and George Washington go get the rest of the books and put one on each of the rest of the desks? Everyone else, stay where you are and raise your hand when I call your name. We have better things to do than play musical chairs for the rest of this period."

Grumbling and the hum of elevated conversation greeted this pronouncement. "Hey, lady, this was your idea!"

"Gee, she's testy!"

"Make up your mind!"

"Does that mean you're not assigning seats? Can I go sit by Angela?" Marie Firabello, the long-haired girl who had shoved her way into the room an eternity ago, called from her assigned seat in the second row and indicated her friend across the room.

"No, uh . . ." Barbara consulted her seating chart. "No, Marie, stay where you are. Sarah Larsen? Is Sarah here?"

"What a bitch!" Marie's reply to Barbara's refusal was clearly audible, but Barbara decided to let it go. By now the seven minutes left in the period seemed like forever.

Sarah Larsen raised her hand, and Barbara checked off her name. "Edward Minot?" Barbara looked around in vain and was about to pencil an X by that name when George Washington came around from behind her with his arms full of textbooks. "Yo!"

Barbara smiled and mustered the little good humor she felt she had left. "Nice to meet ya. Name's Mrs. Parker." Barbara checked off Edward's name and called out the next; with four minutes to go she had identified every student and taken attendance. She put the clipboard down on the desk and stood straight, facing the class.

"This is ninth-grade Afro-Asian studies. I am Mrs. Parker, and I am looking forward to a fruitful year. Tomorrow when you come into class, I want each of you to take the seat you are now sitting in, and I want you in your seats by the bell. I do not have many rules, but promptness is one of them." As she spoke, Barbara realized that she was again competing with the sounds of student conversations in the room. She reached for the pointer and whacked the desk. Heads turned; some students laughed, but most became quiet.

"This course will begin with the study of countries in the Middle East. If you look at the table of contents in your books, you will see that we are also going to study Africa, Asia, China, and Japan before the year is over. I think you will find these cultures . . ."

A scuffle and muted laughter distracted Barbara and captured the attention of the class, which turned en masse to look toward the sounds at the back of the room. Lincoln had apparently grabbed Edward's book when Edward tried to open it, and a page was ripped halfway out of the book.

"Lincoln, sit back in your seat. Keep your hands to yourself." Barbara refocused on the rest of the class. "I do not usually go over class rules explicitly with my high school students; most of my classes are old enough to behave. But I see that I must start by teaching you all how to act in high school. Tomorrow we will begin with a review of my class rules and what you can expect if you do not follow . . ."

The harsh air-horn sound of the bell drowned out Barbara's words, and the students rose as a unit to make their escape. Desks scraped linoleum, papers shuffled and books banged, and thirty-one students began uninhibited and unrestrained conversation. Barbara just watched them go.

* * *

Barbara heard the bell signaling the beginning of the seventh period and looked up from her preparations. About half of her twenty-eight students (she had mercifully lost two to transfers and one to the American Beauty Academy) were seated. Others cruised the room or hovered, talking and laughing, just outside the room.

Barbara marched purposefully toward the open door and waved the students into the room. "All right, inside. Names will go on the board. Let's move!" To herself, she thought, "Lord, I hate this class." With a sigh, she donned the mental armor she would need to face another day with these students.

After her dreadful first day, Barbara had spoken to friends who taught at the Littleton Middle School. They were astounded that so many difficult students had been placed in a single class. Barbara had to contend with several distinct groups of troublemakers, and since none of these groups looked to the others for leadership or direction, what worked to quiet one group seldom worked with the others.

In the two months that had passed since the first day of class, Barbara tightened control and established a routine. Rules were explained and posted: Come to class on time; come prepared; speak and listen respectfully. Barbara also introduced a luncheon detention system as a lever to enforce the rules, since school policy required an administrator's decision to impose after-school detention. Lunch detention was not nearly the deterrent for these kids that after-school detention would be, especially since many of the boys were now trying out for junior varsity teams and had practice after school. But it was the best she could do.

Barbara returned to the teacher's desk and stood behind it. "Good afternoon. I see notebooks out and open on only a few desks, and you know that being prepared in this class means being ready to take notes." Barbara was tempted to chastise the class further; it was early November, yet the students were still acting as if it were the first week of school. But she had discovered that nagging often backfired, and she tried to remain as businesslike as possible.

She glanced down at the notes she had spread on the desk in front of her. During this pause, students shuffled papers, retrieved notebooks, and whispered and giggled. Barbara began speaking loudly enough to be heard above this rustle. "This week we are going to begin our study of Iraq and Iran. Last week we completed our study of the history of this region, and you know that the Tigris and Euphrates rivers, which flow through modern-day Iraq, formed the cradle of civilization, which was . . ."

"Miz Parker, I don' got no pen." Lincoln Maxwell waved his hand wildly from his seat smack in the center of the room.

"Oh, Lincoln, again? All right, get up here." Lincoln uncoiled his long legs from underneath the tablet desk and strolled forward. When he reached her desk, Barbara handed him a pen from the top drawer and asked, "Where's your collateral?" She had begun "selling" supplies in this class as a relatively efficient way to minimize the delay caused by unprepared students. Students could use her supplies as long as they gave her something to hold as collateral; they would get their collateral back when they returned the borrowed item.

"Uh, like what?"

"Come on, Lincoln, you know the drill. You are wasting time." Barbara thought there might be some hope for Lincoln, but he was so often a source of delay and distraction in the class that she had little time to encourage the possibility. Lincoln came from a single-parent family, and when Barbara telephoned his mother, the woman mumbled something about her job and Lincoln's job and said that class matters were Barbara's job. Lincoln wasn't as blatant as some of the other characters in the class, but he was frequently a cause of disruption.

Behind Lincoln's back the class was getting more and more restless. "While we're at this, does anyone else need a pen?" Barbara had been interrupted more than once on many days, and she decided to get it over with. Two more students raised their hands, and she waved them forward.

"Here's a Whitney Houston tape," volunteered Angela as she tossed the cassette onto Barbara's desk.

"God, that's mine. Don't give her that!" Marie Firabello, whom Barbara had placed at the front desk in the center row, could clearly see the transactions going on at the teacher's desk.

Barbara ignored Marie and smiled at Angela. The two girls were friends, and Barbara thought Marie was a terrible influence on Angela's behavior in class. Barbara had decided on a divide-and-conquer strategy with the pair.

"Don't worry, Angela, you'll get it back," Barbara said as she met Angela's gaze with a genuine smile. "I already have that tape." Angela looked both surprised and impressed and smiled back at Barbara hesitatingly. "I'm not so bad after all, sweetheart," Barbara thought to herself as she watched Angela return to her seat.

When the other students had returned to their seats, Barbara tried to pick up the thread of her introduction. "All right. What was the name of the ancient civilization we first studied, which was located here?" As she spoke, Barbara pointed to Iraq on the map of the world that hung in front of the chalkboard. The class stared back at her in stony silence, except for two boys who were passing notes in the back of the room.

"Come on, people. We just had a test on this last week. Edward, what civilization was located at the Euphrates River?" Barbara addressed the question this time to George Washington, who was half of the pair passing notes in the back. She walked down the aisle toward him as she spoke.

Edward looked up blankly. "Uh, could you repeat the question?"

"Never mind, Edward. Give me the note." Barbara held out her hand, and the boy surrendered the torn slip of paper he had crumpled in his fist. She walked back to the front of the room and wrote Edward's and Robert's names in the leftmost corner of the board, beginning her lunch-detention list for the day. Then she turned to the class.

"Mesopotamia, class. Mesopotamia was the civilization we studied three weeks ago that was located where Iraq is today. Present-day Iraq is governed by . . ." Barbara began her introductory lecture, discouraged as usual by the class's lack of interest in participation. In other classes, Barbara sometimes used grouping, creative assignments, and projects in addition to lecturing to communicate content, but with this class any deviation invited bedlam. The students seemed to think that if she wasn't "telling," she wasn't really teaching, and they would take advantage of what they thought was an "easy" day.

So she told them about Iraq, making notes on the board as she spoke. The students were to copy the notes into their notebooks, and Barbara periodically spot-checked and graded their notebooks for neatness, thoroughness, and accuracy.

Barbara was discussing the recent hostilities between Iraq and Iran when Lincoln interrupted again.

"Miz Parker, Miz Parker?"

"Lincoln, raise your hand to speak in this class. I can see I'm going to have lots of company tomorrow." Barbara wrote Lincoln's name on the board alongside Edward, Robert, and the three others she had added to the list during her lecture.

"Oh, Jeez, Miz Parker, why you always pickin' on me? People's talkin' all the time in this class."

Barbara ignored Lincoln's complaint and tried to steer the class back to the topic. "Did you have a question about Iraq, Lincoln?"

"Well, yeah. Who was that Ayatollah guy, anyway?" Lincoln looked genuinely curious but a little embarrassed to be asking a "real" question.

Barbara was delighted. "You know who the Ayatollah was?" she asked with a sincere smile.

"Yeah—that religious nut. Who was he anyway?"

"The Ayatollah Khomeini was the religious and political leader of Iran until his death last year," replied Barbara. "That was a good question, Lincoln, and we will talk more about the Ayatollah starting on Wednesday, when we'll talk about Iran in more detail. Let's get back now to where we were in chapter 9 so that we can finish the introduction and do the worksheet on Iraq today."

After five more minutes, Barbara completed her comments and reached for the pile of worksheets in her book bag. "I want you to complete these individually while I walk around the room to look at your notebooks." A collective groan greeted this announcement, since several of the students hadn't opened a notebook during her overview (which was precisely why Barbara had decided to grade them today). She began handing papers to the students at the front desk of each row.

Marie Firabello, the student at the front of the middle row, was Barbara's biggest problem. Marie came from a large and extended Italian family; most of her relatives lived in North Littleton, and she had many cousins in the school. Barbara had spoken to Mrs. Firabello, who was timid and resigned and no help at all: "Oh, I know, Mrs. Parker. I'm having so much trouble with her—it's the age." Barbara suspected that Marie led a wild social life and was experimenting at least with liquor if not drugs.

Marie's challenges to Barbara's authority were so frequent and so brash that Barbara bluntly encouraged the girl to transfer out of the class. But Marie elected to stay and harass her.

Characteristically, Marie was ready when Barbara approached. "I don't want to do no dumb worksheet again. My boyfriend Rick is in your morning class, and he said they did some deal where they wrote a letter home from visiting some shrine or something?"

Marie was referring, Barbara knew, to her honors Afro-Asian studies class, which was as different from this class as night from day. There were only fourteen students in the class, and they were lively, interested, and motivated. They were a chapter ahead of the seventh-period class, studying .the tenets of Islam, partly because they moved through material more quickly and partly because Barbara had abbreviated her coverage of ancient history with them in order to focus on current events in the Middle East. Rick had told Marie about the assignment in which the students pretended they were visiting Mecca and wrote home about their experiences.

"Marie, I'm glad Rick liked that assignment. Maybe we'll do that or something similar when we get to our study of the Moslem religion." Barbara smiled, handed Marie the worksheets for her row, and turned to move on.

"You think you're hot shit, don't you?" Marie snarled to Barbara's back. The ten or so students within earshot hooted and laughed, and Barbara began to feel real anger. "I hate that girl, and she hates me—period," she thought. Aloud, she said, "All right, Marie, that's it. Not another minute in my class."

"What'ya mean?" asked Marie indignantly.

"You may not stay in this class after that outburst. Stand in the hall, right now." Barbara indicated the door to Marie and crossed to the telephone, which hung on the wall by the door. Barbara waved Marie toward the hall as she lifted the receiver to call the office.

Marie slammed her books together in a show of bravado designed to mask her embarrassment and flounced out of the room. Barbara completed her conversation with the school secretary and then followed Marie outside to ensure that she stood where Barbara could see her through the open door until a staff member arrived.

After Marie was settled, Barbara returned to the classroom, resigned to the inevitable disruption that this episode had caused. As she reentered the room, a paper airplane made of the Iraq worksheet sailed by her head. Conversation and laughter swirled throughout the room. Several students were standing by the open windows, sailing airplanes outside and calling to friends.

"All right, ladies and gentlemen, quiet down." Barbara no longer hesitated to raise her voice to the level required to compete with this group. "We've had enough excitement for one day." Barbara crossed purposefully to the other side of the classroom and shooed the standing students to their seats, closing the windows as she did so. "Back to work. These worksheets will be collected in ten minutes so you'd better get busy."

"Hey, Babs, I ain't got no book. How'm I gonna do a worksheet?" cried Jackson loudly. Barbara sighed as she turned to the board and wrote Jackson's name in the detention space; then she retrieved her own book on her way back to his desk. Barbara really liked this kid, but she couldn't tolerate disrespect. "My name is Mrs. Parker, and next time remember your book!" she said as she handed Jackson hers.

Barbara gradually got the students settled. As they worked on their task, she managed to review notebooks—or annotate the absence of same—for seven students. Soft conversation permeated the room, but that was all right. When completing worksheets, students were allowed to ask each other for help, as long as the answering student gave only the number of the page where the answer could be found rather than the answer itself. Barbara assumed that the hum of conversation out of her direct hearing was productive, for she hadn't the energy to mount a challenge now. She kept one eye on Marie, sulking in the hallway, at all times; it took about five minutes for Sandy, a school secretary, to come for the girl.

Barbara completed marking a notebook grade in her grade book and scanned the room. Lincoln, she saw, had fallen asleep. Barbara generally left Lincoln alone when he dozed off in class; the periods when he slept were among the class's more productive ones. "Probably drugs," Barbara thought sadly, remembering his expression of shy curiosity when he'd asked about Khomeini.

Without warning the bell rang and the students scrambled for the door. Lincoln lazily stretched and sat up, closed his book, and rose to go. Several incomplete worksheets littered desks and the floor, and two texts had been left in the classroom.

Barbara walked slowly to the front of the room and began to erase the board. Angela came to reclaim her tape; the others either forgot or didn't care about whatever they'd left in exchange. As Barbara watched Angela go and gazed at the empty room, a feeling of malaise crept upon her. She wondered unhappily what she might do to break this class "or when this class will break me."

PART TWO

LEARNING

CASE 6

THERESE CARMEN

A first-grade teacher in her second year of teaching is presented with a new districtwide science curriculum that she finds unteachable.

Therese Carmen looked out over her class of seventeen first-graders and smiled as she watched them prepare for the science lesson.

"Maybe I love first-graders so much," she thought, "because they are so defenseless, so needy." Therese walked up one aisle and down the next, helping one child make a place for his math book in his desk and another fit her crayons back into their box. The children, while fidgety and noisy, were responsive to Therese's attention, and their immature behavior and dependence did not bother her.

Once all the desks were clear, Therese began her introduction to the lesson. She perched at the edge of her desk and held up several circles of different colors and sizes. "What are these?" she asked.

Some children responded. "Balls, dots. . . ."

"Yes, these look like balls and dots. What *shape* are they?" Therese emphasized the word *shape* and pointed to a bulletin board that showed circles, squares, and triangles.

"Circles." Most of the children called out the answer.

"Good. These are circles. Are all the circles the same?"

The children were quiet. Some were no longer watching Therese. William called out, "Some are different."

"How are they different, William?"

"Some are red."

"Yes, some are red. Let's put the red ones here." Therese put the red circles on the flannel board and looked out at her students. Three or four had opened their desks and were looking inside. Other students were bouncing in their seats or talking to the children next to them. Fewer than half of the students were watching Therese.

"It's this damn science curriculum," Therese thought as she observed her students. The curriculum seemed poorly matched to the needs of her students and to their maturity levels. It was written by a new science coordinator, Carol Miller, who had been appointed two years earlier. The elementary level of the new science curriculum evolved from her work with a committee of elementary school teachers. It took them a year and two summers to produce the curriculum that Therese was now trying, unsuccessfully, to use. She wondered which of the teachers on the committee had decided that first-graders would be ready, in October, to begin a two-week unit on classification. Regardless, she plunged ahead.

"OK, everybody. Eyes front. Look at Miss Carmen. Rosa, Anthony, Jacob." As she called the names of several students, all the children turned toward her.

"William told us that some circles are different because they are red. Kelly, how are some other circles different?"

Kelly shook her head but didn't answer.

"Tiffany, do you know?"

"Some are round."

"Yes, all circles are round. How are they *different*?"

When none of the students responded, Therese answered her own question. "Some of the circles are yellow," she said as she placed the yellow circles underneath the red ones on the flannel board.

"What color do I have left?"

"Blue," several students responded.

"Good," Therese said enthusiastically as she put the blue circles on the flannel board. "We have circles that are different *colors*. What colors are they, class?"

A few children answered, but most were no longer looking at the teacher or the flannel board. Again, Therese thought about what a poor idea it was to teach classification in this way to first-grade children. It occurred to her that tomorrow might be better because the lesson involved animals, and she knew that the children would be more interested in animals than in circles.

But she had to get through today's lesson before she could introduce tomorrow's, so she again sought the children's attention to continue the discussion.

* * *

Two weeks after the classification unit, Therese went to see Marie Sharp, the third-grade teacher whose classroom was next to Therese's. Marie had been teaching for more than twenty years, and she was a wonderful resource for her new colleague. In the year and two months that she had been teaching, Therese had come to see Marie as her mentor: Marie was able to help when Therese wasn't sure what to do with a problem in her classroom, and Marie's years in the district had "sharpened her eye," so she was also Therese's source of advice about political issues. Since Therese considered her problems with the science curriculum as both academic and political, she was again turning to Marie for counsel.

Marie smiled as Therese walked into her classroom. "Hi, how was your weekend?"

Therese returned the greeting and went on: "Actually, my weekend was lousy, since you asked. I spent hours working on my lesson plans for the next science unit. I thought I'd get some help at the grade-level meeting on Friday, but I seem to be the only first-grade teacher having a problem with the curriculum. You should have heard the other teachers when Carol asked how teaching the new curriculum was going. I couldn't believe it. I can't be the only teacher having trouble with the lessons, but no one said anything except how well the classes were going. I was the only one to bring up problems."

"What did you say?"

"I explained that I felt some of the lessons were impractical for young students. Remember the lesson on classification I told you about? The manual called for the students to use animal crackers as part of the lesson. The kids ate the cookies as soon as I handed them out. I told that story."

"And what was the response?"

"That's just it. No one agreed with me. I said that I thought some of the units were unrealistic. I also talked about how elaborate some of the lessons were and how much time I'm spending making the 'props' I need for the lessons. First-grade classrooms aren't equipped for science. And not one other teacher said anything. I really felt like a fool."

Marie looked sympathetic, so Therese went on. "What's going on, Marie? Why the silence?"

"Don't forget Therese, Carol's got a lot invested in the new science curriculum. She's still pretty new as science coordinator, and the science curriculum is her first big project. The teachers are probably changing the lessons. I'd guess that they've figured out how to work around the curriculum, and they're just not talking about it."

Marie's last comment actually gave Therese some relief. "Then I really don't have to use this curriculum," she thought to herself. "I can pretty much do what I want."

Therese hadn't told Marie that she was going to be observed the following week and that the principal had specifically told Therese that she wanted to see a science lesson. But now that she and Marie had talked, she knew what to do for the principal's visit. She was feeling better already.

LITTLETON SCHOOL DISTRICT
K–2 Science Program

TEACHERS' GUIDE
Lesson Plan Ideas

Level: K–2 Science Curriculum
Topic: Science Skill—Classification
Week: 6

Lesson 1

Objective: To enable students to see that objects can be grouped and regrouped according to certain characteristics.

Method: In this lesson the teacher will model the skill of classification. Using one or more shapes familiar to the students, demonstrate how to sort the shape(s) by different characteristics. These characteristics may be color, size, texture, etc.

Once the initial classification is understood, demonstrate that the shapes can be reclassified by another characteristic.

Lesson 2

Objective: To provide guided practice in grouping and regrouping objects according to certain characteristics.

Method: Using animal crackers (or something similar), have the students sort the animals by different characteristics, such as the number of legs, the length of tail, the humps on body, etc.

Once the initial classification is understood, help the students to see that they can reclassify the shapes by a different characteristic.

Lesson 3

Objective: To give students independent practice in grouping and regrouping a variety of objects according to certain characteristics.

Method: Using materials available in the classroom (erasers, pencils, chalk, books, etc.), have the students sort the objects by different characteristics. These characteristics may be shape, size, color, usage, etc.

Then have the students reclassify by another characteristic. Be sure that the students understand the characteristic that is common to each sorting.

JOYCE DAVIDSON

*A high school English teacher is not making much progress with
a remedial English class and is particularly concerned about an
extremely shy student.*

Joyce Davidson gazed unhappily at the folder of papers on the table in front
of her and then raised her head to scan the study hall she was monitoring.
Students were whispering quietly or working. Joyce knew that she should
concentrate on grading the papers she had brought, but the next period was
her ninth-period remedial English class, and she often used this study hall
just to regroup mentally and try to find the reserves of energy she would
need to manage the class. "This just wasn't such a problem last year,"
Joyce thought ruefully. "Maybe Beth's lack of participation is getting to
me."

This was Joyce's second year teaching in the English department at
Littleton High School. Joyce enjoyed her job partly because it was demanding, but dealing with this particular English class for ninth- and tenth-graders
was a special challenge. The class was loud and boisterous and tough to
control, except for one quiet little girl. Beth Martin had been in the same
class with Joyce last year, as had six others of her thirteen students, but
this year the child seemed increasingly withdrawn and indifferent. Joyce
herself was an outgoing, gregarious person, and a withdrawn child caused
her concern.

"Well, for one thing," Joyce thought, "last year I had this class first
period. Ninth period is the worst time of day for everyone." It wasn't so
much that Beth was tired or difficult at the end of the day; it was that the
rest of the class was so much louder and intimidating. "At 7:45 in the
morning they've hardly woken up," Joyce thought with a smile.

Beth was a short blond girl of 16. She had a slow gait and a timid manner;
she entered the classroom every afternoon with her books held tight to her
chest as if it were the first day of class. All the students in Joyce's class
were reading well below grade level, but Beth seemed to have the most

difficulty. Most of the rest of the class exhibited more behavior problems than academic ones. Beth's file reported a slight speech delay, which Joyce thought was a considerable understatement, since Beth almost never spoke in Joyce's class. Beth was not an independent thinker and worked best on worksheets or with rote material. Her reading grade level was about 4.5, and her written work matched her reading level.

Joyce thought that Beth was immature in her outside activities as well and that this contributed to her isolation. Beth seemed to be overprotected by her parents. Joyce's mental image of Beth being picked up at the bus stop by her mother, going home, having a snack, and watching cartoons crystalized for her the challenge of getting this 16-year-old girl to interact with a class full of loud and rambunctious teenagers in order to learn.

Last year, Joyce had wondered whether assignment to a special education class might serve Beth better than the remedial track she was now in. She had inquired about Beth's placement and learned that Beth had been evaluated in middle school and that the test results indicated that she was not eligible for special services. Joyce agreed in principle with the concept of regular classroom instruction whenever possible, and she had vowed to make Beth's time in her class productive.

There were four levels of classes in most academic subjects at Littleton High, which the administration tried not to refer to as "tracks." Joyce's ninth-period English class was a remedial class. Most of the students in it were in remedial classes all day except for art, music, and gym, which were not grouped by ability. Joyce's class this year was also larger than the one in which Beth had been placed last year: Last year Joyce had had only ten students in the sophomore remedial English class. She knew that had been a real luxury; in fact, she was lucky to have only thirteen students this year. The class was made up of eleven boys and two girls; the other girl was as flamboyant and aggressive as Beth was reserved. Angela was Peruvian and, at 17, was one of the oldest students in the class. She had confided to Joyce that when she first arrived in the United States four years ago, she had been as quiet and shy as Beth, a claim Joyce thought preposterous. Angela was Beth's antithesis.

The boys in the class were an engaging mixture of personalities: enthusiastic, friendly, loud, and occasionally hyperactive. There was one other shy student in the class, but his reserve was very different from Beth's. Rao, who was West Indian, was intellectually alert and conscientious; his assignment to Joyce's class was the result of difficulty with English as a second language. Rao's withdrawal was probably due to fear of being drawn into misbehavior by his peers; Beth's isolation seemed to be the result of indifference.

The boys in Joyce's class were black or Hispanic. All were sophisticated and worldly; their poor reading skills had not prevented them from becoming social creatures who participated actively in life outside the school. This participation was not all positive: Pedro, for example, was fond of flashing wads of bills and occasionally wore a beeper in class.

LITTLETON HIGH SCHOOL

Class: Tenth-grade English

Teacher: Joyce Davidson

Period: Ninth

Name	End of ninth grade MAT scores*	Total reading†	Reading compre- hension‡	Vocab- ulary‡
Antiero, Angela	33	4	6.7	6.9
Ayagari, Mahon-Rao	55	6	7.9	8.1
Booth, David	31	4	6.4	5.5
Bowen, Harold	9	2	5.0	5.1
Diaz, Ernesto	18	3	5.8	5.0
Espitia, Luis	49	5	7.7	7.8
Fernandez, Carlos	8	1	4.9	4.9
Lawson, Jesse	28	3	6.0	6.1
Martin, Elizabeth	5	1	4.4	4.6
Maxwell, Leon	30	2	5.1	5.2
Sanchez, Pedro	10	2	5.4	5.8
Washington, Tyrone	35	4	6.0	6.4
Wilson, Anton	11	2	5.5	5.6

* Metropolitan Achievement Test scores, reported in percentiles.

† Stanine scores; 1 = low, 5 = average, 9 = high.

‡ Grade-equivalent scores; 6.7 means seventh month of sixth grade.

Joyce worked hard to ensure that her students were comfortable in her class so that they could participate freely. While the price of this atmosphere was an occasional behavior problem, Joyce felt that it was crucial to establish a positive, risk-free climate if her students were to learn.

Joyce actually jumped when the bell rang signaling the end of the eighth period, and she thought once again what an irritating sound it was. She sighed as she stuffed her unopened folders into her book bag and headed toward ninth-period English. "Still all questions and no answers," she thought.

Joyce opened the solid, heavy door to the small classroom and immediately saw Beth sitting at a desk. Beth was always the first to arrive. "Hi, Beth," Joyce said with a smile. "How was your weekend?"

Beth did not answer, at least not audibly, and Joyce quickly began setting out materials for the day's lesson. Not having a room permanently assigned made teaching much more difficult. Joyce could not decorate, post students' work, or otherwise personalize the classroom. The L-shaped room was longer than it was wide, making seating difficult, and it seemed crowded even though furnished with only fifteen desks. By ninth period, the desks were awry, the wastebaskets were full, and the air was thick with the smell of lunch recently served in the cafeteria next door.

For weeks, Joyce's class had been working on nouns and adjectives: What are they? How are they identified? How are they used? Joyce was permitted some latitude in course content, and she tried to choose reading and writing activities over grammar whenever she could. But at least two-thirds of the sophomore curriculum was mandated, and parts of speech were unavoidable. Joyce was having trouble getting her students to focus on these lessons, and she found it difficult to make the material interesting and meaningful.

Today, Joyce planned to review the subject *again* and then group the students for an exercise designed to give them practice in what they had been learning. As usual, she had tried to design a lesson that would hold her students' attention in spite of their distractibility and boisterousness.

"OK, settle down and listen up," Joyce said loudly enough to be heard as soon as the bell rang and the last student let the door slam behind him. "I know everyone had a good weekend, but it's time to get to work!"

"Yo, Miss D, what are those magazines for?" called a tall boy who lounged comfortably at a desk by the window.

"They're for you, Tyrone, and your teammate, after you come up here to the board and help me out," replied Joyce with a big smile. General laughter greeted Joyce's invitation to Tyrone, as he groaned and affected great reluctance. In fact, it was no easy matter for him to pull his long, powerful legs from beneath the desk to come to the board.

When Tyrone was beside her, Joyce handed him the chalk and said, "Write an example of a noun, Tyrone."

Tyrone took the chalk and turned to look at Joyce. "I can't think of no noun."

"Sure you can, nouns are everywhere." Joyce gestured widely with her arm.

Tyrone's eyes followed Joyce's gesture, and then they lit up as an idea occurred to him. Joyce just loved seeing that look on her students' faces. Tyrone turned to the board and wrote the word *air* with a flourish. Looking pleased with himself, he pivoted to return to his seat. "Wait, Tyrone. That's fine," said Joyce, and she put out a hand to keep him with her. He rolled his eyes good-naturedly. Joyce knew he loved the spotlight. She turned her attention to the class. "*Air*—that's a noun, right? Luis, tell Tyrone a sentence to write using this noun."

Luis's desk was at the back of the classroom, and he was leaning back in his chair, pulling at the cord of the telephone on the wall near the door. He pulled it and let it snap back a few times as he thought. "Tyrone is a air head," he finally said solemnly. The class erupted in laughter, and Tyrone threw the chalk in Luis's direction as he, too, laughed.

Joyce was smiling even as she tried not to laugh. She mentally rehearsed the sentence in her head and contemplated a response. She realized that Luis had stumbled upon one of the few possible usages of the word *air* as an adjective, and she could not resist the urge to use his contribution positively. Joyce knew she risked fanning the fire with these students, since insults were the "stuff" of their constant confrontations, but she couldn't let the opportunity pass.

"Write it," she said to Tyrone, gesturing toward the board and handing him a new piece of chalk. Her students loved to write with new, long pieces of chalk.

"No way," Tyrone laughed, and he refused the chalk. Joyce was laughing with her students as she went to the board herself and wrote "Mr. X is an" and "head" around the word *air,* which Tyrone had already supplied. As Joyce turned to the class, the students were still laughing. Joyce held up her hand and waited, indicating to Tyrone with her eyes that he could return to his seat. In a minute the class quieted down enough for her to be heard.

"*Air* in this sentence is not a noun, Luis," Joyce said matter of factly. "What is it?"

Luis looked at Joyce blankly. Joyce persisted. "Luis, how is the word *air* used in your sentence?"

Luis looked around, as if trying to find the answer on the walls or the ceiling, and Joyce waited. Slowing herself down had been one of her biggest challenges in this job, but she had learned. Only when Luis reached for the phone cord again did Joyce help him out. "Luis, look at the board." When he was looking up, she continued. "Everyone look at the board. Is air what the sentence is talking about? Luis, what is the sentence talking about?"

"Mr. X," Luis replied slowly. He and the other students were following Joyce now. Joyce saw that Beth was looking in her direction also, and Joyce thought about calling on her. But it was unlikely that Beth would respond, and these moments came too rarely with this class to break her momentum now.

"Right!" Joyce exclaimed. "*Mr. X* is one noun in the sentence. We know it's a noun because it's the name of someone." Joyce underlined *Mr. X* and continued. "What else is the sentence talking about? What other word is a noun? Angela?"

"Head!" Angela shouted. The class laughed at Angela's style as much as at her answer, and Joyce waited again.

"OK," Joyce said when she could be heard. "You are right. *Head* is a noun because it is the name of something. Now, listen, here it comes. What kind of head? David. What kind of head?"

"Air head!" David answered.

"Right. Luis, what is the word *air* in this sentence? It tells us what kind of head we are talking about. How is the word *air* used in the sentence?"

Luis was really concentrating as he looked at the sentence. "It's an adjective!" he said. The class was looking at the board with him.

"Right!" Joyce smiled. She sat on the corner of the teacher's desk and let her shoulders drop a little. Her relaxation seemed to touch the class. As the students sat back in their chairs, she repeated Luis's words. "*Air* is an adjective in this sentence, not a noun. We are not talking about air in this sentence. *Air* tells us about the word after it. *Air* describes the next word; it modifies the next word. *Air* is an adjective here. Usually, in most sentences, *air* is a noun, but in the sentence Luis made up, *air* is an adjective.''

Joyce got up and went to the board. She erased the sentence and wrote ''Beth flies through the air.'' ''Beth, where is a noun in this sentence? Beth?''

Beth was looking at Joyce, and Joyce made eye contact, but she was not sure the girl had heard her. Tyrone called out from the rear, ''*Beth* is a noun.''

''I want to hear from Beth,'' Joyce said. ''Let's give each other time to answer. Beth, Tyrone was right. The word *Beth* in this sentence is a noun— a proper noun because it is a person's name. What is another noun in this sentence?'' Joyce leaned a little toward Beth as she held her left hand under the sentence on the board. This time the class waited, although as the seconds passed, the inevitable whispering, shuffling, and laughing began. Finally Beth softly said, ''I can't fly.''

As her class broke into new peals of laughter, Joyce glanced at the clock. By now she was running short on time. The class's earlier laughter had been for a good cause, but it was time-consuming. Joyce knew that Beth was not trying to be obtuse, but she was slowing the class down.

''Quiet down,'' Joyce admonished. She took a deep breath. ''Beth, pretend you can fly. Think about the sentence here on the board. Your name, the word *Beth* [Joyce underlined the word *Beth* as she spoke], is one noun in this sentence. What other word in the sentence is a noun?''

Beth looked a long time at the board. Noises from outside the room filtered in. (The school dismissed some students early to catch buses, and the bus stop was right outside the classroom windows.) Joyce prayed she wouldn't have to wait so long that the rest of the class would start throwing things at the kids outside.

Finally Beth spoke, so softly that Joyce had to read her lips to hear her. ''Air?''

''Louder, Beth. Say it so that the class can hear you.''

''Air?'' Beth repeated, still hesitatingly.

''Right! Air! *Air* is a noun in this sentence. It was an adjective in the sentence before.'' Joyce scanned the class to look for expressions of comprehension or confusion. ''Do you all understand?''

Sure enough, the delay in waiting for Beth to answer had broken the other students' train of thought. Joyce saw a few quizzical looks and a few expressions of understanding, but the rest of her class had forgotten the topic. Joyce felt frustrated: Learning had been happening a moment before, but now she had lost the students. Joyce seldom proceeded without ensuring complete understanding, but she had to move on if she was to get her next activity done.

''Now we are going to pair off. I want each of you to work with one other person. We have a project to do about nouns and adjectives." Joyce began to pair students sitting next to one another. "Angela, you work with Pedro. Beth, you work with Tyrone. Luis . . ."

"I don' wanna work with her," Tyrone interrupted.

Joyce used grouping often in her class, and she usually allowed students to work with whomever they chose, especially when they were working in pairs. Most of the time the students were fairly tolerant of Beth, seeming to recognize her differences, but they did not socialize with her and seldom wanted to work with her. Joyce did not tolerate rudeness, but Beth was often so blank and indifferent that Joyce thought simple remarks like Tyrone's went right over her head. In any event, Joyce elected not to challenge Tyrone. "You may work with whomever you want." Tyrone happily rose and walked over to Luis. Their earlier exchange had apparently made them fast friends.

"Miss Bartino, will you please work with Beth?" Joyce indicated Tyrone's vacant seat for her assistant, who had been watching quietly from the back of the room. Joyce often used Anita Bartino to work individually with Beth, anyway. When they were working in pairs, Joyce needed Anita to round out the number, and Beth certainly needed the extra attention.

Joyce got all the students teamed and explained their assignment. They were to search for examples of nouns or adjectives in the magazines she had brought and were to cut them out and paste them onto construction paper in an appropriate arrangement or design. Joyce gave the students some examples, showing them how they could choose just nouns, just adjectives, or nouns and adjectives all on a certain theme (all about fashion, for instance). She told them that supplies—scissors, glue, markers, crayons— were available at the center of the room on a supply table. Joyce usually orchestrated projects in this way so that the entire class was required to cooperate in order for individual teams to obtain materials.

The students were more or less occupied with their task as Joyce walked from pair to pair. She worked for a time with Tyrone and Luis, and then she turned and saw Beth sitting alone, looking quietly at the magazine on her desk. Anita had partially turned her chair away from Beth and was answering a question for another group.

Joyce approached the girl and spoke softly. "Beth, do you need something?"

Beth looked at Joyce without much expression. "Scissors," she answered softly.

"You know we have to share materials in this class, Beth," Joyce said. Beth did not reply. "How do you get supplies that you need?"

"Ask?" Beth asked quietly.

"That's right, Beth," Joyce replied. "Ask the other kids for what you need. We have to share."

Beth looked doubtfully at Joyce and then spoke in the general direction of the rest of the class. "Can I have the scissors, please?"

"Louder, Beth" persisted Joyce. "You have to speak up to get what you want in this class." Anita turned away from the other group and began to move her chair toward Beth, but Joyce stopped her with a glance. Beth remained mute.

"Beth, this is a loud, noisy class. You have to talk loud enough for the others to hear you and ask them for what you need. Just ask again so that they can hear you."

Finally Beth repeated the phrase. "Can I have the scissors?" Her voice was still soft, but Pedro, her nearest neighbor, heard her. He handed a pair of scissors back to Beth without turning around.

"There! See!" Joyce spoke brightly, verbalizing her pleasure with Beth's accomplishment. "You just have to ask!" Joyce nodded toward Anita, who then moved her chair around to work with Beth.

Joyce walked back to the front of the room to collect the students' work and dismiss the class. She was really worried about Beth. Joyce thought her approach and personal style were beginning to work for the rest of the students, and she did not want to jeopardize their progress. But after a year and a quarter she still had not found the combination that would unlock Beth's mind and bring her into the group.

SCOTT DONOVAN

*A high school English teacher discovers that four of his students
plagiarized parts of a lengthy writing assignment.*

Scott Donovan closed his briefcase and walked toward room 209 anticipating
a good class. He enjoyed his second-period sophomore English class, and
he was pleased with the assignment he planned to give the students this
morning. Scott had taken a book which he found personally dull and arcane,
but which was part of the required curriculum, and he had created an
assignment designed to make it palatable. He was anxious to get the reaction
of his class.

Scott was a second-year teacher at Littleton High School. He had been
one of eighty-five applicants for the position he now held, and his credentials
and experience made him the most competitive candidate. After graduating
from an eastern university, Scott worked for fifteen years as an editor and
reporter for an aerospace newspaper and for an information service company
in the metropolitan area around Littleton. He recently completed a master's
program in education, and he embarked on his second career, as a teacher,
with enthusiasm as well as with the realism that comes from experience.

Scott's second-period English class was one of his favorites. It was an
above-average-level class, which meant that the students were generally
college-bound, although not as proficient as those in the honors or the
honors AP classes. There were only fifteen students in the class, and they
were as involved as he could expect high school students to be with
sophomore English.

There were ten boys and five girls in the class, and their ethnic mix was
fairly typical of the community: two black students, one Hispanic, and the
balance Caucasian. Scott conducted all his classes with an emphasis on
discussion and writing, and this class participated intelligently in the
discussions, which were a pleasure to mediate. But the students' writing
was less commendable. Their composition skills were weak and their

grammar atrocious. At the beginning of the year, Scott gave the class a grammar pretest, and he was shocked at the poor results. Of the three passing scores, two were earned by German students who had learned English in Germany as a second language.

Since writing was his field, Scott had resolved to help his students improve. To date he had done a lot of remedial work on grammar and some short essay work. The class had read two of the six novels required by the curriculum, and Scott had led some lively discussions about them. He now felt the students were ready to undertake a more challenging writing assignment based upon the next novel they would read.

Three of the novels in the sophomore English curriculum were identified specifically, but Scott could exercise his discretion on the other three. The three required texts were *Giants in the Earth*, *The Red Badge of Courage*, and *The Scarlet Letter*. The class had already read *The Old Man and the Sea* and *Of Mice and Men*, two of Scott's favorite novels. Now Scott had decided to bow to the inevitable and tackle *Giants in the Earth*, the novel he considered the worst of the three mandated texts.

Scott reached the room in which he taught this class—he shared it with other teachers and found this mildly inconvenient—and pulled out the attendance roster and other materials that he kept filed in the room. He greeted the students as they entered, and he dispensed with his opening procedures quickly.

"Now I am going to tell you about the assignment that will keep us occupied for the next five weeks," Scott began. "We are going to read the novel *Giants in the Earth*." Scott held a copy of the book aloft as he walked to a corner of the room and brought back a cardboard box. He placed it on the desk of a young man in the front row. "Hand those out, will you, Tom?" he asked.

Scott continued as Tom took several books from the box and began to distribute them. "This book is by O. E. Rolvaag, a Norwegian. This is probably the only novel you will ever read that was translated from Norwegian. The book evokes a strong feeling of how hard life was for Norwegian immigrants on the American prairie—not unlike novels about the experiences of other Americans as they moved west. You know, you can almost feel the bleakness of the surroundings. Major themes that you will find in the novel are the struggle of man against nature and man against man."

As Tom distributed the books and the students had a chance to leaf through them, a few groans became audible and a few pupils exchanged stupefied looks.

"Mr. Donovan—it's so long!"

"Five weeks! How about five months?"

Scott smiled at the students' gripes and continued: "Listen, reading full-length novels is an important step in becoming fluent consumers of the written word. While you're working through *Giants* at home, we'll continue our composition work in class, so you won't have much other homework."

Scott moved back to the desk at the front of the room and pulled a folder from his briefcase. "I am handing out a pacing schedule now. It will guide you as to how far you should have read by certain dates. The schedule calls for reading two chapters each week. I've left the two weeks of Christmas break open, so you can use that time for catch-up. But you can expect a reading check test at each milestone on this schedule, so don't let it slide too far."

A girl waved her hand from the back of the room. "Yes, Amy?"

"What will be on these tests?"

"Oh, one might be on key characters or events that occur in the chapters you have read. Or I might give you a quotation quiz—identify who said a particular line or speech in the book." More groans greeted this explanation.

"Don't worry. I'll be more specific about each check test before we have it. The tests are really just to keep you honest about time. I don't want you to fall behind, because I haven't told you yet about the best part of the assignment."

"You mean there's more?"

"We do take other courses, you know!"

Again Scott smiled as the class objected. He was anxious to tell them about the assignment and refused to let their mostly good-natured objections dampen his enthusiasm for his next idea. "Listen, now. This is important. The reason it is so crucial for you to keep up with the reading is that I want each of you to keep a journal as you read. As you complete each chapter, I want you to write a personal response to the text."

"What do you mean, a personal response? Like, did we like it?" blurted Tom.

"Well, yes. But be organized about it. Start each journal entry with the title of the chapter. Summarize what the title means literally and speculate about its meaning in the context of the rest of the book. Then write a personal reaction: Did you like the chapter? Was it realistic? Did each character seem logical? Things like that. Look at the bottom of the pacing sheet. I've included directions for the journal."

"Mr. Donovan, there's ten chapters in this book," complained a boy in the second row, who had his novel open to the table of contents. "How long is this journal supposed to be?"

"Well, you'll obviously have ten journal entries, one for each chapter. Even though your journal is due when you've completed the book, it will be much easier for you if you write each entry as soon as you finish reading each chapter. Don't wait until the night before it's due to write it all."

"Yeah, but how long should it be?" persisted another student.

"Well, each journal entry should probably be about 250 words. That's only one page, typed," replied Scott. He had anticipated this question, knowing that high school sophomores were very uncomfortable without concrete quantification of assignments. In this case the length of each student's writing sample actually was important. He planned to use a coding scheme that he had developed as an editor to critique and analyze writing styles. Scott wanted to help the students improve their writing, and he needed a long-enough writing sample to make it worthwhile. Ten entries of about 250 words each would give him a rich view of each student's writing; he would be able to isolate faults in composition or identify characteristics of the individual writing styles. But Scott wanted the students to write naturally, so he had decided not to tell them about his intended use of their journals.

Amy was looking at the pacing sheet and holding the book in her hand as if weighing it. "This journal is due January 15?"

"Right. Seven weeks from today, counting the holidays. No excuses and no extensions. The journal is due when the pacing sheet says you're to have completed reading."

"How much of our grade is this worth?" asked Harry from the back of the room. Harry was slouched down in his seat and looked distinctly depressed.

"Oh, thanks for reminding me, Harry. All the parts of this assignment— the journal, our class discussions of the book after you've read it, and the reading check tests—are worth 400 out of 700 grading points for this quarter. In other words, the book and the activities about the book are worth more than half your grade for this marking period. So be serious here."

Resigned silence greeted this final directive as the class digested the information and seemed to realize the futility of further objections. "Any other questions? Are you clear on this?" A few students nodded, and the rest remained noncommittal. "Well, as you proceed with your reading, please ask me if you're confused about my intentions. Now let's turn to page 63 in your composition books and pick up where we left off yesterday." Papers were shuffled as students switched materials, and a new topic was undertaken.

* * *

Scott scraped back the chair from his kitchen table so abruptly that he almost fell backward. He could not remember any time that he had been so angry—not even at secretaries or reporters or copy editors, all of whom routinely irritated him in his previous job. He was infuriated.

Six hours ago, Scott sat down at his kitchen table and faced the mountain of papers in front of him with a combination of resignation and anticipation. He had thousands of words to read, analyze, and grade, and as he looked at the stack, he wished that he had asked the students to hand in their journals periodically rather than only at the end. But this regret was quickly brushed aside by Scott's curiosity and interest in the students' thoughts and opinions.

Now, however, his curiosity was replaced by anger and incredulity. Scott leaned forward to study the journal in front of him. "Tom!" Scott actually spoke aloud, "How could you do this?"

Scott had just read the last of the fourteen journals his students had submitted, and the frustration that had germinated on the due date now grew into wrath. On the day the journals were due, two students came to class without them and two were absent—suspiciously so, in Scott's opinion. One of the students who came to class empty-handed turned his journal in the next day, as did the two "sick" students, but Harry simply admitted that he had neither read the book nor written a journal.

Yet Scott's irritation over these events was minor compared with his disappointment now that he had read the papers. For while ten of the journals were acceptable, he was sure that four of his students had copied significant sections of the commercially published *Cliff Notes* into their journals. They had even copied the same sections—in collusion or not, Scott did not know. The similarity of the passages was Scott's first clue that something was awry. On rereading he was sure, as the writing style of a high school sophomore abruptly changed to the smooth prose of a professional writer in each of the four journals.

Scott's anger was dissipating as he gazed at Tom's paper, but it was replaced by a feeling much harder to bear: defeat. Scott had sincerely wanted to teach using this assignment. Even though he did not particularly like *Giants in the Earth,* he thought he had designed a meaningful assignment around a required part of the curriculum. Now, if the plagiarism meant that these students had not read the book, then a third of his class would be unable to participate in the class discussions Scott had planned for the coming week. Obviously, critiquing their writing was out of the question; what was the point of analyzing a professional writer's pat synopsis?

Furthermore, Scott's personal code of ethics and his professional training and experience made him view plagiarism as the worst crime a literate person could commit. His first reaction was that he should fail the four students who had acted so irresponsibly; in fact, he had already marked a large red F on the cover page of the journal in front of him. But then he began to wonder if he had somehow encouraged their dishonesty by the way he constructed the assignment.

Scott picked up Tom's entry for chapter 3 and read it once more. It did seem as though Tom had read the chapter; there were passages reporting on his personal reaction that were recognizably his work. But the section of the entry which summarized the plot was clearly not original.

"Damn it," Scott thought, "I gave these kids a grown-up assignment, and they blew it. Was I off base?"

Scott noticed that he had knocked over the salt shaker, and grains of salt were sprinkled over several papers. With a sigh he rose and switched off the kitchen light, leaving his briefcase open on the floor and the papers strewn about. Scott walked slowly upstairs, wanting to react firmly, even angrily, but also wanting to be fair. Nothing in his experience or training had prepared him for this. He did not know what to do.

ALICE PETERSON

*An experienced elementary school teacher is having problems with
a prefirst-grade class in which every student brings unique (and
difficult) problems into the classroom, leading her to wonder if
she is reaching anyone.*

Alice Peterson drove to work mentally agonizing over the same dilemma
that faced her every school day: how to help her students learn. Alice taught
a class of prefirst-grade children at the Mason Elementary School in Eastvale,
a small town outside Chicago. This year was proving to be the most
challenging and the most frustrating of Alice's twenty-eight-year career.

The Eastvale school district served a heterogeneous school population.
More than 40 percent of the students were black or Hispanic, and about a
quarter of the school population qualified for the free or reduced-cost lunch
program. There were also many students from middle- or upper-middle-
class families.

Three years ago the school district introduced a prefirst class in an attempt
to serve developmentally latent children. Over the past ten years or so, the
kindergarten curriculum had become more academic, with less attention
paid to readiness and group social skills. For some children, an academic
kindergarten was not the best preparation for formal schooling; they needed
more time before they faced the demands of first grade. On the basis of
testing and the recommendations of their kindergarten teacher, such children
were placed in a prefirst class rather than first grade at the end of their
kindergarten year.

Alice held strong opinions about the prefirst concept, both as intended
and as actualized. If it was used properly by parents and educators together,
she knew that the opportunity to spend another year growing and developing
could work magic for some children.

But many parents, particularly well-educated ones, saw assignment to
prefirst grade as an indication of failure; they argued adamantly to have
their children placed in first grade, despite test scores and teacher recommen-

dations. Parents' attitudes were crucial to the success of this program. If a child detected a negative attitude about prefirst grade from his or her parents, the child would be likely to develop the same attitude and might benefit less from the extra year. Accordingly, the district often accommodated parents' wishes.

Since it was typically the middle-class parents who rejected the prefirst class for their children, the students actually placed in these classes often came from poor, disadvantaged, minority backgrounds. Furthermore, since there was only one prefirst class in any school, all the least mature 6-year-olds were placed in one classroom rather than distributed throughout several first-grade rooms. Despite these two drawbacks, Alice initially had seen the prefirst assignment as a challenge and believed that she could make a difference in these children's lives.

Alice tried to ensure that her students developed a sense of confidence and self-worth, which the experience of "failing kindergarten" had already undermined. She began the school year using kindergarten curriculum and in January began to introduce first-grade materials. In this way, she hoped that her students would have a head start relative to their peers when they entered first grade the following fall. Alice had followed her game plan this year and started using more advanced materials after Christmas, but she knew it wasn't working. This class just didn't seem ready for more advanced academic work.

Minority children were usually overrepresented in prefirst classes, but the presence of a few white students assured Alice that placement was based on age, maturity, or stage of development rather than race. This year, however, Alice thought her class configuration made teaching almost impossible. The two white children in her class were not simply immature; they each had serious deficits, physically, mentally, and emotionally. Therefore, the other children, all of whom were black or Hispanic, saw the "normal" white children being promoted to first grade and saw themselves placed in prefirst with other minorities or with white children who had obvious handicaps. Alice felt sure that these children had internalized a negative self-image as a result. Because they believed that they were dumber, slower, and naughtier than the other children in the school, Alice thought, they performed below their individual potential and ability.

At 6 years of age, these children were still enthusiastic and endearing; they each very much wanted to learn to read, for instance. But their home environments and individual histories had made them emotionally needy, and they often "acted out" to gain attention. Alice knew that children this age all craved a teacher's attention, but most children wanted to be noticed for positive things. It seemed to Alice that her students this year were happy even with negative attention. As a result, her class was often rowdy, rude, and inattentive.

Alice turned into the staff parking lot, which was framed by mounds of dirty snow plowed aside after last week's storm. As usual, she was the first to arrive. The February morning was cold, and Alice walked briskly to escape the chill. She unlocked the school door and headed toward room 105.

As she unlocked the door to her classroom, Alice was already beginning to rehearse the opening minutes of the phonics lesson she was going to conduct with her students this morning. She tried to arrive at least an hour and a half early every morning in order to finalize preparations for the day's instruction. Throughout her career Alice had invested long hours in order to teach effectively, but the fact that the results this year were so disappointing made expending the effort increasingly difficult.

Alice Peterson began her career teaching in the Chicago school system, and after three years she moved to Eastvale. She had taught every elementary grade, although most of her experience was in third and fourth grades and kindergarten. She accepted the position teaching prefirst at Mason last year because she was promised flexibility and control over the choice of curriculum. Increasingly, however, Alice felt that even though she had the flexibility to design unique instruction, she did not have the time.

Alice took off her coat and sat down behind her desk in the back of the room. She scanned the empty classroom, which she could view clearly from this vantage point, and enjoyed the peace and quiet, which would end soon.

Alice had carefully designed the arrangement of furniture and supplies in the room. The twelve desks at which the children sat for instruction all faced the front of the room, where they could see only the chalkboard and an alphabet banner above that. All the toys, art supplies, and decorations, as well as the bulletin board, were in the back of the room near the play rug. Alice had planned the room in this way in order to minimize distractions for the children as they sat at their desks and listened to lessons. For the same reason, she had their desks arranged in four rows of three each, far enough apart to minimize each child's opportunity to irritate others. Alice would have liked to group the children at tables in order to foster better cooperation and communication, but she was sure that this would only lead to arguments or collusive misbehavior.

Alice knew that she should review her objectives for the morning's lesson, but she sat instead just looking at those twelve desks, so neatly aligned and soon to be thoroughly askew. She let her mind wander, thinking of the children as she looked at their desks.

Barry sat at the front of the classroom, at the desk to Alice's right as she faced the students. She had purposely placed Barry at arm's reach so that she could physically assist him if necessary. Barry was one of the two white children in the class, and he had muscular dystrophy. Although he could walk, he was much slower than the other children and fell down five to ten times each day. He had been placed at Mason because it was the only elementary school in the district without stairs.

Alice thought Barry was a spoiled brat. He was self-centered and did not adjust well to the social environment of the classroom. Barry did not display much respect for authority and was very headstrong. He had temper tantrums when challenged, complete with screaming and kicking.

Yet Alice was most concerned for his safety. Barry would topple over with the slightest shove from a classmate, and Alice found herself constantly maneuvering to be near him in order to catch him if he fell. This, of course, was an unacceptable situation, since the frequently rowdy misbehavior of the other students also demanded her physical proximity.

Realizing this, Alice had requested an aide for Barry after the first two days of the school year. Yesterday the aide had arrived, but Anna Brown was only 17 and the mother of an infant. After her first day Alice was concerned that Anna would be more of a distraction than a help. In any event Alice would have to take time to train her explicitly in what she needed her to do. "They'll put me on the committee to hire the principal, but they won't give me a say in hiring my own aide," Alice thought as she gazed at Barry's desk.

Theresa sat at the desk behind Barry; she was a quiet, cooperative girl who generally did as she was asked. Alice's thoughts, though, quickly skipped to the last desk in the row. In a few minutes, she knew, Peter would sit there, constantly disrupting class, calling out, and harassing her.

Peter inspired Alice's sympathy when she thought about him objectively and out of the context of his misdeeds. He was a black 6-year-old whose family situation was truly sad. Peter's mother was handicapped. He was cared for by his aunt, but she could not speak because of a stroke. Peter had two brothers, one of whom was recently jailed; the other one was in the army. Peter was very attached to his 18-year-old sister, but she was living in a halfway house for drug abusers.

Peter was a chronic behavior problem. He was loud and impulsive and had developed few inner controls. He was very jealous of other children and tended to bully them. His sense of humor and his affection for adults were the traits that kept Alice trying with Peter. She had found that he responded to physical affection and to gentle teasing, and she hoped to help him develop the self-discipline he would need to succeed in school and in life.

Shoma sat next to Peter, in the last desk of the next row. Alice nearly grimaced when she thought of this child. Shoma represented an escalating problem for Alice. She was a black Haitian-American who was very tall and looked about 8 years old even though she was only 6. She was jumpy and easily distracted and displayed little interest in schoolwork. Alice thought of Shoma as an angry child. Shoma often reacted defiantly to Alice's instructions, and Alice worried about the constant frown on the child's face. Shoma's mother had so far been unavailable for a conference in spite of Alice's repeated attempts to solicit her help.

Alice's gaze continued along the desks at the rear of each row. Don, the other white child in the class, sat at the desk to Shoma's right. Alice thought Don might have a neurological problem. He was deficient in his small motor skills—he couldn't hold a pencil correctly, for instance—and he just didn't seem to make mental connections. All his work was rote, with no evidence of thinking taking place at all. Even in behavioral issues, Alice could not reach him or break through to reason with him. It was not that he was purposely dense; he seemed unable to understand the relationship between his behavior and consequences. Alice would never forget the time when Don screamed an obscenity at another child, was sent to the office, and still asked for a star at the end of the day. Alice had been unable to communicate to him the relationship between his behavior in the morning and his reward in the afternoon.

Don's parents were trying not to panic over their obviously handicapped oldest child, Alice thought. Don had two sisters, ages 4 and 3, who could do more than he, and this was having an impact on Don's self-confidence. There had been some discussions between Don's parents and school personnel about special testing at a private rehabilitation center in town, but they were all concerned about the messages that this additional testing would send to an already insecure child.

Alice realized that special education placement was a possibility for Don, but she hoped, along with his parents, that this could be prevented. In fact, Alice knew that prefirst was in some instances an attempt to make the regular curriculum and the mainstream system work for children on the edge. She wanted very much to make it work for her students.

Thinking about special education made Alice's mind wander to Luis, who sat in the desk next to Don. Luis was Hispanic, and even though English was spoken in his home, he was practically nonverbal and very shy. Alice had heard rumors that Luis's mother was on crack and that she supported her habit through prostitution.

Whatever his true home situation, Luis did have difficulties in school. His shyness made it difficult for him to relate to the other children, and when he did engage them, it was often in a belligerent or impulsive way. When he expressed himself verbally, it was often by cursing.

Luis sometimes lapsed into silly moods in which he could not control his giggles or his need to rock in rhythmic patterns. At these times, Alice would ask Luis to help clean the room. His interest in picking up toys or sweeping the floor was the antidote for his private pain.

Alice tried to shake her reflective mood and reached into her desk for the phonics worksheets. But as she did so, her mind traveled involuntarily from thoughts of Luis, in the back of row four, to little Darryl Washington, in the front. Darryl's birthday was in August, which made him one of the youngest in his grade; he was born four months prematurely to a mother in her forties and a father in his fifties. Both Mr. and Mrs. Washington were retired employees of the school system.

Alice thought that both of Darryl's parents were overprotective of him, and it seemed that they were in school almost daily checking on him. Darryl was in occupational therapy for fine motor skills and was in private counseling because of his behavior problems.

Actually, Darryl's behavior had improved since the first of the school year, although he still had lapses such as sneaking around behind Alice's back or being physically disruptive by jumping or yelling. Alice thought he perpetrated these antics mostly to attract friends. Like almost all her students, Darryl had a temper tantrum from time to time, and his typical reaction to discipline or even mild correction from Alice was, "I'm gonna' tell my mama on you!"

Alice began to hear the sounds of children in the halls and bus traffic at the front of the building. "Where did the time go?" she wondered as she moved from behind her desk to look at the clock in the back of the room. It was 8:40.

The students in Alice's class were beginning to line up in the hallway outside the door. She opened it to invite the first three inside. "Good morning, Shoma. Hi Don, Darryl," she said pleasantly as they entered.

Alice had found that permitting all the children to enter the room at the same time invited bedlam. The lockers were inside the room, and the process of removing outerwear inevitably led to pushing and shoving if the children were shoulder to shoulder when they took off their coats. Children were placed in this class in part because of language deficiencies, and they tended to express themselves physically rather than verbally. Although the students might jostle and argue in the line outside the room, Alice preferred that to misbehavior in the classroom.

Shoma, Darryl, and Don moved toward their desks. The children knew that after they put their things away, they were to go to their desks, where work was waiting for them. Last night, Alice had set out a copying exercise, designed to practice handwriting.

Alice, who still stood at the classroom doorway with one eye on the hall and the other on the room, gestured to the next students in line. "Barry, Peter, good morning." She then greeted the new aide. "Oh, hello, Anna. I'm glad you're here."

Just then Peter stopped short in front of Barry at the lockers, causing Barry to bump into him and teeter to the left. Anna had been looking at Gumdrop, the class rabbit, and she noticed too late that Barry was about to fall. She reached out to catch him but missed, and Barry hit his hip on a desk as he fell to the floor. The desk, luckily, was fairly insubstantial, and it was pushed noisily to the side by the force of Barry's fall.

Barry looked momentarily as though he might cry, but he visibly held his feelings in check and began to collect his things, which had scattered when he fell. As Barry picked himself up with Anna's help, the children waiting in the hall pushed forward to investigate the commotion. Peter turned and laughed, enjoying the fact that he had captured the attention of the other children.

Alice had not been sure that Peter's abrupt stop was intentional until she saw his expression. She put a hand out to signal that the children in the hall should stay put, and then she went to Barry and Peter.

"Peter, what you just did to Barry was mean and rude," Alice admonished. "Turn around and apologize."

Peter was facing his locker, acting as if he had not heard Alice. A little louder, and with a touch of impatience, Alice repeated herself. "Say you are sorry, Peter!"

Peter turned to Barry, who was now on his feet and trying to escape any further notice. "Sorry," he mumbled. Barry looked up fleetingly at Peter and headed toward his desk. Anna followed him and pulled a small chair beside it for herself.

Alice ushered the rest of the children into the room and glanced at the clock as they made their ways haphazardly to their desks. By the time the last students to enter were seated or standing in the vicinity of their desks, the children who had entered first were now out of their seats and talking. Alice moved to the front of the room to begin her day.

She started each day with a routine the children could depend upon. She noted that Luis was absent, made her introductory comments, and walked back to her desk and located the phonics worksheets. The instant she left the front of the room, the conversation and activity that were a constant in her classroom escalated. Alice walked from desk to desk, handing a worksheet to each child, and began to speak more loudly than usual in an attempt to recapture the group's attention.

"Let's start by looking at the blue side of this paper," Alice said. Most of the children turned to the correct side. "On this worksheet we're looking for the *eh* sound. Look at the first picture. What is that?"

As Alice began talking, the din subsided somewhat, but there was still noise in the room. Peter was humming quietly at his desk; Shoma was alternating between rocking in her chair and jumping up and down in her seat. Other children were just talking—sometimes to themselves, sometimes to each other. Alice was used to the constant hum in her classroom and usually addressed it only when it became overpowering.

"Darryl, what is that in the top picture?" Alice repeated.

Darryl had been sitting sideways at his desk, but now he turned to the front to face Alice. "A elephant," Darryl answered.

"What sound starts that word?" Alice continued, looking at the entire group. "Do you hear the *eh, eh, eh* sound? Circle that elephant. Now what is the next picture?"

About half of the children were involved now with Alice's lesson, either watching and listening to her or focusing on their worksheets. A few of these mumbled an answer to Alice's question. "Bird," she heard faintly.

"It's a special kind of bird," Alice replied. "An ostrich. *Oh, oh,* ostrich. Do you hear the *eh* sound there? *Eh, eh, eh?* No. Get rid of that ostrich. Now what is the next word? Barry?"

Barry had his head on his desk, and Anna sat beside him craning her neck to see over his head in order to follow along. Barry's eyes were on Alice even though he was bent over. "An egg," Barry replied.

Before Alice could respond, she heard Peter speaking from the back of the room. "My teeth are falling out," he said.

Alice walked back toward Peter's desk. "I know they are falling out,

Peter. And there is nothing I can do about it, unless I knock them out."
She smiled as she reached Peter and playfully touched his chin with her fist.
"I could knock them out." The rest of the children laughed loudly. Alice
particularly heard Don, laughing more raucously than the joke justified.

"Shh," Alice said gently as she turned to walk back to the front of the
class. "I know your teeth hurt, Peter, and I'm sorry they hurt. But there is
nothing I can do about it."

When she was back in front, Alice tried to pick up where she had left
off, momentarily hunting in her book for the picture she had been asking
about. "*Eh, eh,* egg," Alice said. "Right. Circle that egg. Now the next
word—what is the next picture?"

As she spoke, Alice realized that the noise level in the classroom was
slightly higher. She also saw that Shoma was becoming a real distraction in
the back row as she bounced in place or stood up, leaning her elbows on
her desk, and wiggled her hips.

"Shoma, what is the next picture?"

Shoma took a minute to find the picture. "A apple." Shoma seemed to
spit her reply at Alice.

"*Ah, ah,* apple. Do you hear the *eh* sound?" Alice was again addressing
the entire class. "No. Throw out that apple; get rid of that apple. Now what is
the next picture? An igloo, right? Do you hear the *eh* sound in the word *igloo?*
No, not in igloo. Now the next picture—Peter, what is the next picture?"

Peter looked up at Alice with a vague expression, and Alice walked down
the row of desks to his. She gestured toward the picture in question on his
worksheet. "What is that, Peter?"

Peter answered promptly, "A elevator."

"*Eh, eh,* elevator. Hear it? Yes! Circle that picture. Now what is the last
picture?"

"An arm," Darryl called out exuberantly.

"No, it's a special part of your arm," Alice replied, holding her right
elbow with her left hand as she bent her arm. "An elbow," she said. As
she spoke, Darryl said "elbow" with her simultaneously.

"*Eh, eh,* elbow. Hear the sound?" Alice was now walking up and down
the rows between the desks as she spoke. "Circle that picture."

"You should each have four circles on your papers. Do you have four?"
Alice bent over each paper as she moved from desk to desk. "Sit still,
Shoma," she said as she came to Shoma's desk.

When Alice had glanced at most of the papers to see that the children
were following her, she walked back to the front of the room. "Now I don't
know if we should do the green side of the paper. It's awfully hard." Alice
looked doubtful. "Let's turn to the green side."

Barry said something unintelligible, which Alice took to be "no." With
a smile she said to the class as a whole, "Don't you like trying hard things?"
She got no answer from the five or six children listening to her, but she did
see Peter's hand waving in the back.

"You didn't check my paper," Peter called. Without commenting, Alice walked back to his desk and drew a star on his worksheet; she then pivoted to look at Shoma's paper and drew a star on it also.

"Do you remember last week when we were doing word families?" Alice asked. She got no response. She moved to the side of the room where a large poster hung on the wall from a previous lesson, in which like-sounding words (*mix, fix, six*) were written in groups. Alice thought briefly of drawing a parallel to an earlier lesson but then thought better of it. She walked back to the board and picked up the chalk. Alice wrote the word *bed* on the board.

"Now are you looking at the green side of the worksheet? Now look up here. See this word? *Bed.* Hear the *eh* sound in the middle of it? Now if I erase the middle letter [Alice did so with the heel of her hand] and change it [Alice wrote an *i* where the *e* had been] the word becomes *bid.* 'I bid my mother hello.' " Alice smiled, acknowledging the stilted sound of the sentence she had used. "The sound we are listening for is in the middle of the word."

Alice wrote a series of other words on the board: *bud, bed, bid, bad.* Don called out from the back of the room, "I know! Bug!"

"We are working with the sound in the middle of the word," Alice said, not really in reply to Don's contribution but to the class as a whole. She drew a line on the board and a circle in the middle of it. "Not the sound at the beginning and not the sound at the end; the sound in the middle.

"Now look at the picture on the top of your worksheet. What is that picture? A bed, right? See the bed?" Alice left the front of the room and walked from desk to desk as she spoke. "*Eh, eh,* bed. Hear the *eh* sound in the middle of the word? Circle the bed."

"Now what is the next picture? Theresa?"

"Sock," said Theresa.

"Sock," repeated Alice. "Sss . . . oh . . . ck. Hear an *eh* sound? Who hears it?" Alice gestured a thumbs-up sign with her hand, indicating to the children that they should signal with their hands if they heard the sound. She had found that any physical activity she could weave into a lesson helped them listen and remember. But too few children were with her this morning. "It's always worse on a Monday," Alice thought to herself as she persevered. "Who doesn't hear it?" she asked, gesturing thumbs down. A few children responded. "Who isn't really sure?" Alice got no response. "*Eh, oh.* No. Get rid of that sock."

Alice realized as she paced the rows that nine of the eleven children were lost. Several were engaged in conversation with their neighbors, and the rest were looking out the window or at the wrong picture on the paper. "Let's finish this another time," Alice said as she walked back to the front of the room. "I'm going to collect your papers now. We'll do the green side later." Alice walked to each child's place, collecting worksheets.

As she walked to the back of the room to deposit the worksheets on her desk, Alice said, "Please take your storybooks out now." A few groans greeted this request, which Alice ignored. She exchanged the worksheets for her storybook guide and went back to the front of the room.

The children shuffled possessions inside their desks, looking for the right book, and the general din increased. Suddenly Don spilled a plastic container of Cuisenaire rods onto the floor, and they bounced on the linoleum, scattering under desks in the back third of the room. Don laughed and began picking them up, crawling around on his hands and knees. Alice had found there were too many of these interruptions for her to wait for their resolution, so she continued in spite of the distraction Don was causing.

"Turn to page 30. Are you all on page 30?" Alice went to a few desks to help each child find the right page. The picture on the page was entitled "Dressing Up" and depicted children in an attic playing with old clothes. Alice saw, out of the corner of her eye, that another boy had joined Don on the floor, but they were almost finished picking up the rods, so she let it go.

Alice began the picture story by asking the children to define an attic. As usual, she got no immediate response from the class, but this time she didn't know if it was due to the children's language deficiencies or the fact that most of them had never heard of an attic. She went to the chalkboard and drew a house, placing a big star under the roof.

"This is an attic, children," Alice said. "It is right under the roof, and sometimes people store old things up there. Do any of you have an attic in your houses? Barry, do you have an attic in your house?"

"I don't know," said Barry.

Alice decided to go on. She looked at her teacher's guide for another item to discuss, but she couldn't immediately locate anything that would be familiar to the children. The picture in the guide was only a black and white outline of the picture in the children's books. Alice walked to the back of the classroom, toward Luis's empty desk. "I'll use Luis's book, since he's not here. My book doesn't have the big colored picture that your books have, and I can't see everything we are talking about."

"You can have my book," Don volunteered.

"No, that's all right. I'll use Luis's." Alice sat down at Luis's desk and resumed the lesson from there.

Alice returned to the conversation about attics by asking the children where, in their houses, their parents stored old things. "Where does your mother store your old baby clothes, Theresa?" she asked. The children indicated various storage spots in their homes or said that their parents didn't store things at all. Alice then asked the class to identify various things in the picture: a dresser, a trunk, a rocking chair.

By now, Alice was again on her feet and walking up and down the rows. "What else is in the picture?" She heard no reply. "Name some things you would use to decorate the walls of a house."

The conversation about the picture continued haltingly for a few minutes, until Alice glanced at the clock and saw that it was almost 9:45. She closed her book and walked back to Luis's desk to replace his.

"Tomorrow we will talk about the picture on the next page and do some rhyming," Alice said. "We will have fun with that. For now, you may close your books and put them away. Take out your reading workbooks." The children began closing their books and putting them away in their desks.

Alice walked from desk to desk, getting each child started on a workbook exercise. A few children sat still at their desks and began to work, and Alice went to sit at the round reading table. One child, then two, then several left their desks. Some of the children stood talking in small groups; a few others stood at the reading table, waiting to speak with Alice. Shoma, who was still at her desk, began to call out, to no one in particular but generally in Alice's direction.

"I need help!"

"You know how to do that page," Alice called back. She turned to Darryl, who was first in line at the table.

"I need help," Shoma repeated. She looked around the room and saw everyone occupied, either in work or play. She began to walk about aimlessly, carrying her workbook.

Alice helped Darryl with his question and then spoke to Theresa, who had completed her current workbook and so needed a new one. Peter was next in line. "OK, Peter, read to me, sweetheart."

As Peter read haltingly from a paperback storybook, seven other children also stood around the little table, listening to him and waiting their turn for help. Alice began sorting books and other materials into piles on the table as she listened to Peter. Occasionally she heard him stumble and looked over to his book to help him with a word. When he had finished three pages, she stopped him.

"OK, Peter. Do you want to work in your blue phonics book?" Peter's expression was her answer, and Alice relented. She saw that Darryl was in line again at the reading table. "You and Darryl can go read together." Alice looked up to see if Anna was available, but Anna was still sitting next to Barry, working with him and another boy. They were the only children still sitting at their desks. Shoma was standing behind Anna, trying to get her attention. "Ask Anna to get you mats."

Peter bounded over to a tall cabinet and tried to climb onto a chair to reach the carpet samples which served as mats. "No, you're not tall enough," called Alice. Anna looked up, saw the activity, and stood to go help Peter.

Peter and Darryl happily grabbed their mats and ran to the opposite corner of the room. They pulled the chair back from Alice's desk and crawled in under the desk. Peter reached out and pulled the chair back into the opening, enclosing the two boys in the space underneath.

Alice noticed that Shoma was again roaming the room, occasionally asking a child to look in her book and identify a picture. "What is this?"

she would ask. Alice waved her back to her seat and then turned to the next child waiting at her elbow. Alice listened as he began to read. "Page 7 is a hard one, isn't it, honey?" she said after a moment. "You keep working on page 7. Go ask Anna to help you read if you get stuck." Alice turned to the next child, and the student she had dismissed carried his book toward his own desk. He saw that Anna was busy and looked momentarily confused. Then he tossed his book onto the top of his desk and went to talk to Tyrone.

Alice quickly spoke to the remaining children at the table, answering their questions and steering them back to work independently. Shoma came up behind her as she finished with the last child in line.

"Can I have a snack now?" asked Shoma.

"No, you may not have a snack," replied Alice sharply. "Get back to your desk and get some work done!"

Alice was ready to work with Barry, but she saw that he was still engaged with Anna, so she sat quietly at the reading table, observing the groups of children talking or playing in various corners of the room. The two boys who had been hiding under her desk now surfaced and began to wander around the room. They headed toward the lockers and opened them. Alice thought about getting them back on task but realized that snack time was imminent and that any new activity would probably be interrupted. Alice generally resisted the urge to rein her children in too tightly, believing that the opportunity to pursue self-directed activity was a gift for children who were unable to control much else in their lives.

In a few minutes Barry brought his book to Alice at the table. As Alice bent over the workbook with Barry, Anna walked to Shoma.

"Have you done any work yet this morning, Shoma?" she asked.

"Yes. Mrs. Peterson checked me out already, just now."

Anna looked at Shoma skeptically and glanced toward Alice, but Alice was busy, so Anna turned away to help another child.

"That's good, Barry," Alice said to Barry as he finished the exercise. "You and John are the hard workers in here today. Bring me your other book now." Barry smiled and walked back to his desk. Alice called loudly to the class as a whole. "All right, children, I am still waiting for some work from Barry, and I think Theresa is doing extra work today. The rest of you can go get your snacks." Alice sat as Barry returned with a second book, and they looked into it together as the children gradually disengaged from their various conversations and activities and went to their lockers.

Some of the children took lunch boxes or bags from their lockers and sat down with their treats. In a few minutes Alice finished with Barry, and she walked back to her desk to retrieve a package of graham crackers. She walked from desk to desk and offered a cracker to those children without a snack. She also took one for herself. The class was fairly quiet as the children ate and spoke softly to each other. Alice began setting out cards that the children would use to indicate what they wanted to do during playtime.

As the children finished eating, they moved toward the toys and began playtime activities. Some of the children first went to the front of the room, where a large poster entitled "Playtime" was hung. Alice had set out cards on which were printed the available playtime activities: "Blocks," "Lego," "Puzzles," etc. Each child chose a card—sometimes with Alice's help, as the children could not yet read—and then went to find the item named on the card chosen.

Alice went from desk to desk, wiping up crumbs and straightening the mess from snack time. Don had spilled raisins all around his desk, and she enlisted his help to pick them up.

Playtime was centered in the back of the classroom, where Alice had placed a large, colorful, inviting rug, patterned with letters and numbers. Most of the children were now busy at some activity. Two boys were playing together with wooden blocks, and three others were playing with Lego blocks, building airplanes and flying them at each other. Three girls were in the front of the room, using a Bright Lite toy.

Darryl and Don wanted to play with Lego when playtime began, but since all the cards for that activity were gone, Alice told them to find something else to do. Instead, the boys wandered back to the rug and slowly injected themselves into the Lego activity. Gradually the noise from that corner became more and more irritating. Darryl and Don's conversation was escalating.

"Darryl, Don, I want you to stop shouting!" called Alice. She was sitting at her desk trying to grade papers, but she knew she wan't going to get much done.

Just then, Luis walked into the room. Alice stood up and helped him off with his coat, noting the time as she did so: 10:20. Luis stood in the center of the room and seemed to need a minute to get oriented.

"Did you miss the bus?" Alice asked sympathetically. Luis nodded. "Did you have breakfast?"

Again, Luis nodded affirmatively, but Alice was doubtful. She went to the snack supplies and brought back a graham cracker.

Alice offered the cracker to Luis, who took it and began to eat. "What do you want to do for playtime, Luis?" she asked. Luis looked thoughtful and then walked over to the big box of waffle blocks next to Alice's desk.

"Do you want to do waffle blocks?" Alice asked. "Could you say that for me?"

Just then Alice heard shouting from Darryl and Don, who were arguing over a tower one of them had built. Alice walked quickly to the scene of the altercation. "Darryl, I want you to put that down and go sit at your desk. I told you before to stop shouting!" Darryl suddenly looked cowed, and he complied, walking quietly to his desk.

Alice turned back to Luis and saw that he had built a large maze from the giant waffle blocks. She walked over to him. "Do you want me to get Gumdrop?" she asked quietly. Luis nodded, so Alice gently lifted the rabbit's cage from a table by her desk to the floor next to Luis's structure.

Ensuring that the rabbit could not escape at the point where the cage met the blocks, Alice opened the door.

"She got really scared this morning, Luis," Alice cautioned. "We have to be especially gentle with her now." Luis watched as Gumdrop sniffed at the open door of her cage and then tentatively hopped to the rug inside the maze he had constructed. Alice smiled at Luis as they watched together.

Alice used animals extensively, not only by selecting stories about them but also by providing real experiences whenever she could. She had found that sometimes the children could relate better to animals than to people. Inner-city children, in particular, often had no other opportunity to learn about nature or to know what "cuddling" a bunny felt like.

Sometimes Alice wished Gumdrop could know how important she was to the children in the class and how instrumental she had been in helping Alice make connections with some of them. Luis, for instance, really seemed to love the animal. He helped Alice take care of the rabbit, and he often built a pen for it out of the plastic waffle blocks, as he had this morning. On those mornings when the other children joined him in this activity, Alice felt that she was really making progress.

The classroom had gotten very noisy, and several of the boys were chasing each other. Alice felt ambivalent about restraining their play, for she knew that they had nowhere else to run or to pretend. Often Alice let the play escalate as long as she could, drawing the line only when safety became a concern.

Alice witnessed a near collision between one of the boys and a desk and reacted. "Don, Darryl, stop that running around! If you're going to play with Lego, you get back on the rug!" The boys returned to the rug.

Alice saw that it was 10:55 and almost time for the children to leave for gym. The school was on a six-day cycle, and the children alternated between music, art, and gym at this time each day. Each of these special sessions was conducted elsewhere in the school.

"It's time to clean up, children," she called. Some of the children began to pick up their toys, but others continued to play. Still others stopped their games but sat without helping to straighten the room. Alice put a carrot in Gumdrop's cage to lure her back in; after the rabbit was inside, she closed the door and picked up the cage. As she tried to step over the waffle blocks to put the large cage back on its table, she banged the cage against the side of her desk.

"Oh, I'm sorry, Gumdrop," said Alice sadly. She opened the cage and petted the rabbit. "Now you're scared again. It was my fault, Gumdrop," she crooned.

Anna was helping the girls put away the Bright Lite toy, which had at some point spilled, showering tiny pegs over the floor in the front half of the room. Alice helped Luis pick up the rest of the waffle blocks and then walked to the classroom door.

"May I have Shoma and Barry at the front of the room, please?"

she called. The two children quickly complied, gladly interrupting their contribution to cleanup. "Now the rest of you line up behind them," called Alice.

By eleven o'clock most of the toys had been put away, and the children were in two lines behind Shoma and Barry. "Now I want a good report from gym, do you hear me? I want no problems with gym," Alice admonished. Several of the children nodded and grinned. "Now everyone follow me."

After escorting the children to the gym, Alice returned to room 105 grateful for the opportunity to collect her thoughts and take a mental break. Teaching always required constant vigilance in the classroom, but Alice found managing these children even more mentally exhausting than usual. As she opened her grade book to annotate comments on the morning's activity, she wondered if she could approach the problem differently.

ELIZABETH RHODES

A high school math teacher is frustrated by her advanced-placement (AP) calculus students, who want to work only for solutions to problems and do not want to apply higher-order reasoning skills.

Elizabeth Rhodes sighed as she unplugged the overhead projector and wound the thick black cord around her hand and elbow. "Well," she thought, "at least when I do all the talking it is easier."

After pushing the overhead to the back corner of the room, Elizabeth picked up the styrofoam cup on her desk. "Only two months until the calculus exam," she mused aloud, swirling the cold, muddy coffee. She put the coffee down and tore a page from the calendar on the closet door. "Will they be ready?"

This question was one that she asked herself every year at this time; it was always accompanied by the same uncomfortable uncertainty. But this year, her cause for concern went deeper. "Am I really reaching my students?" she wondered. She looked again toward the back of the room and the projector. "Am I really helping them by standing in front of them day after day talking to them?" As she left the room and headed toward the faculty lounge, she caught herself shaking her head.

"Hi, Liz," greeted Clare, Elizabeth's long-time friend from the English department. Over the eighteen years they had been at Littleton, each had served as sounding board and confidant for the other. Clare could immediately tell something was bothering her colleague.

"What's the matter?" she asked, making room at the big, messy table.

"It's those kids in my AP calc class again," responded Elizabeth. She plunked herself down next to Clare with a fresh cup of coffee.

"What did they do now?" Clare asked, leaning back in her chair.

"Well, nothing," Elizabeth smiled ruefully. "But I still don't think I'm teaching them all I could be. Here it is three-quarters of the way through the year, and all I'm doing is assigning homework and giving them tests.

They seem happy that everything is teacher-directed, but I don't think that's the right way to teach this class.''

"So just tell them what you want, then. What do you want, exactly?"

Elizabeth leaned forward and spoke earnestly. "What I want—these kids are seniors, after all—is to make them independent thinkers and problem solvers. Math is a tool for philosophers and explorers. These kids are smart enough to use math to create and discover, not just to pass tests.''

"They must be pretty bright," ventured Clare.

"You know, several of them are much quicker with math than I am," admitted Elizabeth. "I'd so like to see these kids achieve to their potential, and a few of them really could be the next generation of research mathematicians. But they just don't seem motivated to ask questions using math; their only goal is to answer them." Clare was silent as Elizabeth pensively sipped her coffee. "I thought group work might motivate them, but that opens up a whole new can of worms.''

"How so?" prompted Clare.

"Well, they see group work as a waste of time, since they're only interested in the quickest answer and they want to ignore the process. When I suggest collaborative work, forget it; they start to whine and complain. They just won't work together!''

"Sounds like the word *together* might be the problem," suggested Clare. "If I remember correctly, Ted Ryan had a similar problem with some of these kids when they were in his global studies class last year. He had a confrontation with some parents who complained that a group grade wasn't fair. Some of these high-powered kids resented a grade based on an average from the group. Most of them are so competitive, they think only of themselves.''

"They are terribly self-centered," nodded Elizabeth. "But they don't realize that I'm trying to help them compete. When they get to those high-priced colleges they're headed for, they'll have to take responsibility for their own learning. If they can't be more independent of their teachers and more communicative with their peers, they'll be at an academic disadvantage.''

"Have you tried telling them that?" asked Clare.

"Yes, but they don't believe it. They can't understand how one person's success could be intertwined with another's.''

"Great attitude. They've just been graded on a curve for too long!" laughed Clare. Suddenly she glanced at the wall clock. "Look at the time! I've got to go, Liz. Listen, if I know you, you'll stick to your guns. If you think that these kids could win Nobel prizes and learn something about discovery from group work, then my advice is to persevere! Sure, they'll complain, but you're the teacher. Remember, you have the final say!" Clare pointed her finger at Liz's grade book. "See you at lunch.''

Elizabeth pushed herself away from the faculty-room table but remained seated, thinking about Clare's advice. As she pondered her problem, her thoughts turned to individual students in AP calc.

She thought first of Melissa, a talkative and popular girl in the class. While Elizabeth would be explaining homework answers from the overnight work to the class, Melissa was one of several students who would be ignoring her, trying to complete the long-range assignment that was also due the same day. When subsequent quizzes covered material on the daily assignments, Melissa would swear that some of the material was never explained in class. Elizabeth supposed that Melissa's many obligations (she was on the yearbook staff and active in dramatics) were taking priority over homework; she thought this was a shame, since Melissa was so naturally proficient in math.

Melissa acted in school plays with Karen, who sat near Melissa in AP calculus. Karen was adamant about working alone; she did all her figuring at home and complained about minor distractions in class even when students were doing independent seatwork. The hum of group activity exacerbated her concentration problem, and so Karen was one of Elizabeth's least cooperative students.

Another contestant for that description was Bill, Elizabeth's most obnoxious student. Bill always had an answer for everything. He was impatient with mistakes on the part of his classmates and often provoked heated arguments during group work with his sarcastic remarks. Bill also had an irritating habit of asking his classmates for their test scores while not divulging his. If he perceived that he did not have the highest score in the class, he would corner Elizabeth and try to negotiate more points, in spite of the fact that he was already in the upper-A range.

Ralph was Bill's best friend. Elizabeth felt that he was the more even-tempered and good-natured of the two. In fact, she noticed him explaining problems to some of the girls from the class during lunchtime. In class he seemed to restrain himself, but Elizabeth found his desire to seek alternate methods of solving the problems to be proof that he was actually interested in getting something more from the class than just a grade.

Elizabeth stood up, resolved. "Stand by your guns" kept echoing in her head. She would give it another try.

* * *

"Are the tests corrected yet, Ms. Rhodes?" Ralph spoke politely as he and Bill burst through the classroom door.

"Yeah, how'd we do?" asked Bill with a smile as they both made a beeline for her desk.

Shooing their riffling fingers from the pack of corrected papers, Elizabeth replied, "Yes, yes, they're corrected, but first we have some work to do. Take a seat, OK?"

At this, Bill and Ralph turned and noticed the configuration of desks in the room.

"Oh, not again," moaned Bill under his breath.

"Come on, Bill, it might not be so bad. Maybe you'll get in a group with

Marlene!'' Ralph laughed at Bill's embarrassed look and shoved him good-naturedly from behind. They trudged toward a group of desks in the rear.

Karen and several other students were now entering the room, and the looks on their faces made Elizabeth begin to feel uneasy. "We aren't working in groups again, Ms. Rhodes, are we?" asked Karen. "It gets so noisy in here that I can't think!"

"Yeah . . . no groups . . . forget it!" grumbled a few other students as they wandered to the center of the room and then looked around in confusion, trying to decide where to sit.

Elizabeth had known this would not be an easy period, but her class's behavior was already irritating her. "Sit anywhere you like for now, class; later we'll count off by numbers and get into groups. I have your tests from yesterday, but I'll return them at the end of class so that you won't be distracted from our activity."

The mere mention of tests brought the class to attention. The students not yet seated sank into the clustered chairs, and several hands shot into the air. "Yes, Melissa?" acknowledged Elizabeth.

"Could we please see them now?" entreated Melissa. Her question prompted several others to join in.

"What was the grade range?"

"How many A's?"

"What was the top score?"

"No, no, I said later!" smiled Elizabeth, holding her hands out with palms down as if to physically calm her class. "You did not do badly, any of you, so relax. But I do think you will all benefit from some exercises that force you to consider options and to discuss alternative solutions. So we're going to work together today to do just that. Count off by fives: Bill, you start."

The students grudgingly complied, and with some cajoling and directing, Elizabeth shepherded them to their new seats. "OK, listen up. There are several reading problems in the packets on your desks. Work on them alone for a few minutes, and then compare your work with that of your group-mates. You might find that one person in the group used a different procedure but arrived at the same result. I want each group to determine the best approach for solving each problem and to be prepared to defend the choice. Clear?" Elizabeth scanned the room for signs of understanding. Some of the students were already hunched over the word problems on the desks, writing equations. Others weren't even in their seats; they were perched on desks in their assigned clusters or were leaning against the wall near their clusters. Elizabeth sighed and began to cruise the room.

The students seemed more or less on task during Elizabeth's first circuit, and she returned to her desk to organize her own notes about the problems they were working. As she pulled one folder from her case, she glanced at another and realized she hadn't yet recorded the students' test grades in her grade book. Elizabeth glanced up and, comfortable that the students were busy, sat to record the grades.

In a moment or two Elizabeth heard the hum of conversation; she looked up and saw Karen and Melissa conferring quietly in their group. Peter, their group-mate, was still bent over his paper. At other clusters students were beginning to converse, glancing at one another's papers as they spoke. "Maybe this will work yet," thought Elizabeth hopefully. She rose to listen to their conversations.

"How can you even think that way?" Elizabeth heard Frederick challenging Ben at the group nearest her desk.

"Well, if you know it all, how come you got *xy?*"

"Come on, guys, there's no right or wrong, just better or worse," interjected Elizabeth. "Work it out together."

"Yeah, yeah, OK," grumbled Ben as the two boys shifted their bodies away from Elizabeth. She noticed that Paula, the third member of that group, wasn't even listening to the interchange, and she circled the cluster to the girl's side.

She saw that Paula was working on the long-range assignment which was due that day; the packet of group word problems remained untouched by the girl's notebook. "Paula, put that away!" whispered Elizabeth quietly. "If you haven't finished the weekly assignment, you must hand in whatever you have finished," she continued. "Class period is for new work!"

"Oh, sorry," replied Paula apologetically. Obviously embarrassed at being discovered, she shuffled papers and turned toward Ben and Frederick. Elizabeth scanned the room, suspicious now that others of her apparently engaged students were working on the long-range assignment. She headed for Bill's table.

"Give me a *break!*" she heard Bill exclaim as she approached. He was looking at Angela's work.

"Easy, Bill," cautioned Elizabeth on her way past his desk. Comfortable that his group was at least on task, Elizabeth kept walking.

She heard Melissa and Karen deep in conversation as she approached their desks:

"Have you finished your yearbook copy?"

"No. I got the stupid assignment of covering French club and Spanish club and Latin club and all that boring bullshit. How about you? How's advertising going?"

As Elizabeth reached their sides, she asked innocently, "Could I see your conclusions, girls?"

"Oh, Ms. Rhodes, I'm going to do these tonight," offered Karen, without missing a beat. "I can't think with all this talk and noise. Peter did the problems for us anyway." Melissa indicated the third member of the group, who was bent over his text and the packet of problems.

"No, girls, the point is to discuss your work with your group-mates. You may not do them tonight." Elizabeth stood erect and noticed two students heading for the classroom door. "Joe, Robert, where are you going?" She had to call across the room in order to catch them before they were out the door.

"To the john," called Joe over his shoulder. The two boys were gone before Elizabeth could reply.

"Ms. Rhodes, I'm sorry to interrupt but could we see the tests now?" Ralph had left his group to approach Elizabeth, on a mission for Bill, she suspected. "Class ends in ten minutes."

"How are we going to be graded on this group stuff?" called Frederick from the front of the room.

"Oh, this is graded?" another student exclaimed.

"You can't grade me on this; Bill never shows his work!" exclaimed Angela.

The mention of grades had a visible effect upon the class: Students literally pushed their tablet chairs back from their groups, trying to physically distance themselves from their peers.

Elizabeth was surprised. "Please, class, don't worry about it!" The students quieted somewhat, but their frustration remained evident. "All right, I refuse to give up on this. Believe it or not, you have something to teach each other and I intend to make you try. Your homework for tonight is to complete those word problems on your own and to come to class prepared to share your approach with your group."

"Do we have the same groups?" called Alex.

"Yes. Now, I do want to return your tests and to talk about some mistakes that several of you made; they might have been avoided if you'd thought in just the way I'm asking you to do in your groups. Some of you jumped at the first right answer without thinking through the best answer." Elizabeth walked around the room placing papers face down on students' desks. "When you get your papers, turn to problem 4. Many of you indicated *d,* which is a possible correct answer, but *b* is the better solution."

Most of the students had their papers now, and the chorus of complaints again increased.

"Ms. Rhodes, *d* is right! I checked it three times!" protested Bill. "Point 003, 162!"

Elizabeth returned to her desk and picked up her own copy of the test. She turned and wrote problem 4 on the board:

4. The graph of $y = 5x^4 - x^5$ has a point of inflection at:
   a. point 00 only
   b. coordinate 3, 162 only
   c. coordinate 4, 256 only
   d. point 003, 162
   e. point 004, 256

Elizabeth turned back to the class. "Can anyone share an alternative idea about the best answer to this problem?" She scanned the room for volunteers but saw, from the expressions on the students' faces, that she might easily wait forever.

"All right, then, listen. In this case, *b* is the better answer because it is phrased as a coordinate, not a point, and when dealing with graphs . . ." As Elizabeth was finishing the explanation, the students interrupted her.

"You're kidding!"

"That's just a trick question!"

"One answer's the same as the other! Anybody with either answer ought to get credit!"

"How about half credit?"

The bell rang before Elizabeth could attempt an answer, and five or six students immediately headed for her desk as the rest gathered books and papers and rose to leave. As the line of students asking for extra points formed, Elizabeth sank wearily into her chair. She looked past her students and gazed at the room: clusters of desks disbanded and awry, problem packets strewn about, and the overhead projector sitting silently and invitingly in the rear.

PART THREE

EFFECTIVE TEACHING

MARIE DUPONT

A college student observes a high school French class and learns how a good teacher handles all the events of a typical class.

Debby Barton ran down the central hallway at Littleton High School, wanting to absorb the scenes of adolescence around her but rushing because she was late for her field placement observation. Debby was a sophomore at Metropolitan University, majoring in English with an education minor. Her assignment this semester was to observe and assist for twenty hours at the high school as part of an educational psychology course. She was savoring, even as she ran, the "feel" of a high school again; the two years since she had been a senior seemed an eternity.

Debby was irritated with herself for being late; she found room 233 less than thirty seconds after the bell rang and opened the knob without stopping to catch her breath. Marie Dupont already had her class of twenty-two freshmen settled and was saying something to the students in French. She turned toward the opening door, smiled, and said, "Bonjour."

Debby wished immediately that she had thought about this assignment enough beforehand to conjure up some of her own high school French so that she could have replied. In fact, she had forgotten that this was a French class, if she had ever been told. Her adviser at the university had simply given her Ms. Dupont's phone number and told her that she would see a pro in action. He told her that Marie Dupont graduated from Metropolitan's education program two years before, having pursued another career for several years before entering teaching, and that the faculty thought very highly of her when she was at the university.

"Good morning," Debby murmured, and then she felt sillier than she had from being late; this was the eighth period, and it was one o'clock in the afternoon.

"This is . . . I'm sorry, I've forgotten your last name," Marie said. "Perhaps you could introduce yourself to the class."

"Sure." Debby gathered her thoughts and smiled at the terribly young-looking faces staring at her expectantly and a bit irreverently. "My name is Debby Barton. I am a student at Metropolitan University, and I am studying to be a teacher. Ms. Dupont has been kind enough to let me watch your class today. . . ."

"Because you guys are such a great class!" interrupted Marie. The students burst into raucous applause, during which Marie smiled at Debby and indicated an empty desk at the back of the room.

The chairs were arranged uniquely. While the room itself was standard high school issue—beige cement-block walls; metal-framed crank windows at the rear; green chalkboard at the front, with the teacher's desk in front of the board; bulletin board on the right—the usual arrangement of tablet desks in rows was replaced with what looked like an upside-down *v*. The point of the *v* started at the teacher's desk, and the legs of the *v* angled backward toward the two rear corners of the room. The desks on either side of the *v* were angled inward slightly, so that the students faced each other across the *v*, although their general orientation was to the front.

Debby's first reaction was that the room looked messy, and in fact the desks were askew by this time of the day. But she also felt a pleasant air of informality in the classroom, and she noticed that the students were addressing each other as well as Marie when they spoke.

Debby made her way down the outside of the *v* to an empty desk in the back. As she took a seat, Marie resumed her conversation with the class. Debby caught "Giants" and "Browns" between Marie's fast and fluent French and intuited that this was a conversation about the pro-football playoff games televised over the weekend. The class was trying valiantly, with mixed success, to understand and answer Marie's questions.

"Maintenant. Qu'est-ce que vous avez fait ce weekend? Ellen?" Marie changed the subject with this question, and Debby tried to translate along with Ellen. During the pause as Ellen thought, Debby heard "weekend" and "I went skiing" from the opposite side of the *v*. Two girls on that side of the room began a quiet conversation in earnest, and a general hum, which Debby now realized had been present all along, escalated until it was distracting.

"Sshh . . ." Marie put her hands out at her sides in a gesture for quiet and sidestepped two paces toward the noisiest perpetrators. After a moment it seemed apparent that Ellen wasn't going to answer, and Marie turned to one of the girls who had been talking. "Denise, qu'est-ce que vous avez fait ce weekend?"

Denise immediately assumed that self-conscious look of a novice speaker of a foreign language. "Je . . . I went skiing."

"En français: J'ai fait du ski. Où est-ce que tu es allée?" Marie caught the look of confusion on Denise's face and relented: "Where did you go?"

"Stratton." Denise was obviously relieved that she needn't translate a proper name. Marie was not ready to move on, however. "Est-ce qu'il y avait beaucoup de neige?" Marie was smiling and nodding with an expectant look of encouragement, but Denise returned the gaze with an expression of befuddlement. She was rescued, however, by an audible "snow" from one of the seats behind her. "Ahh, oui." Again, Denise was relieved, this time at getting away with a one-word answer.

"Oui, il y avait beaucoup de neige." Marie phrased the answer in a complete sentence as she returned to Ellen. "Maintenant, Ellen, qu'est-ce que vous avez fait ce weekend?" This time, of course, Ellen was ready and seemed pleased to be able to respond fairly fluently.

"Comment est-ce qu'on dit *babysitting?*"

"J'ai fait du babysitting," answered Marie promptly. "Répétez."

"J'ai fait du babysitting," obeyed Ellen.

"Bonne réponse!" Marie turned toward a source of conversation on her left. "Manuel, qu'est-ce que vous avez fait ce weekend?" She addressed a slight Hispanic boy who sat in the front row on the side of the *v* to her left. He had been intermittently leaning toward a long-haired, pretty girl on his right, making comments and remarks during the class conversation.

"Uh . . . Je slept and went to a movie."

"En français, en français," encouraged Marie. "Je suis allé au cinéma." She nodded toward Manuel expectantly. "Répétez, répétez. Je suis allé au cinéma."

"Je suis allé au cinéma," repeated Manuel loudly. Manuel displayed none of the sheepishness of his classmates when he spoke French; rather, he affected a bravado that Debby found endearing considering the atrociousness of his pronunciation and the hesitancy of his delivery.

"Quel film?" asked Marie. Even as she asked this, another general hum had begun around the room as students spoke to each other about movies they had seen. *"Baker Boys," "Friday the 13th," "Back to the Future II"*—Debby heard snippets of conversation underneath Marie and Manuel's exchange in French.

"I saw *The Little Mermaid* on Saturday," a blond girl directly in front of Debby whispered to her neighbor.

"Oh, you're kidding. That's for kids!"

"Well, I had to take my little brother," said the girl as she realized her grievous social error and hurried to backtrack.

"Sshh, let Manuel answer. Laissez Manuel répondre." In spite of the din Marie stuck with her question and moved closer to Manuel in order to hear him.

Manuel replied confidently in English, obviously anticipating the reaction he was sure to receive. "I saw *Leatherface: Texas Chainsaw Massacre!*" The class did not disappoint him.

"Disgusting!"

"Oh, yuk!"

"How could you watch that?"

"Ohh, I saw that. It was gross!"

"I couldn't watch it—too bloody!"

Again Marie motioned for quiet and spoke softly to regain the students' attention. "One at a time, en français, en français. You may talk if you talk in French. Vous pouvez parler, mais en français." She turned abruptly toward the overhead projector, which was placed in front of her desk, and her motion quieted the class as much as did her words. "Take out some paper for writing." Marie spoke as she turned on the projector: "What am I asking you to do here? Jesse?" As she spoke, Marie looked up and realized that the white screen had not been pulled down. She circled the teacher's desk and pulled back the teacher's chair to stand on it and reach the screen. By the time she had pulled it down, the hum of conversation was again audible.

"What am I asking you to do here?" she repeated. Some of the students quieted as they looked with concentration at the page projected on the screen:

Traduisez les phrases suivantes:
1. The players won the game.
2. The teacher answered the question.
3. The Yankees are a baseball team.
4. Littleton lost the basketball game.
5. Do you see well?

"Jesse?" Marie walked back around the teacher's desk and all the way down the center of the *v* to address an older-looking Hispanic boy who sat in the back. Marie's physical proximity further reduced the chitchat. Manuel, however, resumed speaking softly to his neighbor in the front.

Jesse had been slouched over, resting his head on his hand, which was braced on the tablet-desk surface. "Translate," he said as he straightened up.

"Bien. Translate these sentences into French. Everyone do that now while I come around and look." Marie began to circulate, leaning over individual students as they worked. A few students pulled out textbooks, and whispered help became audible between neighbors.

"Players . . . players," murmured the pretty girl next to Manuel as she riffled the pages of her text.

"Le match," Debby heard another student volunteer to his seatmate from the other side of the *v*. Debby figured this was not a quiz, for Marie did not take notice of these various forms of assistance as she continued from desk to desk. After visiting two students, Marie looked up at the class as a whole from her location at the rear of the room. "Don't spend too much time looking up vocabulary in the book. Just write what you do know. For instance, if you don't know *players,* just write the rest of the sentence with *game*. Show me what you do know."

Marie had walked toward the teacher's desk during these instructions and pulled a folder from her book bag as she spoke. While the students continued to talk and write, Marie began to return papers, which Debby could see were graded homework assignments. The students took little notice of the papers they were receiving, other than to emit an occasional groan.

After a few more minutes, during which whispered collaboration had grown into whole-class discussion, Marie returned to the front of the class. "Bon. Commençons avec numéro un. Anna?" Marie addressed the object of Manuel's affection. "Start us out."

"Les joueurs . . . uh . . . I don't know *won* . . . le match."

"Bien. Let's see . . ." Marie wrote Anna's contribution on the chalkboard to the left of the white projection screen. "*Les joueurs* . . . good! Now what if this were an all girls' team? Anna has given us boy players. What if the players were women?"

Debby heard the increased hum of several simultaneous replies and assumed that Marie heard what she was looking for, for she nodded and wrote the words *les joueuses* below *les joueurs* on the board. "Right—les *joueuses* if you decided you were writing about a female team. Now, who knows the verb *to win?*" Again Marie waited for volunteers and seemed willing to acknowledge spontaneous answers.

"Gagner," called out a girl in front of Jesse.

"Bien. How do we say it in the passé composé? How do we say *won?*" Marie continued her patient coaxing and coaching until the rest of this sentence and the next three were on the board in French.

"Maintenant, numéro cinq?" No one answered, and Marie smiled impishly at her class. "I fooled you, didn't I? We haven't done *to see* yet, but . . . voila!" With a flourish, Marie removed a piece of paper that had been covering the lower half of the transparency on the projector, and revealed the verb *voir:*

VOIR—TO SEE

Je vois	Nous voyons
Tu vois	Vous voyez
Il voit	Ils/Elles voient

The students greeted this revelation with slightly less excitement than their teacher, but several of them did laugh appreciatively at her dramatics. Marie did not pause but quickly recited the verb. "Listen to it, now. Écoutez. To see." Marie's fingers went to her eyes. "Écoutez: Je vois. Tu vois. Il voit. . . ." As Marie pronounced the words, it seemed to Debby that the constant hum in the classroom was an increasing distraction. Just then, however, Marie commandeered her students' vocal chords.

"Say it with me . . . répétez!" Marie began to repeat the conjugation, and gradually her class fell in, until the chattering was replaced with quiet choral recitation: "Je vois, tu vois. . . ."

"Bien. Now, what do you hear here?" Marie pointed to the first column of the conjugation. "It sounds the same, right? Now say *ils voient*. What do you hear? Robert?"

"The same," replied a freckled boy in the front row, whose posture and manner suggested that he was an infrequent volunteer.

"Bien. Let's say it." Marie nodded encouragingly at the boy, and he hesitantly repeated, "Je vois, tu vois. . . ."

"It's the boot rule!" shouted a husky black boy on the opposite side of the room.

"Aha—the boot!" laughed Manuel loudly.

Marie ignored, or didn't hear, these contributors as she encouraged Robert to pronounce each verb in the conjugation. When he was done, she turned again to the class as a whole.

"Now, I say it in English, and you reply in French: *I see*."

Marie was waiting for the class to respond, and a few did begin: "Je vois."

"It's the boot rule!" insisted Manuel.

Marie did not appear irritated by this interruption; she dealt with his comment according to its content. "Well, I'd rather not get into that, because the boot rule really applies in different situations. But if it helps you to remember it, then remember it as a boot."

"Yeah—they all start with v-o-i," called out one of the girls sitting in front of Debby.

"OK, use it if it works for you. Now say it in French: *I see*."

"Je vois."

"You see."

"Tu vois."

"He sees."

"Il voit."

Marie continued through the verb until everyone was responding in French to her English prompts. Then, without a pause, she held up a hand: "Now one at a time: Anna—I see."

The students seemed familiar with this drill and responded quickly. Anna called out, "Je vois."

"Bien. Manuel—you see."

"Tu vois."

"Très bien. We see—Jesse." Marie peppered the class with versions of *seeing* and pointed to students to request responses. Individuals answered promptly, and the stumbling in their replies now seemed the result of their lingering unfamiliarity with the new word rather than lack of attention. Manuel, however, continued intermittently to address Anna on his right and the boy on his left. A particularly audible outburst caught Marie's notice as she was rehearsing the verb on the other side of the room, and she glanced sharply at Manuel with an expression that clearly conveyed her displeasure. Still calling for responses, Marie crossed to the front of the room and wrote

Manuel's name on the board in a square, already drawn at the far right, entitled "Warning."

"Oh, man!" grumbled Manuel good-naturedly, and then he at least temporarily quit talking.

Marie's pace did not falter as she turned from the board and switched tactics. "Bien. Maintenant, écrivez. I'll say it in English, and you write it in French." As she spoke, Marie turned off the projector with a flip of the switch and circled in front of the class. It seemed to Debby that this woman was flying. "I see."

"What?"

"Do what?"

Sounds of confusion greeted this change. "Write it in French after I say it in English. Come on—*I see.*"

Students began to write, and Marie danced around the room checking their work as she spoke.

"Bien. *We see.*" A slight pause. "Très bien. *They see.*" As Marie called out words, students listened, talked to each other and to her, and wrote. Marie, too, whispered in side conversations with students who had written the verb incorrectly and who needed redirection. Debby sat back and listened to the constant hum peppered with Marie's called-out English ("*You see. . . . We see*") and occasional student remarks ("I got it!" "Aha—you didn't get me!" "Agh, I was right and then I changed it!").

"Now, no more translating. Just write what I say." Marie materialized at the front of the room, and she waited to see that her class was listening. "Sshh . . . sshh . . . I will say something in French, and you write just what I say—in French. Get it?" A few nods in reply persuaded her to proceed: "*Le professeur voit.*" Marie was on the move again. "Write it! *Le professeur voit.*" Marie cruised from desk to desk glancing at her students' efforts to record her words.

"*Les élèves voient.*" The phrase produced more writing, conversing, and occasional laughter.

"*La classe voit.*" A devilish look overtook Marie's face as she called out this phrase.

"La classe . . . that's plural," whispered Denise to herself.

"No, it's one class." Students now conferred without inhibition about the mystery Marie had introduced.

"Can you get it? The verb sounds the same, doesn't it, so which is it? La classe voit." Marie continued to move from student to student, offering individual feedback. "Bien. . . . No, try again. . . . Bien. . . . Très bien. . . . OK, everyone, what is it?" Marie walked purposefully toward the board and gestured to Robert as she passed: "Robert, you've got it. Which form of *voir* do we use?"

"La classe v-o-i-t," he replied with an imperceptible smile.

Marie wrote "La classe voit" on the board, to the accompaniment of groans and cheers. The black student next to Manuel clasped his hands over his head in a gesture of victory and exulted, "I'm the French champion!" Other students similarly registered their success or failure.

"Did I get you? I know it seems as though it should be plural: There is more than one person in the class. But that's the way the French are. The word is singular—one class. That's what the *la* tells you—one class. OK, more: *Les garçons voient*. Write!"

Marie resumed her circuit as Ellen called out. "Le garçon or les?"

"Les garçons. Les garçons voient." As she replied, Marie headed back toward Ellen to lend further help.

"No, v-o-i-e-n-t."

"But it sounded the same. I thought you said *le*."

"That's why we're practicing listening. It is hard to hear the difference." Turning to the class as a whole, Marie said, "Now here's another tricky one: *Ton ami voit*."

"Them's fightin' words," joked Manuel with a laugh. Just then Marie, who was in the back near Ellen, happened to catch Jesse's eye, and he rolled his eyes and winked at her conspiratorially, as if commiserating with her about the immaturity of his classmates.

Marie smiled ruefully at Jesse and marched toward the chalkboard. Since either confusion or indifference seemed to greet this example, Marie quickly intervened. She wrote the words *ton ami* on the board. "What is the noun, here? What are we talking about?"

"Friend!" called Anna.

"Bien—ami." Marie completed the phrase by writing *voit*. Anna half turned in her seat and displayed her notebook for Manuel and the class beyond him: "You see—I was right! Haha!"

Marie ignored this boasting and pressed on. "Maintenant: *Tes amis voient*. Écrivez."

"Oh, you're not going to get me this time," called Denise. The students by now had turned this exercise into a lighthearted competition of sorts between themselves and their instructor, and Marie played along happily, moving again from seat to seat. "Did I get you? No? Bien!"

Finally, with a flourish, Marie walked to the board, wrote "Tes amis voient," and dropped the chalk. "OK, no more writing. Sit back, relax, and listen."

In immediate reaction to this invitation the class loudly and physically relaxed: The students dropped pencils and books, scraped desks, and groaned as they relaxed their shoulders, put out their feet, and leaned back into their seats. Marie grinned broadly. "This class always takes me so seriously!" she laughed. "OK, now listen. Écoutez. Qu'est-ce que tu vois à Paris?"

The class resumed the halting conversation with which Marie had opened the period; the students attempted to reply to her questions about what they would see in various locations: Paris, the classroom, the local shopping mall. During this exchange Marie added three more names to the "warning" box on the board, as students again used the class conversation as a chance to chatter privately.

"Well, now you're experts in seeing, right?" Marie smiled as she headed for her desk and retrieved the chalk she had dropped in the tray. "Tomorrow, when this is 'le verbe du jour,' you will all get 100, right?" A few groans greeted this observation, but Marie continued. "Tomorrow we will learn the passé composé of this verb. Now you know how to *see,* but tomorrow we will learn *saw* and *will see*. Now, here is your homework." Marie wrote "Les devoirs" on the board, followed by a page number.

Marie turned her head toward the sudden sound of laughter. She frowned deeply but spoke softly to Manuel, who had again been caught in conversation with Anna. "Manuel, see me after class." From Debby's vantage point, it seemed that Manuel's transgression was no worse than his classmates' behavior, but he did not argue; he just rolled his eyes and was quiet. Debby doubted that most of the students had even heard Marie's directive, as they griped loudly in response to "les devoirs."

"You mean we got homework?"

"This is the first class I got homework in today!"

"Homework—agh."

Marie, of course, was undeterred. "This activity is more practice of what you learned today, so you will be ready for the passé composé tomorrow." Then, finally, Marie dropped her vigilance and allowed the last few minutes of class time to be consumed in the wave of chatter that had constantly threatened to flood the more purposeful conversation in the room. After two or three minutes the bell rang, and the students made for the door. Several students stood in line to speak to Marie, and she dealt with them in turn until only Manuel was left waiting.

Marie looked at him expectantly. "Yes?" she said. Then, almost instantaneously, she remembered. "Oh, yes!" Marie bent to speak to Manuel, and Debby suddenly felt like an intruder. She busied herself putting her notebook away and tried to let Marie speak to Manuel privately. Debby could not hear Marie's words but assumed that Manuel was happy with them, for he agreed loudly and sauntered from the room.

Debby rose with mixed conclusions to greet Marie. She wasn't sure what to think of what she had just witnessed. For one thing the time had flown, and Marie had moved from one activity to another so quickly that Debby hardly had time to make notes on one exchange before Marie went on to the next. In addition, the class had seemed awfully noisy. But Dr. Goldman had told her that Marie was one of the best teachers Metropolitan had graduated, and Debby had been trying to remember her high school French as she listened to the class. In any event, Debby decided to compliment Marie and sort it out later.

"That was great. You made me feel like taking French again!" As she spoke, Debby realized she was sincere in her flattery: She did wish she could take French again, this time with a few more years of maturity and motivation.

"Well, thanks. This class is always a challenge, but I try." Marie's smile was as warm and friendly up close as it had been when directed at her class. She headed for the door, weighed down with books, book bag, and purse. Debby followed her down the hall and through a corridor to a large study hall area. "I monitor this study hall for the last period; we can talk," invited Marie.

"Were those first- or second-year French students?" asked Debby.

"Second year, average level," replied Marie. "All but three in the class are freshmen, and they all took a year of French last year in middle school. Most of them are just finishing the second year as a requirement for graduation. They were in heterogeneous classes last year, and many of them felt left behind by the end. Several of them entered this year with a pretty bad attitude. You know: 'I can't do this; French is hard; I'm not the type who can learn a language.' "

"So they need two years of a language?" asked Debby.

"Right. Two years of average level is the basic graduation requirement. For an honors diploma they need three years of above-average-level language or four years at the average level. Actually, some of the kids in the class are feeling better about French now, and some are thinking of going on for the honors diploma."

"Gee—doesn't that make you feel great? I mean, isn't that sort of the ultimate litmus test, in an elective, that they want to take more?" Debby fleetingly felt relief that students had little choice about English.

"You're right, I guess. I never thought of it that way." Marie smiled pensively, and Debby could almost see her file the thought away for further contemplation.

"Are all your classes average level?" wondered Debby.

"No. I have another class like this one, a remedial class, and two classes that will take the honors exam this spring. So I have four preps, although it's almost five, since my other average class is so different from this one."

"How so?" prompted Debby.

"There are half as many students, for one thing, and eight of them are A or B students. So they move through material pretty quickly."

"I counted twenty students in this class, right?"

"Well, twenty-two; two were absent. But here is an example of my point: I introduced the same verb this morning in my other average class, and the students had mastered it after ten minutes. They were bored with the rest of the drill. So I went into this period expecting to shorten the rehearsals, but you saw what happened. These guys really needed the practice. They were just beginning to respond reliably when the period ended."

"So what will you do tomorrow with them? I heard you say something about the verb of the day?"

"Oh yes, 'le verbe du jour.' They hate that." Marie flashed the now-familiar grin at Debby. "Usually I don't tell them which verb it will be, but on a new verb like this they'll know it's coming. So there's no reason, if they'll just go home and study it, that they can't get 100."

"What is it—a quiz?"

"Well, sort of. All they have to do is conjugate the verb and use it in context."

"What else will you do, say, for the next several days?"

"Well, my goal today was for the students to recognize, hear, and write the verb. The homework they're doing tonight uses *voir* in sentences, so tomorrow I'll have volunteers write their sentences on the board and, in that way, correct their homework in class. I usually collect the homework after we do it together, and I let them make corrections to their work during our class discussion before they hand it in."

"So everyone can get 100?"

"Yes, if they've done it and if they bother to make the in-class corrections. If they're not paying that much attention, I give them a zero."

"How do you grade, anyway?"

"One-third is based on exams, one-third on quizzes, and one-third on homework and class participation. It actually takes several 'verbes du jour' to add up to a quiz grade."

"Ok," murmured Debby, taking notes as she spoke, "so after you correct homework in class . . . ?"

"Well, if it seems as though they're comfortable with the basic verb, I'll add on some new information—the past tense. That will tie into a general focus we've had lately on speaking and writing in the past tense. So it ought to strike a familiar chord for them. Then . . . let's see, I haven't thought this all the way through. . . . Their homework tomorrow night will be to write their own questions in the past tense. . . ."

"Using *voir*?" Debby interrupted.

"Not necessarily. We'll all be sick of *voir* by then," laughed Marie. "The questions will be their own sentences; they can write what they want. Then, the next day, I think I'll organize the class into pairs or groups."

"Do you use groups a lot?"

"Yes, I like to get the students talking to each other—not that that's hard to do!" Marie laughed at her own words. "Talking to each other in French, I mean. But I'll have to see how they're doing before I divide them up. If enough of them are 'getting' a particular subject, they can be very helpful to each other. If that's the case, I'd have them ask each other the questions they wrote for homework and record one another's answers. Something simple like that."

"Is it hard to keep them under control during group activities?"

"This class is never quite under control," laughed Marie again. "I'm always exhausted after I finish eighth period. The 'warning' system you saw today is yet another attempt at keeping them on task without harping at them all the time, but as you saw, it had mixed results. I always feel as if I'm doing a balancing act with these guys.''

"In what way?" prompted a rapt Debby.

"Well, I could control them if I just wanted to shut them up; I could make them write conjugations all day. But I don't want to. I want them to speak French to me and to each other and to get used to hearing it. And I think they'll be more interested if we talk about things they care about, like the playoffs or whatever. But this class is all chatter; a single question is an invitation to general discourse."

"Is Manuel your worst offender?"

"No. No one in this class is really impossible. Manuel is friendly and outgoing; he thinks he's cool and fancies himself a ladies' man. He craves attention, but he doesn't really want to get into trouble; he won't push the limits too far. He's a smart boy. He could be in an above-average class if he were willing to work hard enough. He often skips his homework in my class and still does B work on tests."

"Does he speak Spanish?"

"Yes, fluently. That makes it easier—for all the Spanish-speaking students, for that matter. There are a lot of similarities between the Romance languages, and that gives them a head start."

"Is the boy who sits in the back Hispanic too—the one who winked at you?"

"Oh, yes, Jesse. He's a junior, and he sometimes tries to act superior when the freshmen act up. He emigrated from Peru three or four years ago, and he was in my class last year for beginning French. Before that he was in ESL classes."

"You mean Spanish is his native language?"

"Yes, but he speaks English very well. And I think taking French gives him a feeling of confidence. I've told the guidance counselors that they should encourage Hispanic students to take another language. These students are often good at it, and it's an opportunity for them to excel. My class is at least one place they can take on majority kids and do as well or better. In the rest of the school environment, students from different cultures aren't on such equal footing."

"Well, I think it's neat that you have so many minority students in that class so involved in a foreign language."

"I guess I feel an affinity with some of them. I grew up in this country, but my parents were French, and I can remember times when the culture in my home conflicted with the one in school. My mother would say, 'You don't need to do that'—whatever it was—'it's dumb.' Well, it probably was dumb, but it was what everyone else was doing, so I wanted to do it too."

Just then the bell rang, and the few students in the large room collected their belongings and bolted for the doors. "Where do you go now?" asked Debby as she closed her notebook and reached for her coat.

"Home. This is the end of the day," replied Marie cheerfully. "Have we covered everything you wanted to ask?"

"Yes, I think so. I don't know yet how Dr. Goldman wants me to use these observations—whether I'll write a paper or what—so I may have some more questions. Thank you very much for letting me see your class and take so much of your time."

"No problem. It was nice to meet you. Just give me a call if you want to come again or talk some more, but wait until after nine, when my kids are in bed!" Marie held out her hand, and Debby shook it appreciatively.

* * *

Two nights later, Debby retrieved her notebook from her book bag and unfolded the assignment Dr. Goldman had distributed in class that morning. She reached for a handful of the popcorn on her desk and reread the first item: "Comment upon those elements of teaching theory that we have studied to date which were operative in the classrooms you observed or which were notable in their absence. Analyze and evaluate the instruction you witnessed on the basis of these principles."

Debby leaned back in her chair and reflected upon Marie Dupont's eighth-period French class. For almost an hour she reviewed the notes she had made that day, and then she reached for a pen and began to write.

HELEN FRANKLIN

An experienced first-grade teacher who uses parent volunteers to help her run her unique class sees that one of the volunteers will work only with the white students and discovers that one of the black parents is aware of this.

"She said what?" Helen exclaimed.

"She told the superintendent that her daughter was not being challenged and was spending her day doing busywork. That's practically a direct quote. I was sitting right next to her!" replied Doris Baxter.

Helen Franklin was a first-grade teacher at Roosevelt Elementary School in Littleton, and Doris Baxter, the mother of one of her students, had been helpful and supportive of Helen's efforts all year. Doris served as a minority representative on one of the district superintendent's parent committees. It was at a committee meeting that she heard the criticism she was now sharing with Helen.

"Well, thank you for telling me," said Helen, trying to decide how much she should tell Doris of her problem. "You know I have lots of parent volunteers in my classroom, and Jane Isaac has been in the class as a volunteer since October. Apparently she hasn't liked what she's seen."

"Well, I knew she was working with you from Tom," Doris offered. "In fact, he said Mrs. Isaac doesn't like him."

"Listen, Doris, I knew I had some problems with Jane, but I had no idea any of it was apparent to the children. If it comes up again, please assure Tom that I don't think that's true. He's a pleasure for all of us to have in class!"

"Don't worry about that part of it," Doris said. "He's a pretty confident kid. But you might keep an eye on her when she works with some of the other black children."

"Good Lord," thought Helen. "There it is. Doris thinks I've got a bigot in my classroom. What a mess." But to Doris, Helen replied, "Oh, I don't think that's it at all. I just think Mrs. Isaac is so concerned with her own daughter's progress that she doesn't pay much attention to the other kids. Anyway, thank you for the feedback.''

As Helen hung up after her conversation with Doris, she tried to control her rising anger. The children would be arriving momentarily, and Helen had to get back to her classroom and begin the day. She remembered with a shudder of distaste that Jane Isaac was scheduled as a volunteer this morning. ''I can't believe that witch has caused me this much grief,'' she thought, realizing as she fumed that she had to calm down and handle Jane Isaac carefully.

Helen understood that she had two problems with Jane and that both of them could affect the children—maybe they already had. Helen was well aware that Jane was dissatisfied with her daughter Emily's curriculum. More than once she had offered a side comment, posed a direct question, or, in conferences, voiced specific criticisms of the job Helen was doing with Emily. Helen felt that the curriculum and instruction she was giving Emily were appropriate, and she had told Jane as much. Helen was really miffed that the woman had taken her complaint to the central office. And now that the specter of racism had been raised, Helen wondered if she had to confront that issue quickly. She struggled to put Jane Isaac's criticism of her and the superintendent's possible reactions in the back of her mind.

While parent volunteers always introduced a level of complexity, Helen had not had a serious problem using volunteers in all her nineteen years of teaching. In fact, the way Helen managed her classes, volunteers were crucial. Every October at Open School Night Helen solicited help from the parents and always took all the help she was offered.

Helen ran what some people referred to as an ''open classroom,'' but she objected to that label because it implied, to some, a lack of structure. Helen felt that her children's days were very structured, and one of her principal goals was to help her students develop a self-reliance and self-discipline that would serve them well throughout their school years.

Each morning when her students arrived, they found their work waiting for them on their desks. After welcoming the students, Helen would present their desk work for the morning. She would explain to them their reading lesson, their math lesson, a language arts assignment—whatever she had planned for that morning. Sometimes the work centered on reviewing material Helen had taught the previous day, and sometimes it involved practicing new information. If the latter was the case, Helen would teach the new material to the class as a whole and then explain the worksheet assignment, which provided practice in applying the new concept.

After taking her class through each assignment, Helen would encourage the students to ask any questions they might have and then she would turn them loose to do the work independently. As they did so, Helen and her volunteers reviewed the children's homework by moving individually to each desk. Concepts practiced in homework, such as mastery of new vocabulary words, were often crucial to the children's ability to complete their seatwork for that morning, and Helen had to be sure that each child understood one concept before expecting him or her to work independently on the next. This tour of the room was also Helen's opportunity to differentiate seatwork assignments if necessary. The slower students might be given extra explanations or even different worksheets, and the brighter children might be assigned extra activities on which to work if they finished their other lessons early. Helen spoke Spanish, and she always offered instruction and explanation to her bilingual students in Spanish at this time.

The children could work at their desks, on the floor, or back in the "private corner," but Helen expected them to do the work they had been given on their own. They could do the lessons in any order they chose; her only rule was that they were not to work on the same thing as their neighbor at the same time. Once her students were peacefully occupied at their desks, Helen began reading groups or gave individuals special instruction.

The help of volunteers was the magic that made this system work. While Helen was busy conducting a reading circle or giving individualized instruction, volunteers in the classroom could go from desk to desk helping children with their work or could do special drills for certain children. They also helped Helen "check out" each student's desk work as he or she completed it, after which the child could do special activities like work on the computer or play in "puppet alley." Essentially, the volunteers helped Helen keep this system of organized chaos organized. It had always worked beautifully, until now.

The twenty children in Helen's class represented a broad range of backgrounds and abilities. The school served affluent and working-class neighborhoods, and Helen's class had a healthy socioeconomic and racial mix. The families of the children in her class represented a range of incomes, but there were no very rich or very poor children in the class. Racially, the class was approximately half white and half minority; of the minority children, half were black and half Hispanic. She also had some children who were not yet comfortable with English.

Unlike most years, when the students in Helen's classes had a gradual range of abilities, this year she had some unusually slow children at one end of the continuum and three extraordinarily bright children at the other. Jane Isaac's daughter, Emily, was one of three girls who had known how to read when they started the year. After only one week of classes, Helen had telephoned the parents of the three girls and had explained that she recognized their children's abilities and didn't intend to waste their time. She was using more advanced readers with the girls and expecting more of them in general. That should have pleased Mrs. Isaac, but unfortunately it wasn't that simple.

Of the three girls, one—Kate Delbrook—was particularly advanced.

Helen had decided by November that Kate could easily complete two years in one, and she had told Kate's mother of her plan by January. Helen provided Kate with individualized academic instruction and extra homework; she believed strongly that if a child showed unique capability, she should "go with it" and help the child fulfill his or her native potential. But neither Helen nor Mrs. Delbrook had breathed a word to anyone of the plan to have Kate skip a grade, and Helen was sure Mrs. Isaac knew nothing of it.

Meanwhile, Helen had recognized early in the year that Emily Isaac had some unique emotional needs, which Helen had tried to meet. Emily was nervous and meticulous to a fault; she would work too slowly in a misplaced need to color exactly within the lines or to keep a letter precisely between lines on the paper. Emily seemed insecure and pressured, and Helen felt that sometimes just drawing a picture or doing other nonacademic work was a welcome relief for Emily. The child needed her curriculum customized socially as much as Kate needed hers customized academically, and Helen wanted to help Emily learn to relax and enjoy school.

"But is Jane jealous of the time I spend with Kate?" Helen wondered as she sat down in the teachers' lounge and looked out at the winter landscape. The fact was, Mrs. Isaac seemed interested only in the work that her daughter and the other high achievers were given on the days she volunteered. Therein lay the other problem.

Helen honestly didn't know if Mrs. Isaac's motive was racism or a preoccupation with what Emily was doing, but Mrs. Isaac refused to work with the low-ability groups in Helen's classroom. If Helen asked Mrs. Isaac to do something with one or another of the low achievers as they started the day, Mrs. Isaac would assume a slightly pained expression. Although she would begin to do what Helen asked, she would soon find an excuse to work with the brighter children, leaving the slower ones unsupervised.

After observing this several times, Helen started ducking the issue by asking other volunteers who were in the room to work with the slow children or by working with them herself. But the fact that some of the students in the lower groups were black and that all three of the brightest children were white now sowed a bitter seed of doubt in Helen's mind. She had been willing to give Mrs. Isaac the benefit of the doubt and believe that she just didn't have the patience to work with the slower children—after all, Mrs. Isaac was an uptight, nervous, hurried type—but Doris's comments now forced Helen to face the other possibility.

Helen looked at her watch. This morning was going to be difficult. Mrs. Isaac and another parent were the volunteers. Helen had to manage the two of them, her children, her own anger, and a charge of racism. Should she continue to try to ignore Mrs. Isaac's refusal to help the slower children? Her other volunteer would gladly help them instead. Should she also ignore Mrs. Isaac's continued criticism of her work with Emily? Helen felt that she was the professional and that she knew what was best for Emily, but if the superintendent was involved, maybe she should change Emily's work. Should she confront Mrs. Isaac on either issue, or try to let the matter slide? Accusing Mrs. Isaac of racism now might look like retaliation for her criticism to the superintendent. As Helen stood up and headed toward her classroom, she searched for answers.

CHRIS KETTERING

A first-year high school social studies teacher finds to his dismay that his white, middle-class students are uninterested in becoming involved in social activism and suffer from narrow-mindedness.

Chris shut the classroom door immediately after the third-period bell rang; his students knew that his prompt action meant he would begin the class right away rather than let them take a minute to settle in. He walked into the middle of the semicircle of desks, where he usually stood to teach the class; quickly scanned the group of twenty-one seniors; and raised his voice a bit, as he always did when he began.

"How many of you know someone who has died from AIDS?"

Whatever quiet chatter there had been in the classroom stopped. After a moment, a few students shifted in their seats. Several looked around. No hands went up.

"That's good," Chris said, looking over the row of startled faces. He thought that for the first time in the ten weeks he'd been teaching this course, he had everyone's attention. "How many of you know anyone who has AIDS now?"

More silence. Several more students turned their heads to see if any hands were going up. None did. "We have a very lucky group of people in this room," Chris said.

"We're going to begin the second unit of this course today. We spent the first ten weeks researching and proposing solutions to what we've called 'public policy issues'—apartheid, the death penalty, abortion, teenage pregnancy. While we were researching and writing, several of you asked me why, if this course is called 'Participation in Government,' you weren't *doing* anything. You asked when you would start participating. The answer to that question is *today*.

"We spent ten weeks researching public policy problems so that we would have an understanding of what they are and how people work to solve them. For the next several weeks, we are going to take a few small

109

public policy problems and work on them, not on paper but in real life. I have some ideas for projects we can work on. I want your ideas too.''

Chris glanced around the semicircle at his students. They were looking at him curiously. He continued, "Obviously, we can't solve the AIDS epidemic. But there is an annual walkathon that raised $3 million last year to help fight AIDS. I called the people who organize the walk, and they told me that twenty-five high schools sent teams last year, and they expect even more this year. Abbott Tech had the largest team last year. They sent about sixty students and teachers, and their team raised $5000.''

Chris took a deep breath and continued. "I'd like to see this high school send a team to the walk this year. It's on Sunday, May 20. It's not too early to start planning for this, because all the projects will require a lot of work. We'll need to get the administration's approval for the things we decide to do, arrange for publicity in the school, figure out transportation. . . .''

Chris scanned the room again and felt he still had his students' attention, although he wasn't sure he had their interest. He glanced at the clock and saw he had thirty minutes remaining in the period, plenty of time to describe the other projects that the students could choose from to meet the participation requirement for the course. Among them, he suggested running a voter registration drive, designing and implementing a program to collect wastepaper from classrooms and offices for recycling, and organizing a Saturday morning footrace to raise money for the school's athletic department. He talked about the tasks that would have to be done in each of the projects.

There were five minutes left in the period when Chris finished, enough time to gauge his students' interest and to tell them to come to class the next day with their own ideas for projects. He answered a few questions and then asked students to indicate their preference for the projects discussed so far by a show of hands. They divided pretty evenly among three of the four projects. No one chose the AIDS walk.

Thirty minutes later, Chris was seated in the school's main office waiting for his appointment with Steve Helms, the principal at Fallstown High School. He'd need Helms's approval to go ahead with any of the projects in his government class. Waiting for the meeting, Chris went over his thoughts about the class. He was glad for the interest the students had shown for three of the projects, but he was disappointed that there had been no interest in the AIDS walk.

Chris found some clues about his class's response as he watched the faculty and student traffic move through the main office while he waited. The Fallstown school district was 98 percent white and solidly middle-class. Besides teaching the senior government class, Chris had three ninth-grade global studies classes at the high school and was an assistant coach on the school's track team. In all, he taught or coached 170 students, about 10 percent of the high school's enrollment. In his classrooms and at track practice, Chris's face was the only black one.

The town of Fallstown was insulated, Republican, and Roman Catholic. Although the town was located midway between two major cities in the northeast, about 50 miles from each, it remained mostly untouched by the social ills that had plagued its urban neighbors throughout the recent decades. Schools in the nearby cities were being overrun by crack and other cheap cocaine derivatives, but other than discussions about drinking and driving, school officials expressed little concern about drug abuse at Fallstown.

The town wasn't wealthy, but neither was there much poverty. Its small homeless population was housed in a handful of motel rooms, all of them out of town. Only one or two AIDS cases had been reported by local health officials. Indeed, the greatest threat to public health in Fallstown was the deer tick and the Lyme disease it carried.

The high school's curriculum was an indicator of the community's conservatism. English teachers long ago gave up trying to teach *Catcher in the Rye* because of the annual battle that would result with parents. *The Christian Science Monitor, USA Today,* and *The National Review* were available in the school library. *The New York Times, The Nation,* and *The New Republic* were not. The sex-education courses were the minimum required by the state and were taught separately to boys and girls. A well-attended Christian fundamentalist school in the town competed with the Fallstown public schools for students, a fact that department heads and administrators were keenly aware of when they planned curriculum.

Watching the stream of white faces and fashionably dressed bodies flow through the main office while he waited for his meeting, Chris thought of his own contrasting background. He was born and raised in the Red Hook section of Brooklyn. He earned a bachelor's degree from Howard University in Washington, D.C., and a graduate degree from Columbia University in New York. He spent seven years covering urban issues for a newspaper just outside New York; then he left the paper two years ago, thinking he could have more of an impact by teaching in a high school than by writing in a newsroom. This was his first year of teaching.

Chris knew a handful of people who were sick with AIDS or had died from it. Some of them he'd met while writing about AIDS; others were friends from college or graduate school or from the newspaper. Recalling them, Chris increased his resolve to have a group of his government students organize a team to do the AIDS walk. His thoughts were interrupted as Mr. Helms opened his office door and greeted Chris, waving him in.

* * *

"No."

"No?"

"I'm sorry, Chris," Mr. Helms said, leaning forward over his desk and taking off his glasses. "No. It's not a good idea. There's too much that will need to be done. You wouldn't be covered by the district's insurance policy because the walk takes place more than 40 miles away. And the transportation department schedules weekend buses the semester before. Besides all that, the school board doesn't meet again until May 21, four weeks from Monday. When is this walk?''

"It's on a Sunday. May 20.''

"Well, that settles it, I'm afraid. The board reviews all requests for field trips, and this walk occurs before the board's next meeting. I'm sorry.''

"Doesn't the board usually have work sessions between its regular meetings? Couldn't we present it to the board members then? Or couldn't we poll them by phone about this?''

"I don't think this is the kind of thing we should call board members at home about.''

"OK. That's understandable. Could we call them at work?''

"You're missing my point, Chris. They wouldn't support you on this. I know this district, these parents. I know this school board. And I know these students. They won't support you.''

"I'd like to give my students the opportunity to say so themselves, Mr. Helms. With your permission, I'd at least like to raise the possibility of the trip.''

"How do your students feel about doing this walk, Chris?''

"Honestly, at this point, there's not much support for it.''

"I didn't think there would be. So why are you pushing it?''

"Because I think I can build support for it.''

"I don't think you'll get anywhere with this, Chris. I'm only trying to save you frustration.''

"I appreciate that, Mr. Helms, but I'd like my students to be able to decide for themselves.''

"Go ahead, Chris, if you feel that strongly about the issue. But I want you to know that I'll be talking to the superintendent today about it. I'm sure she'll agree with me that the board shouldn't be contacted.''

"I don't understand, Mr. Helms. You said there would be a problem scheduling a bus to take us to the walk, but you said there wouldn't be a problem scheduling a school bus to operate as a shuttle for our Saturday morning run through town to raise money for the athletic department. And why is insurance a problem when students are walking a few miles in the city but not when they're running 5 miles against traffic on Route 47?''

"You're right, Chris. I don't think you understand. Let me be more clear: This is a very conservative community.''

"Conservative? What's conservative got to do with this? We're talking about raising money to fight a fatal disease.''

Mr. Helms leaned forward over his desk again, and his voice dropped almost to a whisper. "To this community, it's more than that,'' he said. Holding his eyes on Chris, he slowly leaned back in his chair. "I think you should drop the idea.''

Chris gathered his papers and nodded a good-bye. He walked hurriedly from the office, feeling his resolve to do this walk increase once again.

* * *

Later in the afternoon, Chris had lunch in the faculty room with Larry Timber, a union representative and one of Chris's first friends among the faculty. "This isn't how teachers get tenure, Chris, at Fallstown or anywhere," said Larry. "This walk isn't worth it."

"What's tenure worth if you don't have some freedom in your classroom?"

"Tenure for you will be worth about $35,000 a year to start," Larry said. "And academic freedom comes with tenure, not before it. Wait a year, Chris. Then do the walk."

"One million people have this virus, Larry. Even in this county, out here a long way from anywhere, a few people have died. I don't think anybody should be talking about waiting. I think the least this school can do is send a busload of kids to this walk."

"But your kids don't want to do it. You said that yourself. More important for you, Helms doesn't want it. The school board won't touch it."

"Maybe I can change their minds. Maybe this is a chance to educate people, especially my students, about this disease. I feel that's my job. I'm a teacher."

"You're a first-year teacher without any job protection. Push this and Helms will see that the only walk you'll take will be out the front door forever in June. And there aren't many social studies jobs out there. Have you forgotten how hard it was to find a teaching job last fall? Don't be strident about this, Chris. Take Helms's advice. You want to walk? Do the March of Dimes walk. Or have the kids organize a bake sale or a car wash. Damn it, that's what the other government teachers have their classes do."

Chris started to laugh. "Look at me, Larry. I'm not exactly like the other teachers. You know, in a funny way, Helms did me a favor when he turned this idea down. He's helping me make this an object lesson in the political process. I'll bet his rejection of the idea will jump-start my kids' interest in the walk, even though I couldn't get them going. And it could be a great lesson: They'll learn how to oppose the system while working within it. The only way I'll give up on this is if my kids absolutely reject it. I really think I have to go with this now."

"I hope the students aren't interested, Chris," Larry said. "For your sake."

* * *

The door to Chris's government class swung shut again at the sound of the bell. Chris walked to the semicircle and handed a student twenty-one copies of a newspaper column written by a reporter Chris had worked with for several years before he left the newspaper to teach. As the article was being passed around, Chris asked one of the students to read it aloud.

"I lost my brother eleven days ago," Liana began. "He died of AIDS. A year ago today we were together in my car, inching through Easter traffic on the West Side Highway. We were headed home to see my parents. We sat in silence, our small talk swallowed in the blackness of my chest.''

The column described the impact of AIDS on one man and his family. Chris had chosen it because, expecting that none of his students would know anyone with AIDS, he hoped it would help them put a face on one of its victims. As Liana read, Chris wrote these statistics from the Centers for Disease Control on the blackboard:

Total cases in U.S. as of March 30: 124,984
NYC cases: 24,461
Deaths: 76,031
Americans with the AIDS virus today: 1,000,000
Deaths by 1992: 340,000

Chris moved back into the semicircle of desks as Liana continued reading. ''So much has happened in the last year,'' she read, looking up occasionally at Chris. ''My brother died on March 15, at the age of 31. Much of what we all experienced, of course, was horrible. AIDS is most cruel, not only in its indifference to youth but in how it inflicts an endless succession of scourges. Strength goes first, then flesh, then sight or reason—a vibrant person deactivated, one plug at a time. In a condensed span of months, my brother suffered a lifetime's pain and indignity.

''My brother is but one of more than 70,000 who have died of AIDS. Tens of thousands are now suffering as he did. Tens of thousands of families are suffering as we did. And the toll of this epidemic is only beginning.''

Liana put the article down and looked at Chris, tears glistening in her eyes. Chris leaned against a desk and drew a breath, bracing himself for the forty minutes to follow.

''I met with Mr. Helms yesterday to get his approval for the projects we'll be doing, and he gave his okay to all of them except one. He said we couldn't organize a team for the AIDS walk. He said the school board wouldn't approve the project, and he said the community is so conservative that we couldn't get any backing. I know there wasn't much support in class yesterday for doing the walk, but let me ask a theoretical question: If we decide that we want the AIDS walk to be one of our choices, would it be our duty as citizens of the school community to try to change Mr. Helms's mind or to try to find some way to work around him?''

Liana spoke up first. ''He can't stop us from doing this if we want to do it. We can do it on our own outside school.''

''We could, Liana,'' Chris responded, ''but the issue is doing it inside the school, as a project of this class, as a part of the school system.''

Mike spoke up next. ''Well, some of us could meet with Mr. Helms ourselves, or we could have our parents call him.''

''Good suggestions,'' Chris said, marveling at how easy this was. ''Could we do anything else?''

"We could go to the members of the school board. They could tell Mr. Helms to let us do this."

"All right. Possibly we could do all those things. But before we go to the board, we have to go to the superintendent, Dr. Hawthorne. We'll need to call or write to her asking for an appointment. Let's form a small group to do that. Who wants to be part of it?"

A long silence ensued.

"Anyone? Liana? Mike? What's the problem? I thought you were interested in this."

Another silence followed, broken after a minute by a voice tinged with sarcasm. "Thanks for the invitation, but I'm not walking next to any diseased faggots."

"Ron? I'm sorry, what did you say?"

"Those people have done it to themselves," Ron said. "Let them die. Or let somebody else save them. Besides that, it would be against my religion to raise money for those people. Look in the Bible. It says homosexuality is a sin. Sinners should be punished. They're getting what they deserve."

"Those are very strong words, Ron," Chris responded. "There may be others who feel differently." He scanned the semicircle. "What about the rest of you? I'm sure you don't all agree with Ron on this."

Greg spoke up next. "I think it would be dangerous. If we spent a morning with these AIDS guys, couldn't we get it? If we walk next to them, we'll probably brush against them. They're all sick and sneezing. I don't want to breathe that. No thanks. Put me down for the recycling drive."

Several students began speaking, all of them seconding Ron and Greg. Chris let his students talk, hopeful that the remarks would be self-correcting, that others more informed about AIDS would speak up and point out the inaccuracies. But after five minutes, when no one did, Chris cut off the exchange, afraid that the students' fear and misinformation would spread and destroy any chance of doing the walk.

He walked back to the center of the semicircle, angry that he had not been better prepared for this despite all the signals the day before that indicated the discussion might go this way. Under his breath, he cursed the school's health teachers for doing such a miserable job on AIDS education. "Before we go any further, I think I need to correct some misconceptions about AIDS so that we can have a more meaningful discussion," he said.

Chris spent the next ten minutes talking about how AIDS is spread, emphasizing that it is impossible to contract it by bumping into someone with the disease or breathing the same air as an infected person. He spent a few minutes more discussing the communities hardest hit by the disease.

He completed what had become a lecture by saying, "AIDS doesn't affect just homosexuals and drug addicts, although I think your perception that it does explains your reluctance to do the walk. Two thousand children under 5 years old have died from AIDS. Before a test was developed to screen the blood supply, half the hemophiliacs in America had AIDS. Think about Ryan White, the teenager from Indiana; he just died, and all those celebrities went to his funeral. Did he deserve to be punished?"

Chris then distributed twenty-one copies of a brochure describing AIDS and the AIDS walk and asked the students to read it to themselves.

"What's this? The Gay Men's Health Crisis. What are you getting us into, Mr. Kettering?" It was Ron's voice again.

"What are you reading, Ron?"

"Here, on the back. It says that proceeds from the walk go to the American Foundation for AIDS Research, to the AIDS Action Council, to AIDS-Related Community Services, and to the Gay Men's Health Crisis. It sounds like a social club. And look at this! It says this gay group uses some of its money to run a 'buddy system.' A buddy system! I can guess what that is."

"You don't have to guess, Ron. I can tell you what it is. It's a system that provides a 'buddy' to shop or clean or run errands for anyone who's too sick to tend to the details of his or her own life. I also think we need to remember that we're trying to fight a disease, not a lifestyle. I think . . ."

"Why did they choose that name—'Gay Men's Health Crisis'?" said Tara. "If they wanted to raise money, who's going to support a group with a name like that? It's stupid." It was the first time since the semester began that Tara had spoken up in class.

"Hemophiliacs and children with AIDS are innocent victims," Liana said. "Couldn't we raise money just for them?"

"I don't have a lot of prejudices, but this is one of them," said Janet, a Vietnamese girl whose family had immigrated to the United States several years ago and who was one of the brightest students in the class. Chris had thought she would be one of the supporters of the walk. "I think this is disgusting. I'm sorry these people have AIDS. But if they lived moral lives, if they weren't . . . you know, deviant, they wouldn't be sick. I'll do voter registration."

Chris thought of interrupting a second time. But for the few remaining minutes, he let the students express their views, hoping again that some student would speak up for the walk. None did. When the bell rang, he walked to his desk in the back of the room and began making plans for the voter registration drive, the 5-mile run, the recycling program, and the only new idea that had surfaced, a car wash to earn money for the senior class trip.

MARK SIEGEL

*A fourth-grade teacher is irritated by a black parent who visits
him regularly, demanding better teaching for her son. The teacher
believes that he has tried everything and that the problem rests
with the child and the demanding mother.*

Mark Siegel shifted uncomfortably in his chair. This latest conference with
Kyesha Peterson was going no better than the earlier ones. Realizing he had
stopped listening to her, he tuned back in and heard her say, "Karim isn't
learning enough in your class. It's November, and he still isn't catching up.
What are you going to do for him?"

"Mrs. Peterson, we've had this conversation before. I'm continually
trying to help Karim."

"We certainly have had this conversation before. And I don't see any
evidence that you've made things better for Karim in your class."

"You're right. Karim has not made any great breakthroughs since our
last meeting. He isn't responding to any of the strategies I use in my
classroom. He simply shows no interest in participating in class activities."

Mrs. Peterson continued to look out the window. "Well, it seems to me
that it's your job to make school interesting for the students."

Mark gritted his teeth. He tried to recall if he had ever met a parent who
treated him so rudely. He thought, "This woman has a lot of nerve coming
in here and telling me what my job is." And since Kyesha Peterson had
been coming to see him at least once every two weeks since school started,
Mark was feeling both hounded by her and stung by her criticism.

By four o'clock, Mrs. Peterson had said her piece and allowed Mark to
escort her to the front of the school. The conference ended with Mark
assuring her that he would give Karim more attention and make further
efforts to make school more compelling for the boy.

Walking back to his classroom, Mark thought about Karim Peterson. A
part of Mark felt sorry for Karim because, in addition to the child's academic
problems, he seemed like such a social outcast in the class. When the

difficulties with Mrs. Peterson began, Mark went to Paula Fowler, Karim's third-grade teacher the year before. She told Mark a little bit about Karim's background.

Karim was a 9-year-old who came from a stable black family in which he was the youngest of three children. African culture and heritage were strongly emphasized in their home. The mother seemed to be the dominant figure in the family and, according to Paula, her beliefs and values were firmly impressed upon the children. The Petersons celebrated African holidays; American holidays were ignored. The year before, Karim had been kept home the day of the class Christmas party. His mother had explained to Paula that if academics were not going to be taught, Karim didn't need to waste his time at a party for a holiday the family did not recognize.

Paula told Mark that the family seemed to be very conscious of racial issues and that Karim and his siblings tended to have negative ideas about white culture. On one occasion Karim had challenged Paula by rudely asking why there were no black children in the highest reading group.

Karim's father was a bus driver for the city transportation system, and his mother worked in the public library. Paula believed that education and career opportunities were extremely important to the family.

Karim had difficulty socializing with the other children in Mark's class. He could be verbally abusive to the other children, and he seemed to be a loner. The children teased him for talking "like a baby." When he was nervous, he had a habit of smelling his fingers, and the children made fun of him whenever he did.

During the two months that Karim had been in Mark's class, it became obvious that the other children did not like to be grouped with him. When Mark asked the children to choose and work with partners, Karim had to be assigned a partner. Most of the time he was reluctant to participate in activities that involved peer interaction. When the class had free time, Karim usually sat by himself. His classmates did not include him in their activities, and he did not express any interest in joining them in play.

Despite his seemingly antisocial behavior, Karim was a reasonably verbal, bright child. His standardized test scores suggested that he should easily be doing grade-level work. Mark understood why Mrs. Peterson expected better school performance from Karim, given his verbal skills and his test scores. While the boy was working only about half a year behind grade level, his oral reading was slow and labored enough to concern his mother. Mark thought that Karim's limited reading skills contributed to his poor school performance, and he felt that Karim's inability to focus on his work and maintain his attention contributed to his problems. Karim's short attention span and slow reading meant that he worked very slowly, and he often was unable to finish in-class assignments.

Since Karim's mother began demanding that her son receive special attention, Mark had used all the tricks he'd learned in his nine years of teaching fourth and fifth grades. His goal had been to improve Karim's reading skills and bring them up to at least grade level. At first, he thought that if he could spark more interest, Karim would respond with increased attention. Mark tried some high-interest reading materials, using topics like sports, music, and extraterrestrials—guaranteed winners with other fourth-grade students. None captured Karim's attention; he did not seem to share many of the interests of his peers. Mark also tried a reward system, offering Karim free time for completing work within an assigned time. Karim didn't respond. Mark then sat down with him and tried to find out what would act as a reinforcer, but he found Karim uncooperative. The boy seemed unwilling to discuss his interests with Mark or to tell Mark what rewards he would be willing to work for. Mark learned nothing he could use from their meeting.

While Mark was frustrated by Karim, his frustration was exacerbated by Karim's mother, whose demands for after-school conferences were increasing. Since Mark was unable to report any successes with Karim to Mrs. Peterson, these meetings were now making Mark feel particularly anxious. He had had no luck reaching Karim, improving his reading, or getting him to respond to either teacher or classmates. Mark felt he could honestly say that he had tried his best with Karim, but he also felt that there were some kids who could not be reached. It seemed to him that Karim might be one of them.

Mark slumped down at his desk and thought to himself, "I've only got to make it until the end of the year; then Karim will move on to fifth grade and take his crazy mother with him." That thought was not much help, however, since it was now November 4, and Mrs. Peterson was sure to return in two weeks.

DAN TYMKONOVICH

A social studies teacher takes over a high school AP honors class
whose students, he feels, are arrogant. His discussion plans go
awry, and the class falls apart.

Dan Tymkonovich watched Mr. Cochran and wondered when he was going
to challenge the narrow-mindedness of his class. Dan was observing his
cooperating teacher, Earl Cochran, in sixth-period advanced-placement
American government; Earl was leading a discussion of race relations in the
south during the civil rights disturbances of the 1960s. Dan was pleased that
the students seemed so involved and eager to participate in the discussion,
but he thought Earl too often let the students spout unchallenged inaccuracies
and thoughtless generalities in class.

Dan had been student teaching at Raddison High School for three weeks;
although Dan had taken the reins in other classes, he had yet to conduct
this class independently. But he was forming some opinions just from
observation: He found this class of twelfth-grade AP students almost
irritating.

Already Dan had concluded that these AP honors students were the true
embodiment of the "northeastern liberal rich kids." Every student in the
class had a fixed opinion on everything. The debate he was hearing this
afternoon only served to underscore Dan's conclusions.

"Well, white southerners are bigots—period!" Alex was saying.

"Justify your position, Alex," cut in Mr. Cochran.

"Lester Maddox. Governor Wallace on the steps of the University. What
more do you need?" Alex held his arms open as he spoke, as if welcoming
information that would disprove his position. "Even welfare is a vehicle of
racism," he continued. "The white majority invented welfare to keep the
blacks pacified and dependent."

"Welfare wasn't a southern invention," Janet cut in. "And Maddox and
Wallace were just two people. You can't generalize on that!"

"Wait a minute." A third student joined the fray. "They were elected representatives carrying out the wishes of their constituencies. You bet we can generalize!''

"The bus driver on Rosa Park's bus, the other redneck passengers—everyone thought that way. Segregation was a way of life!'' added Mark Petersen. "Blacks were oppressed in the south in the sixties, and they are oppressed in the south today!''

Dan waited with impatience for Earl to say something—anything—to challenge Mark's statement. "There's a black mayor in Atlanta!'' thought Dan. "I don't see any blacks in the Raddison city government!'' Dan had to summon actual physical control in order to refrain from interrupting Earl, who let Mark's statement go unanswered.

In fact, Raddison High School served a homogeneous, affluent, white community near Littleton. The town was divided about equally between middle-class residents whose families had lived in Raddison for years and very wealthy newcomers. Housing prices in Raddison had skyrocketed within the last decade, and since that time only the most affluent could afford to buy a home in the area.

Raddison was a community that took education seriously. The district budget reflected a per-student expenditure which was hundreds more than that spent by the next-closest district in the state, and the high school had the equipment, physical plant, and staffing to prove it. Parental support was very strong; more than 80 percent of the parents of high school students attended Open School Night, for instance. Raddison grouped its students from seventh grade on, and movement between the skills, average, and AP honors tracks was minimal. Parental pressure, as far as Dan knew, was the most likely and perhaps only reason for a student to be moved across tracks.

As a result, this class was a reflection, and even an exaggeration, of the homogeneity in the community. The twenty-four white students and one oriental student in the class had been honors students since seventh grade, and Dan thought they had become accustomed to a deferential attitude from their teachers and less gifted age-mates. Dan thought that the staff at Raddison High coddled these youngsters; he could certainly see arrogance and elitism in the students, which he attributed to years of special treatment. Aside from disliking their conceited attitude, Dan was concerned that these students were not being well-served by the system, which did not prepare them for the competition of college. Academically, the honors curriculum was challenging, but the students' sheltered social existence was not a realistic preparation for the Ivy League, to which most of them aspired. Dan knew that when these youngsters went to college, they would become individually insignificant overnight.

Dan majored in communication at a private eastern university and spent three years working for a media consultant before entering a master's program that would prepare him for a teaching career. He came from a working-class family whose home was in an ethnically and racially integrated neighborhood. Dan felt that he had life experience, aside from his professional experience, which made him a broad-minded person. He understood the value of his colorful background and believed passionately in the advantages of diversity.

Mark had the last word, for Earl took advantage of the silence following Mark's declaration to introduce a new topic. Earl almost seemed to use lectures as opportunities for retreat, giving himself and the students a chance to recuperate after a particularly divisive or emotional exchange. Listening to Earl speak, Dan tried to conquer his frustration as he watched the class settle down. The students seemed to focus on what Earl was saying even as they physically relaxed in their seats. Dan had to admit that it was a mental relief to listen to Earl's soft, plodding voice after a tiring debate.

Earl Cochran had been teaching at Raddison High School for twenty-eight years, and he did seem to Dan to have an intuitive understanding of the pulse of his class and his students' moods. Earl was very much a student advocate, and while Dan thought the honors pupils could manipulate Earl, he agreed with Earl's prostudent orientation. But Dan thought that these honors students had acquired blinders somewhere along the way, either from their families or from their schooling, and that Earl let the blinders stay in place. The purpose of this government class was to produce informed, thoughtful voters. Indeed, Dan thought, these students represented future American leadership: politicians, executives, professionals. But they were not being asked to see the other side of arguments; they were not being pushed to think critically about their preconceived notions. This class was only reinforcing the students' prejudices and hardening their misconceptions. They weren't learning or thinking; they were performing.

* * *

In the two months since the race relations argument, Dan came to know the students in the sixth-period AP American government class better, and they him. The core beliefs that he had formed early in his student-teaching assignment had not changed, but Dan's initial irritation at the students' elitism gradually became tolerance and amusement, for he had simply vowed not to let them "get to him" anymore. Dan had watched these students "work the system" and had been forced to admire their intelligence and "maze brightness" as they manipulated situations to their own ends. Dan did not like these kids much, but he had to admit their techniques worked.

Dan characterized his relationship with the class when he was teaching as a wary one. The students liked it when he took over the class, and on those days Dan sensed a mental preparation and tautness in the group. But there was a tension in the interchanges that kept Dan sharp during class and left him exhausted afterward. These students were alert to any chink in his armor, and if they thought Dan did not know an answer, they would try gleefully to embarrass him. The students almost seemed, as a group, to realize that Dan had seen through their charade, and this both intrigued and irritated them.

Dan much preferred the average-level classes, which he also taught with Earl. Those students, who were also generally college-bound, could far more readily take the other side of an argument or accommodate disparate views. Dan's philosophy, which he tried to share with his students, was "Know thy enemy." He felt that only by comprehending and even advocating the other side of an issue could one fully justify one's own position or understand the weaknesses in the opposition.

The honors students could not do this; they remained myopic and one-dimensional in most debates. In spite of the fact that Earl approved of Dan's work with the students, Dan occasionally returned to his initial reflections that these students were being poorly served. On most days he let it slide, for Earl was happy and Dan had reached a truce with the class. But once in a while Dan still worried about whether or not the honors class was really learning anything.

Furthermore, Dan was determined not to let these kids walk all over him the way they did Earl Cochran. Dan felt that teachers, not students, should control class discussions and debates. These students seemed to believe that teachers should respect their moods; if on a particular day they wanted to relax, they expected the teacher to let them do so. Dan vowed not to be so intimidated.

Dan knew today was his chance to really test his mettle with the sixth period, alone. Earl was attending a three-day conference, and his recommendation that Dan act as his substitute had been accepted by the administration. This particular week, Earl had warned him, would be a tough one, for students were receiving their college early admission results. The students were under tremendous pressure, in terms of their own self-expectations as well as those of their families, to achieve, and college acceptance was a critical cog in each child's self-view and life plan. Emotions during the week ranged from acute anxiety to great joy, and the class as a whole was inattentive and distracted.

Dan had prepared a thorough lesson plan for his first day "soloing," and he felt the adrenalin surge as he walked from the faculty lounge to the classroom after lunch. His topic for the day was a continuation of the class's recent focus on elections; this was a presidential election year, and the entire school was very involved in discussion and commentary on current events in the news.

Today, Dan was going to introduce the topic of third parties in the U.S. political system. He planned to begin with a film clip of a recent mayoral debate, in which the candidates from the two major political parties shared the stage with representatives from the Liberal, Conservative, and Right to Life parties. After using this clip to introduce the topic of third political parties, Dan intended to review with the students the material they had read in their text about the influence of third political parties in the nineteenth century; then he would open up a discussion of the candidates shown on the film and the influence of their parties in contemporary politics. Over the three days he was in charge, Dan intended to have the class compare the third parties throughout history with contemporary ones. When were the techniques they employed similar or different? When were they effective, and when were they irrelevant? How did the political context in which they existed shape their agendas and their influence? Dan was excited about his plan.

"Hi, Mr. T," said Dave as Dan walked into class. Dave was one of Dan's favorite students. Friendly and gregarious, Dave was captain of the soccer team and was involved in the student newspaper; again, Dan thought, a typical "preppie" student. But Dan found Dave a little more open to other opinions than were the rest of the students, and Dan realized that Dave was under tremendous pressure at home to achieve. Dave's father was a powerful corporate attorney, and Dave desperately wanted to attend his Dad's alma mater.

"Hi, Dave. Any word yet?" asked Dan.

"No, still waiting," smiled Dave nervously.

The rest of the students arrived in small groups from their lunch period, and Dan acted quickly to capture their attention after the bell rang. Without comment, he shut off the lights and rolled the film.

In the dark, Dan heard whispering from the back of the room. This class generally had the maturity not to misbehave in the traditional sense of the word; their transgressions were usually attitudinal rather than behavioral. But Dan had no intention of letting any distraction escalate. He walked quickly toward the source of the disturbance.

"Alex, cut it out," Dan admonished in a whisper when he reached the back row. Alex looked up from the paper he was reading, and as he met Dan's gaze levelly and coolly, he handed the letter to his neighbor across the aisle. Dan reached for the paper and, glancing at the letterhead and first line, realized it was a college acceptance letter. He put it back on the student's desk without comment and gestured that both boys watch the film.

When the clip ended, Dan flicked on the lights and addressed the room. "Today we are going to continue our discussion of third political parties. I want to review yesterday's material on the political environment after the Civil War and then come back to this film clip and talk about how today's splinter parties compare with historical ones."

"Mr. T, those parties today are just noise and distraction. They don't even matter. Why bother talking about it?" Alex was always ready to start a fight, Dan thought.

"Alex, that may be your opinion, but let's take a quick look at some historical facts and see if that has always been the case." Dan was privately proud of his combined put-down of Alex and natural transition back to his lesson plan.

"So you agree these parties are irrelevant today?" pressed Mark.

"No, I don't agree they are irrelevant at all," replied Dan. "The third-party phenomenon in American politics has had a meaningful influence throughout history. Candidates don't have to be elected to affect public opinion or legislation.''

A third student refused to let Dan talk history. "But the Conservative party, for instance. And the Liberals, for that matter. They just carry the name of the Republican or Democratic candidate or some unknown guy who no one votes for.''

"Well, the Right to Life party is certainly influential," Allison called out. "The prolife movement is electing lots of adherents in local governments all across the country.''

"How can an electorate vote for somebody on a single issue like that?'' asked Janet. "Especially something so personal as abortion.''

"Hey, you guys," interjected Dan, "let's stay on the subject. Before we can appreciate the influence of political parties today, let's look at the tradition. . . .''

"Abortion is everyone's issue. Murder is murder, Janet," interrupted Alex.

At least half the class erupted at this comment. Several students yelled their disapproval, and a girl in the front row turned around and threw a pencil in Alex's direction.

"Hold it," Janet cried. "If men had to bear children, abortion would be a sacrament! How can you presume to tell me or any other woman what to do with our own bodies?''

Mark laughed loudly enough to be heard above the general din. "You're just a man hater, Janet," he called. "You won't ever have the problem, so don't worry about it!''

"She's a dyke," Alex called, and the two boys doubled over with laughter.

Dan stood in the front of the room dumbfounded. Janet seemed to be on the verge of tears, from anger more than insult, and the students were yelling opinions at each other violently. Dan had never heard such venom, and it had developed so quickly that he had been at a loss to prevent it. He had no idea how to recapture the group's attention, much less teach, after this debacle. He had been prepared, he knew his subject, and he thought he knew this class. But round one was going decidedly in the students' favor, and he had twenty-two minutes until the bell.

KEN KELLY

A first-year social studies teacher having trouble encouraging discussion in his high school classes visits a fourth-grade philosophy class taught entirely through discussion.

Ken Kelly looked out across the four neat rows at his twenty-four ninth-grade students. Each seemed to have one eye on the clock and the other on the door.

After spending a week lecturing about simple economic principles, Ken was trying to engage the group in a discussion of the differences between free and planned economic systems.

Communism had been unraveling in eastern Europe for months, and Ken had asked his students to watch the news each night so that they could see the shortcomings of that system. The students were showing by their written assignments that they understood the issues, but still they were slow to open up in class and discuss them. Ken's questions elicited only simple, two- or three-word answers.

He looked out at the sea of empty faces and pushed on. "Christie, who owns the factories in communist countries, private businesspeople or the government?"

"The government?" Christie answered, hesitatingly.

"Exactly. Very good. Any why's that? Because, as we studied last week, the governments of communist countries own the means of . . ." Ken waited for a second, hoping someone would volunteer the answer. "Of . . . of what? Carlos?"

"Production."

"Exactly. Production. Good, Carlos." Ken got up from his desk and paced across the front of the room.

"And who owns the means of production in the United States? Who owns the factories here? Tell us, Craig."

"Private people do. Lee Iacocca."

"Half right, half wrong, Craig. The stockholders own Chrysler Motors.

Iacocca is president of the company. Remember, we talked about stocks last week? Now, tell us which system you think is better. Should factories be owned by the government or by . . ."

"Yeah. The government," Craig said.

"Hold on, Craig. Don't interrupt. We've already heard from you. Let's hear from someone else. Besides, you should wait until I finish my question. You can't answer a question until I tell you what it is. So, should factories be owned by the govermment or only by the people who can afford to buy them? Should we be able to have private property as we have here in the United States, or should the property belong to the government so that it can be shared equally by the people? Jessie, how about you? You've been quiet all day. What's your answer?"

Silence.

"Jessie?"

"I like it like we have here."

"OK. Why?"

"You should have to earn what you own."

"Excellent. Good answer. Does anybody disagree?"

Silence.

"Anybody?"

More silence. Several students shifted uneasily in their seats or found ways to occupy themselves. Keith, a typically inattentive student who also was captain of the Littleton High School junior varsity track team, stared at the clock with a hand on his wrist, apparently taking his pulse. In front of him, Maria worked attentively on a braid in her hair.

"Keith! Tell us. What are the advantages of a planned economy? The government can control prices, right? Give me another one. Come on. You should have read this in your text last night."

"Taxes are lower? Ah, no. I mean . . ."

"Oh, really? You want to show me where you read that in the text? Tara, Keith said taxes are lower in a controlled economy. Is that right?"

"I'm sorry," Tara responded. "I couldn't hear the question. May I go to the girls' room?"

Ken walked across the classroom and stood behind the lectern by his desk. "This isn't working," he thought. "These kids know this material, but they won't talk about it meaningfully. They're just not interested."

His anger growing, Ken decided to change his tactics. "Maybe if they saw that the alternative to a discussion is a test, it would motivate them to open up," he thought.

"All right. Everyone take out a pen and a piece of paper," Ken said. "Write your name at the top of the paper, and answer the question I just asked. Should property be owned privately or by the government? You've got until the end of the period."

* * *

Ken collected the papers and walked from the classroom when the bell rang, annoyed that he had to resort to the test and bewildered about why his students were pulling back from him. He remembered that discussions in the first few weeks of class were more lively, but participation gradually declined until only one or two regulars spoke up anymore. "These are all bright kids, all in the upper tracks of their class," he thought. "Many of them are friends, which should make them feel at ease in the classroom and facilitate discussion."

Ken was free for the next two periods. He headed for a nearby elementary school, where he usually ate lunch with a friend who taught there. Walking down the hallway on his way to the cafeteria, Ken saw Sybil Avilla, a teacher in the gifted program who had been teaching philosophy to her gifted students in the elementary school and was using the same method in her regular elementary classes.

Ken had been skeptical when he heard that philosophy would be taught to third- and fourth-graders. Now, still festering at the way his last class had gone, he wondered how students that young could be engaged in philosophical discussions if he couldn't get his ninth-graders to discuss simple economic systems. But Avilla's class had been gaining a reputation among teachers. Ken decided to skip lunch and drop in.

He looked into the classroom and waved at Sybil. "Good afternoon, Mrs. Avilla. I'm Ken Kelly. I teach social studies at the high school. I've heard about your class, and I'm free now. Mind if I sit in a corner and watch? I've been meaning to stop by to see how you do this."

"Sit in a corner, or sit in our circle. We're happy to have you, Mr. Kelly," Avilla responded. "I've had several teachers from the middle school in here already. You're my first high school teacher. Take a seat anywhere."

The period was just beginning, and the seventeen fourth-grade students were settling into chairs that had been arranged in a circle. Sybil, sitting with the children in the circle, turned her attention back to the class.

"Last week, I asked you to think about this question: Would you be different if your name were different?"

Several students began speaking at once. "Just one, please," Sybil said, nodding toward a girl with her hand in the air. "Maria?"

"I was thinking about it the other day," Maria said. "Actually, it depends. Because if you have a name and somebody starts to tease you about it, well that might change your attitude. And you might be a different person. Or you might do different things."

From her seat in the circle, Sybil held up a book. "Well, this is a book about a name. And while I read it to you, I'd like you to think about that question—would you be you if you had a different name? The book is called *The Bear Who Wanted to Be a Bear*."

Sybil began reading. "Leaves were falling from the trees. Flocks of wild geese high above were flying south. The brown bear felt a cool wind on his fur. He was feeling very sleepy. . . ."

Sybil read for ten minutes from the book, which described a bear who wakes after a hibernation to find that a factory has been built in the forest over his den. He tries to convince the factory officials that he's a bear, but they say he's only "a lazy, unshaven worker in a fur coat" and order him to work on an assembly line. The bear works through the spring and summer at the factory, coming to believe he may not be a bear. The following fall, as a new hibernation season begins, the bear begins falling asleep on the job. He's fired and eventually finds his way back to a den in the woods to sleep through the winter.

Sybil closed the book and looked up.

"I wouldn't forget I'm a bear," Rita said, leaning forward into the circle.

Sybil asked, "Why?"

"Because even after an amount of years, I wouldn't forget. I'm a bear. I would look like a bear, even if I shaved."

Kathy raised her hand and began talking. "But if you were in a totally different environment, would you still act the same? Would you think you still looked the same? I mean, maybe there weren't any mirrors. Maybe there was just one, to shave or something. So how would you know you were still a bear and not a person working in a factory like everyone else?"

Craig, who had raised his hand when Kathy did and responded to Sybil's nod, spoke next. "If I were surrounded by machines, and all I did was press a button all day long, I really wouldn't think about my normal activities because I'd be concentrating on pushing the buttons. So I'd think I looked the same and acted the same as everyone in the factory."

Rita shook her head. "Well, I'd remember that I was a bear at least."

"But you'd be surrounded by humans," Kathy said.

A chorus of voices filled the room. Sybil raised her voice above the din, nodding toward one of the children. "Go ahead, Camille."

"I know how it feels. I'm surrounded at home by grown-ups and sometimes I feel like I'm a grown-up, and so I do grown-up sorts of things because everybody around my house is grown-up."

"So that brings us to the question we asked last year," Sybil said, turning again toward Camille. "Would you be you if you had white skin?"

Camille thought for a moment. "Well . . . ."

Several students began talking at once.

Sybil held up her hand. "Wait. Wait. Just let her think for a second."

Camille went on, "Yes. You'd have the same personality. It's like on Halloween. When you dress up as somebody else. But you're not that person."

"But that's temporary. It's not for a long time. If it was permanent, would you be you?" Mickey's voice rose as he finished.

Terrell responded, "Yes and no. You wouldn't be yourself because you'd have white skin. But you would be yourself because you'd do what you normally do."

Maya, who had been listening quietly, leaned forward and spoke to Terrell. "What if you were in a completely different environment? Say you moved to California and became a kid star. And every morning you'd go to work. And you didn't go to school. You got a tutor every afternoon, at lunch break. Would you still be you? Would you still run around and play and everything? Or would you be practicing your lines all the time and everything? You'd probably have a different personality if you were always around a different environment."

Terrell started to respond, "Well, yeah, but . . ." and was interrupted as several students began speaking and several hands went into the air. Sybil interjected again. "Let him finish. Then we'll get to you. Put your hands down for a second."

Terrell continued with the series of questions he had been formulating. "You'd forget that you used to live in this town? You would forget that you were white? You'd forget that you have to go to school everyday? You would forget all that stuff?"

Paula spoke next, "You wouldn't forget it. But it wouldn't be a part of you anymore, so you'd change from how you are now. If you lived in a different environment, then your personality or whatever you thought or think would be different."

"When I lived in Florida, everybody was kind of shy and didn't speak up," Allison began. "So I was shy and I didn't speak up. But then I moved to the north, and all the kids say what they think and what they want to do. So that's what happened to me. It just changed my life totally. Because now I can speak out and say what I want to. Before, I was holding everything in. So you change with your environment."

Sybil addressed the whole group, "If that's true, then we shouldn't be surprised that the bear didn't know he was a bear. Can you make that connection with me now? Do you follow me?"

Several students nodded, and Sybil continued, "If what Allison just said is true, if you accept her statement, then we could understand why the bear didn't know he was a bear. Even though we know he was a bear. So is your bearness or your humanness an outside thing or an inside thing? Who determines what you are? Sonya, good to see your hand up."

Sonya smiled at Sybil as she began to speak. "Well, if you have friends that are rich and other friends that are not too rich, you hang around with the rich people. You'll become like them. You'll act like you're rich."

"So is your personality defined by other people?" Sybil asked.

Sally, whose hand had been up for several minutes, said, "No, it's not. Because if you hang around with rich people, it's not like you're rich. You can act like them, but you're only pretending."

Again, Sybil responded with a question. "So then what is it that makes you who you are?"

Sally continued, "Only you should. Yourself. Suppose some kids are from rich families, and you go and hang around with them. Say they're really 'Jappy,' and they talk like 'Like, totally, and for sure.' And say you start to talk like that. That won't be good. If you hang around people that aren't like you and you become like them, then don't try to go back to your old friends. Because they'll see you've changed a lot, and they won't like you."

As Sally paused, Sybil said, "I'm sorry. We have to stop right now. The period is about to end."

Several students spoke up in protest.

Sybil stood and waved her hand to quiet the chatter. "Wait a moment," she said. "Just because we're done with this in class doesn't mean you should stop talking about it later. I would like you to talk about this with whomever you have dinner with tonight. Try to remember the story of *The Bear Who Wanted to Be a Bear*. And I want you to talk about what it is that makes us human. Is it other people who define us, like they defined the bear? Or do we define ourselves? And if we define ourselves, then how come we change when we're with different kinds of people, as we've been talking about? Or maybe who you are can change."

The chatter among the students continued as they reorganized their desks back into rows. A few approached Sybil and began explaining their ideas about the discussion. After a minute, Sybil waved the remaining students toward their seats and gathered her materials as the regular fourth-grade teacher returned to the classroom. Motioning Ken to follow her, she said, "We can meet in my office across the hall."

As they walked from the room, Sybil turned to Ken and asked, "So, Ken is it? How did you enjoy the class? Different, don't you think?"

"There's no doubt you had them going. I haven't heard that much from any of my students, particularly in my ninth-grade global studies class, since the semester began. But . . ." Ken stopped himself short.

Sybil seemed to sense his hesitation. "But what, Ken?"

"Well, where's the teaching? You didn't do anything. You said only a few words, and the kids just . . . talked."

"If you assume that teaching is telling, you're right," Sybil responded. "I tell them very little in this class. But if what you want to do is create a community of inquiry, you have to assume that a teacher's opinion stands as only one. My job is to get students actively talking together and doing their own thinking, not to get my agenda across."

"Agenda? We've got to be realistic, Sybil. The school district and the state have given us an agenda—the curriculum. At the end of next year, my global studies students will have to take the state curriculum exam. I need to cover the world with them in just two years, and I don't think I could do it using freewheeling, open-ended discussions very often."

"Certainly you've got to help your students prepare for the exam," Sybil said, "but you also can use the Socratic technique you just saw. A good teacher needs many techniques. A teacher delivers a lecture when it's important to get a lot of information across in a hurry, but there are times when the teacher has to be more of a coach, a facilitator of information. There are times when it's appropriate for students to listen and take notes, and times when they should participate more actively: talk, respond, react, analyze, personalize, think. That's what these dialogues are for. Every teacher could use them, in any subject.''

"Every teacher?'' Ken asked. "Maybe there's a place for these dialogues in some of the social sciences I teach, but how could they be used in the hard sciences, or math? Kids won't learn long division by sitting in circles chatting with each other about it. C'mon, Sybil. Aren't you stretching the point?''

Sybil started to respond but then paused. She shrugged and said, "Maybe so, Ken. I probably do stretch the point.'' Ken wasn't sure if she was angry or not, and he didn't know what to say next. He watched Sybil organize materials for her next class.

"It's a valid technique, Sybil. I enjoyed watching you work at it. And thanks for talking to me. I don't know if I could ever give up so much control. I don't know if it would work for me.''

"Maybe that's true,'' Sybil responded. "It's interesting, isn't it? The children adore this method, and the teachers are scared to death of it. To make it work, teachers have got to change their point of view, to look at their place in education. They've got to be genuinely interested in asking questions for which they're not looking for the almighty right answer all the time. It's tough to do.''

Ken nodded good-bye and headed for the teacher's lounge, hoping to find the friend with whom he usually ate lunch. He needed another reaction to what he'd just observed, but the room was nearly empty. Ken bought a sandwich and a soda from the vending machine and took a seat at an empty table. He opened the newspaper he carried with him but found his thoughts continually returning to Sybil Avilla's classroom.

"I'm a teacher, not a talk-show host,'' he said half out loud. "I've got to get through a mountain of curriculum—the history of the eastern and western worlds—and she wants me to suspend the lessons every fourth or fifth day so that I can let my kids just chat about it.

"There may be no right answers in Sybil's classes, but when my tenth graders sit down to take the state curriculum exam next June, they'll need to know a lot of right answers. And they're not going to find those answers sitting in circles and talking some bear through an identity crisis.''

Ken picked up the newspaper again and thumbed to the sports pages, but his thinking returned to Sybil's class. "Certainly, there are arguments for what Sybil does,'' he thought. "Clearly, the class was more lively than any of mine have been in a while. But so much of what she does, or doesn't do, contradicts some of the basic strategies I studied in education classes; her lesson had no real advance organizer. It needed more closure. She never praised a right answer. She never corrected an incorrect one. The obvious point of the lesson was that only you can define the kind of person you are. But when a few of the kids said exactly that, she didn't even acknowledge them. Kids need that feedback.

"And the class lasted forty minutes, but only half the kids said anything at all. I'm not sure the other half were even listening. I don't think they got anything out of it. She never called on kids, even those that were obviously daydreaming. And when the discussion wandered, she never stepped in to bring it back. I wonder, really, what Sybil's kids learned today."

Ken looked down at his unread newspaper and then at his watch. He picked up the paper and his trash from lunch, tossed them into the garbage, and headed back toward the high school for his afternoon classes. "She's just too radical," he thought as he swung open the door from the elementary school and let it close gently behind him.

PART FOUR

DIVERSITY

MARY EWING

An experienced high school math teacher moves to the middle school and has problems with grouping in a remedial math class where each of the eleven students is working at a different level.

"Forget it! I have to do my own work!" Joe Johnson's anger at his classmate's interruption was way out of proportion to the concentration he had been investing on his worksheet.

"Well *excuse me!*" Anna Jones affected great indignation to hide her embarrassment at having her request for help rejected.

Mary Ewing was bending over a worksheet of word problems with one of her students, and she looked up in irritation when she heard this outburst from the other end of the room.

"Miss Margolis, would you please help Anna when you have a moment?" Mary addressed her teacher's aide, who was across the room helping Hank with a division problem. Miss Margolis looked up and nodded, although she was clearly frustrated by the number of students clamoring for help. Mary knew that Betty Margolis was no wizard in mathematics and that it took all her concentration to make mental leaps from addition to division to fractions in order to accommodate the four groups into which Mary had divided her class.

"Miss Margolis promised to help me next!" shouted George, who had been waiting more or less patiently with his head on his folded arms. "This stuff don't make no sense no how!"

Mary sighed and marshaled her characteristic patience and understanding. It was six weeks into the school year, and she was enjoying the year in most ways, but she dreaded the constant disruption and noise that seemed endemic to this seventh- and eighth-grade remedial math class. "George, you have been very patient. I will help you when I finish with group B. And Joe, next time someone in your group asks for help, you give it!" Mary realized that this outburst had distracted all the children, and she had exacerbated the disruption by addressing the principals from her seat beside Jesse. But Jesse was so close to grasping the arithmetic operation that had been eluding him since September that she did not want to leave his side until they had finished. Too often with this class Mary wrestled with just such a choice: disrupt her group instruction to control the class or risk overall bedlam.

This was Mary's tenth year teaching math, but all her previous experience was on the high school level. Mary had been excited last spring when she was offered the chance to teach at Littleton Middle School. She saw the change as a chance to meet new challenges and to stay "fresh" in her field. She was assigned four regular math classes, which ranged from general math to honors geometry, and one remedial math class during the second period. The latter was a group of eleven children, ages 12 to 15. The class was nearly balanced racially: six black and five white students, but that was where the symmetry ended. The skill levels and math backgrounds of the children were widely diverse. In this class Mary had some students who were working on two-digit addition and others who were ready for fractions. Individualization of instruction was required in all classrooms, Mary knew, but she had never found it so difficult to accomplish until now.

Mary had known that this would be the case when she first began planning during the summer. She familiarized herself with each child's needs through his or her test scores and other records and devised a plan for math that had worked well in her high school classes. She divided the eleven students into four groups according to their readiness and skill levels. On the first day of class she assigned groups as follows:

Group A: Division and fractions
 • Hank Donovan
 • Sheila Arjoon
 • Sara Black
Group B: Times tables and multiplication problems
 • Jesse Smith
 • Jimmy Lyons
Group C: Four-digit addition and subtraction with regrouping
 • George Sanders
 • Adam Garth
 • Jack Myers
Group D: Simple addition and subtraction
 • Anna Jones
 • Joe Johnson
 • Peter Marks

By the second week, Mary modified her plan, as her personal experience with the children led to a refinement of group assignments. She moved Sheila to group B and Peter to group C. While this rearrangement resulted in groups of different sizes, Mary thought she had like-skilled students grouped fairly closely.

Mary spent the first week of the school year teaching cooperation and group learning skills almost as much as she taught math. Mary had attended a seminar on cooperative learning at her district's Teacher Center a few years ago when the technique was first introduced, and she implemented aspects of the approach with her high school classes, modifying it as she felt necessary to fit the characteristics of her students. Mary duplicated her group formula in most of her classes this year. She arranged the desks in a horseshoe so that she could sit at the open end when working with one group. The children in other groups sat next to their group-mates around the horseshoe, working independently but sitting close enough to each other for help to be exchanged as necessary. Mary also introduced a token system modeled after one that served her well in her high school remedial classes. Each child earned tokens, redeemable for free time, bathroom privileges, computer time, or library time. Tokens were earned by completing one's own assignments successfully and on time, and they were also awarded on the basis of the success of one's group-mates.

By the second week in October, however, Mary was concerned. Total individualization was required, even within groups. Some students responded more easily to word problems; others to arithmetic operations. Some could use the school-supplied curriculum, but others needed customized worksheets and instruction. Within each group, some of the children had yet to grasp the concept of the arithmetic operation under study, while other students were ready for practice and application of the skill involved. Mary often found herself preparing eleven different math lessons each day, drawing upon four different math textbooks, the curriculum used by the regular math classes, worksheets, workbooks, and her own intuition about what would click with each student.

Besides the time required to prepare so many lessons, a big disadvantage of such extreme individualization was its negative impact on group cooperation. When Mary was working with one group and Miss Margolis with another, the remaining two groups were to work individually at their desks, helping each other with questions and explanations as needed. But because the children were working on different operations even within their groups, they were distracted by one another's requests for help.

Furthermore, Mary was not used to the immaturity of children of this age. In spite of her instruction on group behavior, she soon discovered that the children could not work effectively together without an adult present. They would tease each other when they discovered mistakes, and the more advanced students occasionally made fun of those working on more basic skills. Joe Johnson, in particular, was the butt of many jokes, for at 15 he was the oldest student but was working on the most elementary material. Those students who did try to help their classmates often just confused matters with explanations that were unclear or incorrect.

In spite of the fact that general murmurs of conversation were audible around the room, Mary returned her focus to the students in Jesse's group. She forced herself to recall their conversation even as she listened to—and ignored—the escalating din.

"I'm sorry, Jesse. Sheila, put that down and listen too." Mary glanced sharply at Jimmy Lyons to be sure he, too, was paying attention. "Now tell me, Jesse, again. How many popsicles did the Good Humor man sell on Tuesday?"

"Mrs. Ewing, we done this problem yesterday!"

"Sheila, we are going over this again to be sure your whole group understands it, and then we will move on. You know, using multiplication in everyday life takes lots of practice. Listening to this review won't hurt you."

Sheila grumbled something inaudible under her breath and rolled her eyes. Jimmy and Jesse looked at each other with expressions of disdain, but Mary knew they were trying to mask their embarrassment over the fact that they had not completed this assignment. Mary decided to let the boys off the hook.

"All right, Sheila, since you know the answer to this problem, why don't you show the rest of us how you got it."

Sheila looked down at her worksheet and tried to gather her thoughts. "Well, the ice cream truck sold 439 popsicles on Tuesday; 63 of them were ice bars, 244 were frozen eclairs, and the rest were ice cream sandwiches."

"Sheila, what are we trying to figure out in this problem? What is the overall thing we want to know?" Mary wanted to be sure these children really understood the concepts of problem solving behind this example, and so she started again at the top.

"Well, what do you mean?"

"Pretend you are the Good Humor man. I mean woman." Mary smiled. "What do you want to know at the end of the day?"

"How much money I made!" Jimmy was paying attention and even enjoying himself.

"Right, Jim. OK, Sheila, if you want to know how much money you made and you sold different kinds of ice cream bars that sold for different amounts of money, what do you have to do?"

Sheila was on track again. "You have to multiply how many you sold of each kind by how much each kind costs."

"Good! Jesse, do you see what Sheila did? Did she just make sense?" Mary reached for Sheila's paper as she spoke and slid it to the right so that Jesse could see it.

"Uh, yeah, so he sold, um, 63 that cost a quarter and the eclairs cost a dollar. . . ." Suddenly they all heard laughter coming from across the room. Jesse looked up from Sheila's paper and turned toward the sound. Mary turned with exasperation and saw Anna and Peter laughing.

"Hank, look at this!" Peter grabbed a paper from the desk in front of

Joe Johnson and sailed it across the horseshoe. As it fell to the floor in front of his desk, Hank noisily leaped forward in a futile attempt to catch it.

"Slow Joe just added 13 and 38 and got 41!" laughed Peter. "Can you believe it?"

"Group D for *dumb*—I'll never get any chips with Joe on my team," moaned Anna.

"Well you aren't the smartest girl in school either!" shouted Joe. As he spoke, he sent Anna's open book, paper, and pencils flying to the floor with a sweep of his arm.

The noise of the book striking the floor stunned the class into silence, and Mary reacted swiftly and decisively. "All right—*no more!* I am appalled at you! Peter, Anna, I expect you here after school. I will not tolerate this sort of criticism of each other." Mary turned and spoke just as sharply to the rest of the class. "We will all work alone for the rest of the class period. It is obvious you cannot work together today. Miss Margolis and I will do our best to help those who need it, but I do not want to hear one more word from anyone except to a teacher. Is that understood?"

* * *

Mary opened her second-period class the next morning with mixed emotions. She had decided overnight to make some changes in the class in order to structure it more realistically in light of the children's attitudes and abilities. She believed that she was bowing to the inevitable, but she also felt a sense of defeat. Mary had always enjoyed teaching classes that could work well together, and she felt that important skills were learned when children cooperated. But this class was simply not responding to that formula, and math was not being learned. Since she had to individualize so much anyway, Mary decided to capitulate.

"Good morning. I have some changes to explain to you this morning." Mary spoke as the bell rang. The children were arranging their notebooks and taking out pencils, but the tone of her voice captured their attention.

"Each of you is working on different concepts in this class, and I have decided that working in groups is not helping you as much as it is distracting you. From now on, we will have a system for individual work. No more groups."

This sank in for a moment, and then Sara Black waved her hand in the back of the room. "Yes, Sara?"

"Does that mean no more chips? How do we earn free time?"

"You will each earn chips on the basis of your own work. Just as before, you get one chip for turning in work on time, one if you get only one problem wrong, and two if your work is perfect. But you get no chips for anyone else's work. Just your own."

"All right!" Jimmy's comment underscored the general nods of approval visible around the room. The students' reactions made Mary sad, but again she was convinced of the necessity of this action. These kids just didn't like working together.

"You will each have your own work folders, which I will prepare with your assignments." Mary walked around the horseshoe placing closed manila folders on each student's desk. "No one else even needs to know what you are working on." When she got back to her desk, she held up a chart with two columns entitled "Need Help" and "Work Complete." "This chart will always be kept on my desk. If you need my help as you are working on your assignment, get up and write your name in the "Need Help" column; then sit quietly while you wait for me or Miss Margolis to get to you. We will cross off names as we go, so you will know when your turn is coming up."

"What do we do while we wait?"

"You may do other work."

"Even other class work?"

"Yes, as long as you are quiet. When you finish your work, write your name in the "Work Complete" column; I will check your papers when I am free."

"This might be a little boring," ventured Joe. "Can't we . . ."

Mary interrupted abruptly. "Joe, this is our new procedure. Do you have any questions on how we will work?" Joe remained silent, and Mary gazed around the room at the rest of the class. "OK, then, let's do some math!"

ALLISON COHEN

A resource room teacher opens a resource room at an elementary school that has never had any special education classrooms. She believes the teachers are colluding to make the mainstreaming program fail.

No one was sure when the teachers at the Bidwell Elementary School in the Lumberton school district began to refer to themselves as "the old biddies," but the name had stuck, and a short time after Allison Cohen began teaching in the new resource room in Bidwell, she came to the conclusion that the name was appropriate.

The Lumberton school district, located in a suburban area of a large northeastern state, was created many years ago by merging the school districts of seven neighboring townships for purposes of improving the school services they could offer to the children residing in the townships. Currently serving almost 11,000 children in kindergarten through grade 12 with sixteen elementary schools, four middle schools, and three high schools, Lumberton employed 1200 teachers and staff and 60 school administrators.

Bidwell School was different from all the other elementary schools in Lumberton in a number of ways. First, it was the smallest school in the district. There were only two classes at each grade level, with a total of thirteen teachers in the building. (One kindergarten teacher taught both the morning and the afternoon kindergarten sessions.) Because of its size, there had been no full-time special teachers at the school. Art, music, physical education, remedial reading, and computer teachers visited the school weekly, but the regular staff consisted of only the thirteen classroom teachers and the principal.

All thirteen teachers were women, and all had been there for a long time. The "newest" teacher, Theresa Conti, began teaching there fourteen years ago. Mary Edgerly, the principal, had been a Bidwell teacher for twenty-two years prior to her appointment to the principal's position four years ago. The current staff averaged twenty-one years of service at the school, with Margaret Antonelli holding the longevity record—thirty-three years of consecutive teaching at Bidwell.

The teachers' years together and their ability to work as a team accounted for another difference at Bidwell. The teachers were very powerful. For example, there had never been a special education classroom in the building. Over the years, Bidwell principals had successfully argued that it made more sense to bus the few special education students from Bidwell to a neighboring school than to bus many special education students to Bidwell's small setting.

The teachers' power was also seen in the fact that in the past fourteen years none of Bidwell's teachers had been transferred to another school in the district. Bidwell was the only school in Lumberton that had not had recent staff changes. The teachers remained exempt from staff shifts even when Bidwell's enrollment declined in the early 1980s and some classes fell to fewer than fifteen students. Recently, school enrollments had increased, and there were now between twenty-two and twenty-five students in each class.

Some people in the district attributed the power of the Bidwell faculty to Margaret Antonelli. Her family had lived in Lumberton for years, and she was said to be "connected" to local politicians and other powerful people in the community. Margaret, who had never married, still lived in the house where she had been raised. Until recently, she had cared for her aging mother, who died this past spring.

There were other people on the Bidwell faculty with strong connections in the community. The principal was the sister-in-law of the superintendent of schools, and two of the teachers were related to members of the school board. A fourth teacher was married to the scion of one of the wealthiest families in the community.

The most recent challenge to the status quo at Bidwell occurred two years ago when Ruth Greenburg, the director of special education, tried to start a resource room in the building as part of a pilot mainstreaming program. Until then, all mildly handicapped elementary school students in the district had been served in self-contained special education classrooms. When Ruth Greenburg was promoted to the position of director of special education, she initiated resource room programs in the district. At first, as the services to mildly handicapped elementary school students in Lumberton began to change, Mary Edgerly was able to argue successfully that Bidwell was unprepared to test a new program since the teachers had no experience with special education students. But even as Mary won that battle, she knew that a resource room would soon come to her building. Ruth Greenburg had been responsible for changing the special education program in such a way that district policy now called for a resource room in each elementary building. For two years, Ruth had held in-service meetings for all elementary school teachers to prepare them for mainstreaming.

As Mary had anticipated, two years later the resource room became a reality, and Allison Cohen was the teacher assigned to the class. When Allison arrived at Bidwell, she knew little of its history. She had been hired to teach in Lumberton immediately after she graduated from the state university with a B.S. in elementary and special education. Two years before, after teaching in a self-contained LD classroom for five years, she was asked to move to a resource room as part of the pilot program the district was establishing to mainstream many of its special education students. She found the resource room program stimulating, and she knew that her classroom was seen as a model by other teachers. She also knew from attending meetings with other resource room teachers that her relationships with the teachers in her building were better than most.

Now 28, she was married and had a 3-year-old child. A bright, feisty redhead who managed to balance her work and home life with humor and high spirits, she knew that Ruth Greenburg had selected her for this assignment because of her upbeat personality and success in her first resource room assignment. Other than that, she got little information from Ruth about the Bidwell situation.

When school started in September, she found eleven children on her class roll. These were all former Bidwell School students who had been served in special education classes in other elementary schools and who were being returned to Bidwell to enter their assigned grade and receive resource room support. These students had been selected by the Committee on Special Education (CSE) as the most likely to be successfully mainstreamed from among all the children in self-contained classes whose home school was Bidwell. It was expected that Allison's class would be completed as other Bidwell students were returned to their home school and as newly eligible students were scheduled for the resource room instead of being sent to a self-contained class in another school.

Allison began the school year by meeting personally with each of the seven teachers who had a resource room student and talking about the role that she and the resource room might play in helping both the child and the teacher. The teachers were very gracious and listened to Allison with interest. They didn't seem to have any questions or objections, and Allison told her husband that she felt that they probably were going to serve the returning students well, given their years of experience.

But on the second day of school, June Jamison, one of the third-grade teachers, came to Allison to request additional resource room time for Seth, the mainstreamed student in her classroom. As Allison tried to explain that Seth was expected to spend most of his day in the regular class, June nodded and with a smile said, "Yes, dear, and you are quite right to try to follow policy. But don't you think your first responsibility is to the child? Seth so needs your help."

Allison agreed to bring Seth to the resource room for an additional half hour each day and told June that she would check with her at the end of the week to see how Seth was doing. June responded, "I'll be happy to talk with you then."

The following day, Anna Richards, the other third-grade teacher, came to see Allison. "As you know," she began, "I have two resource room students in my class. Third grade is a very difficult year, and neither of these children is able to keep up with the class. They seem very discouraged, and I'm worried about them."

Allison responded, "Perhaps I could observe the children in your class and see how they are doing."

"Oh, no. I'm sure that would upset them. I think they need your help in your classroom." Allison noticed that Anna emphasized "your classroom."

When Allison said she would see the two children for an additional half hour each day, Anna responded, "Half an hour! That won't be long enough. These students need help in reading, arithmetic, and spelling. I was thinking of two more hours a day."

Allison tried to reason with the teacher. "Miss Richards, the whole idea of mainstreaming is for the children to be with other third-graders in your classroom. I really shouldn't see them for two more hours a day."

The two teachers finally agreed that the students would spend an additional hour a day in the resource room. As Anna left the classroom, Allison felt that the worst was over, since third-grade teachers throughout the district were the most concerned about mainstreaming as a result of a recently instituted state Minimum Basic Skills Test, which was given in third, seventh, and eleventh grades.

She couldn't have been more wrong. By the end of the second week of school, she had been visited by four more teachers, each of whom came to request more time in the resource room for her mainstreamed students. Without showing anger or impatience, they all told Allison virtually the same story: The students needed more help than they could give; therefore Allison would have to do something.

Allison decided to try to work with the teachers by suggesting the sort of simple classroom accommodations that had helped the teachers in her previous school. When June told her that Seth could not follow oral directions, Allison suggested that June write the directions on the chalkboard.

June responded, "Well, of course I've tried that, but it just did not help a bit. You know, my dear, you have only five children at a time. Until you've had experience with large groups of children, you really can't imagine what might work in a classroom like mine."

Allison then tried to observe her students in their regular classes. She first approached Margaret Antonelli, figuring that if she could win her over, the rest of the faculty would be pushovers.

"Miss Antonelli." Allison tried to be winning. "Jeff has said the nicest things about your classroom. Since other students are having some problems, I'd like to watch him for a while in your room to see if I can figure out what special things you are doing."

Margaret looked at Allison without smiling. "I really don't think that's a good idea. It would make Jeff and the other children uncomfortable for you to be there."

Another time, Allison had to blink back tears of frustration when a teacher responded to her suggestion that she visit the teacher's classroom by saying, "Perhaps you could run some copies of my worksheets or correct some student work if you are looking for things to do."

And if she went into a classroom without an invitation, the teacher would stop the lesson, speak politely with Allison, and not resume the lesson until Allison left the room.

When Allison tried to discuss the problem with Mary Edgerly, the principal spoke with her in an even tone. "I think you should know that the teachers at Bidwell are the best in the district. I'm sure that every decision they make is in the best interest of the pupils." Allison explained that she respected the teachers but that they were fighting her efforts to mainstream the students. Mary seemed annoyed and responded, "When you have had as much experience with children as these teachers, then you'll understand."

Allison found herself showing her frustration. "But the resource room isn't working!" she told Mary in a louder-than-usual tone.

Mary seemed to sense her distress and responded, "The teachers are very happy with the resource room. The children are getting along well, considering, and I think you should just keep on helping them. If that means spending more time with them in the resource room, then you should do that without getting all upset."

Mary ended the conversation by putting her arm around Allison's shoulder and saying, "In fact, I just saw Ruth Greenburg at a meeting and told her what a wonderful job you are doing. I told Ruth I owed her an apology for resisting the resource room, since it's working out better than I could have imagined. And I made it clear that you are the reason we are so happy with the program. I really think you just need to have a little more confidence in yourself."

"Talk about damning with faint praise," Allison thought to herself. She knew that the resource room was not working and that she was not doing her job. She still had only eleven children in her class, and she was seeing each child for at least three hours a day. She was not working with the teachers, and most of her time in the resource room was spent teaching developmental reading, language arts, and math, since the students were missing instruction in those areas by being in the resource room instead of their regular classrooms.

Allison felt that the Bidwell teachers had entered into a conspiracy against her while maintaining a surface cordiality and friendliness. The first time she mentioned that feeling to her husband, he laughed and said, "Those old biddies in a conspiracy? Allie, you've got to be kidding."

But Allison wasn't kidding. She really had come to think of the Bidwell teachers as evil. She no longer believed that it was a coincidence that their responses to her and the children were so alike. She was convinced that they were trying to prevent the resource room from succeeding.

Beyond that, she felt that Mary had finessed her by lavishly complimenting her to Ruth Greenburg. If she went to Ruth with her problems, Ruth would probably think she was crazy. There was no one in the building with whom she could talk. She needed an ally who knew what it was *really* like in that school and who could give her advice. She did not know where to turn.

CAROL BROWN

*A first-grade teacher, after socially integrating an extremely
heterogeneous class, sees her efforts threatened when a child's
pencil case disappears and is thought to have been stolen.*

Carol Brown locked her car and turned her collar up against the cold January
wind as she rushed toward the school. At the outer doors of the building,
Carol reached down and picked up a red mitten that must have been dropped
as students raced to their buses the night before. She tucked it into her
pocket, making a mental note that later she would take it to the lost and
found.

Her mind was already on a situation that began yesterday in her first-
grade classroom. As the class settled in, John Casey realized that his pencil
case was missing from his desk. Some of the children suggested that it had
been stolen, but Carol assured them that it was probably misplaced and
would turn up soon. However, by the end of the day the pencil case had
not been found, and Carol remembered how upset John was when school
was dismissed.

Hanging up her coat in her classroom, Carol heard an argument just
outside her door. She stepped into the corridor and found two of her students
shouting at each other. Managing to separate them, Carol asked the boys
what the problem was.

"Robert stole my mitten," yelled Brian.

Robert interrupted, "I didn't steal nothin'."

Brian explained to Carol that he had both his mittens in his pocket the
day before. He sat with Robert on the bus going home, and when he got off
the bus one of his mittens was gone.

"He's lying. I never took his dumb mitten." Robert seemed very upset
at the accusation.

"Brian, what does your mitten look like?" Carol asked as she walked
the two boys into the classroom and showed them the mitten she had
retrieved from the sidewalk earlier.

Brian grabbed the mitten and said, "That's mine. That's my mitten. Where was it?"

Carol knelt down and pulled both Brian and Robert to her. She looked at Brian and said, "I found it right outside the building when I came in this morning. Don't you think you owe Robert an apology?"

Brian looked down at his feet and then at Robert. "I'm sorry," he said. Brian spoke quietly, but it seemed clear that he really was sorry.

"It's good that you could apologize, Brian. See how bad you made Robert feel by accusing him of stealing? You guys are such good friends, it would really be a shame to lose a friend because you accused someone unfairly. You won't do that again, will you?"

Brian shook his head to indicate that he would not. Carol turned to Robert. "Do you accept Brian's apology?"

Robert shrugged and said, "Yeah, OK."

Carol hugged the children and said, "Let's seal it with a high five."

Both boys giggled, slapped upraised palms, and left the classroom to wait in the gym for the morning bell.

Carol watched them leave and thought to herself, "Why would Brian automatically suspect that his mitten had been stolen? What a strange reaction from him." But, as she remembered the missing pencil case, she suspected that it was more than coincidence that stealing was on Brian's mind. Carol knew that the children had been consumed the day before with talk about the "stolen" pencil case, and she feared it would not be quickly forgotten.

John had brought the pencil case to school just after Christmas, and the whole class had demonstrated an appreciation for what a treasure it was. John did not hesitate to share the case with other students. It was not unusual to see the other children carrying it around, using the ruler or protractor or stapler that were part of the case. Yesterday morning John came back to school after being absent the day before and found that the pencil case was not in his desk where he had left it.

At first, Carol suggested that perhaps someone had borrowed the case and forgotten to return it. To Carol's dismay, none of the students resolved the problem by bringing forth the missing item. When Carol suggested that maybe it had simply been misplaced, John became frustrated and angry. The child was upset about his loss and in his anger did not hesitate to announce openly to the rest of the first-grade class that someone had stolen his property.

The other children seemed affected by the situation because the missing item was something that they all enjoyed using. The class was quick to rally around the idea that this was a theft, and some children began to name possible "suspects." In only one day, Carol Brown's happy, close-knit class of twenty-four children became accusatory and mean.

In the beginning of the year, this class had presented a real challenge for Carol, because the children came from such diverse backgrounds. Of the fifteen girls and nine boys in the class, eight came from economically disadvantaged homes. The school system had implemented its racial balance program in such a way that this school drew its students from the richest section of the city, where the school was located, and from the poorest areas, from which a sizable number of students were bused. There was only a small representation of middle-class children to buffer these disparate groups. Students in Carol's class who were driven to school in Mercedes sat next to others whose parents could not afford to provide warm winter coats.

At first, as would be natural, the children from the affluent neighborhoods tended to associate with one another, and the children from the poorer areas felt more comfortable with friends from their own neighborhoods. This natural tendency, coupled with the fact that the children shared very few common experiences, made it difficult at first to break down the barriers and create a unified class.

In the first few months of school, Carol implemented as many strategies as she could to help the students interact and to provide shared experiences in the classroom. Early in September, she established cooperative learning groups. She made certain that the groups were balanced socioeconomically and that each group contained no more than three or four students so that small cliques within the groups could not form. The types of activities she created required that the children work together in order to get the most from the tasks. She changed the group composition every two weeks.

Carol also established centers that only a few children at a time could work in. There were centers for playing dress-up games, for building with Lego blocks, for listening to talking books, for working at the computer, for doing art projects, and so on. Children drew lots for which center they could go to, guaranteeing that there would always be a diverse population at each one. Since the children typically had "center time" twice a day, there were many opportunities for the children to interact and to get to know and trust one another.

The classroom also featured what Carol called "the author's seat," which allowed all the children to share stories they had written. This helped the students get to know one another and begin to understand each other's backgrounds. Carol's early efforts paid off, and by Thanksgiving the children were mingling easily and interacting across socioeconomic groups on their own.

This was an accomplishment Carol felt very proud of because her approach to teaching had always stressed respect. In her class, Carol often discussed the importance of individuality and the ways in which all students shared equal rights within the classroom community. But the current incident certainly put her philosophy to the test. In just one day the missing pencil case created an air of suspicion among the students that Carol feared would undermine the integration she had achieved.

Carol began to wonder what had really happened to the pencil case. It was clear that John's friends thought that one of the poor children had stolen it, and Carol nurtured the same suspicion. While all the children coveted the special pencil case, Carol understood that the affluent children had many treasures and the poor children had few.

Carol had been teaching for many years in elementary classes. Early in her career, she spent three years teaching in an economically deprived urban area and encountered many situations involving classroom theft. She understood the pressure and sorrow of poverty and knew that the egocentrism of children could translate envy into action. This very heterogeneous class, however, added a new dimension to this classic problem. Before, she had been able to handle a theft situation without worrying about whether it would undo the foundation of a successfully integrated group.

Carol looked at the clock and saw that class was about to begin. She knew that she had to handle the pencil-case situation today and that she had to do it very carefully. More important to Carol than the $10 pencil case was the preservation of trust among the students. How could she carry on her investigation discreetly in order to solve the problem of John's missing property and perhaps further her agenda of mutual trust and respect?

As the children spilled into the room and began to sit in a circle on the area rug where the class always started its day, Carol resolved to use the pencil-case incident as a means of strengthening the class's unity rather than permit the situation, through inaction, to cause divisiveness. She also knew this was an ideal opportunity to use a real-life situation to help the children grow. "A good offense . . ." Carol thought as she took her place in the circle.

"Good morning, boys and girls. Are you all warm now that we're inside and together?"

"Yeah." "Sure." "It's so cold!" A chorus of replies rang around Carol.

"What day is today, Fernando?"

"Um . . ." Fernando, a dark-skinned Puerto Rican child dressed in an oversize sweatshirt looked toward the poster-board calendar that hung on the wall above the play area shelves. "Um . . . Wednesday."

"And what number day is it?" Carol continued addressing Fernando.

"Numero 15. Of January."

"Good! Would you go put the number 15 in the Wednesday slot so that we can all remember the date?" As Fernando uncurled himself to update the calendar, Carol turned her attention to the rest of the children.

"Today we are going to finish the story we began yesterday about Eskimos, and we are going to make pictures of igloos and snowmen at art time using cotton and glitter. Then after recess we're going to bring some snow inside for science time and look at it and feel it and talk about what happens when we heat it up. But, first, I want to talk to all of you about something I think is on our minds—John's pencil case, which we lost yesterday."

"Somebody took it," a girl with blond pigtails called out indignantly.

"Did you find it?" John Casey asked excitedly.

"No, it was stole. It's gone," Fernando said to John with a "forget it" gesture.

"Well, children, I don't know where it is, and we may not find it. But let's talk about your feeling that the pencil case might have been stolen. Karen, you said you think someone took it. Why do you think that?"

"Because it was so nice and somebody that wanted it an' couldn't buy it would just take it."

"Would you take something that you didn't have the money to buy?" Carol asked.

"Well, maybe, if I really wanted it." Karen seemed to sense she was on thin ice with this admission but obviously answered honestly.

"Then you'd get caught an' go to jail!" cried Brian. "You can't steal, or you go to jail!"

"Why do we send people to jail for stealing, Brian?" pursued Carol.

"Because it's wrong!"

"Yes, it is wrong to steal. But why is it wrong? Yusef?"

"'Cause you might go to jail. My brother is in jail 'cause he tooked some stuff ain't his. He ain't never comin' home!" Yusef's eyes were huge and hurt, and a few of the children looked frightened and subdued as they digested this information.

"That's dumb. Kids don' go to jail," ventured Robert confidently.

"An' if nobody was looking an' you knowed you wouldn't go to jail you might take it," Janey spoke quietly.

"Sure, you only go to jail if the teacher sees," volunteered Arlene.

"Well, we already said that children don't go to jail, Arlene, and certainly teachers are here to help children learn what is right, not to catch children or punish them. But I want you to think about whether or not there are other reasons not to take something that is not yours." Carol's manner was warm and encouraging as she smiled at her class.

There was silence in the circle as the children thought. "Well, just if you get in trouble," Robert finally concluded.

"And if John is sad his case is gone," Brian mused.

"Yeah, if your mother finds it or you get caught!" Another student's elaboration on Robert's point drowned out Brian's contribution.

"What if we all took each other's things whenever we wanted?" prompted Carol. "What would happen then?" Again the students concentrated on their teacher's question. The seconds ticked by, and Carol fleetingly thought about getting through story time and art before recess.

"Well, we'd all get in trouble, I guess," speculated Yusef.

"Yes, that's right," agreed Carol. "Classrooms need rules just like grown-ups do so that students can all work together happily and not worry about their things being taken. We need to trust each other and care about each other.'' Carol studied the open faces turned toward her in an attempt to read the children's reactions. She saw acceptance in their eyes because she was the teacher, but she felt a nagging doubt that they really understood or believed her.

"So who took my case?" John suddenly called, addressing his classmates accusingly. They looked at him miserably, and Carol saw that the discussion hadn't served its intended purpose.

"What," she wondered, "do I do now?"

JOAN MARTIN, MARILYN COE, WARREN GROVES

A classroom teacher, a special education teacher, and
an elementary school principal hold different views about
mainstreaming a boy with poor reading skills into a
fourth-grade social studies class.

Joan Martin looked out on her empty fourth-grade classroom and rubbed her temples. She walked over to Donald's desk, ran her hand over its scarred top, and squeezed her bulky frame into the seat. Despite her concerns, she smiled to herself, realizing she had sat down at Donald's desk hoping to understand him better by putting herself into his physical place in her room. She was looking for a solution to what she had come to think of as "the Donald thing."

Joan had been teaching elementary school in Littleton for fourteen years, and this fall she began her sixth year teaching fourth grade at Roosevelt Elementary School. Now approaching 45, she was distressed to find herself with a problem that she could not resolve, a problem for which her experience and skills had not prepared her.

The previous spring the Committee on Special Education (CSE), principal Warren Groves, and special education teacher Marilyn Coe approached Joan and asked her to mainstream three special education students into her social studies class during the upcoming school year. She agreed without much hesitation. She was flattered that they had chosen her from among the five fourth-grade teachers in her building, and she believed at the time that she needed and could handle the challenge of these students. Sitting at Donald's desk, she wondered how she could have so seriously misjudged her own situation.

Joan completed her teacher preparation program at a small private college in New York more than twenty years ago. She taught for the two years following her college graduation and then left teaching to marry and raise a family. She returned to the classroom when her youngest children (twin sons, now juniors in college) entered first grade.

Since her return to teaching, Joan had been working in a system in which students with serious learning problems were served in special classes. Therefore, her classroom problems were limited to an occasional outburst of frustration or anger or to the prepubescent silliness associated with 9- and 10-year-olds. One of the reasons she enjoyed teaching in Littleton was the quality of the support services available to students with real needs. Joan's feeling was that these services enabled her to be more effective with the students assigned to her classroom. Over the years she earned a reputation in the district for being a creative, demanding teacher who was able to challenge her students successfully. Parents of gifted fourth-graders often requested her, feeling she would enrich their child's curriculum.

For Joan, fourth grade had become somewhat boring, and she was considering asking for a change of level. When she was approached to mainstream the special students, she readily agreed, partly to have a new challenge in her teaching. While two of the mainstreamed students, Barry Frederick and Michael Neafe, were not presenting many problems, Donald Garcia was proving to be more of a challenge than she anticipated.

Donald was a learning-disabled (LD) student who had spent most of his school years in a self-contained classroom for students with learning disabilities. Joan knew that he, Barry, and Michael were being mainstreamed for the first time and that Donald was the least skilled of the three. She had been "briefed" about the students by the CSE and Marilyn Coe at a meeting the previous June, just before school ended for the summer.

Aware that the students might feel a little awkward in her class, Joan made sure each had a desk "right in the middle of the action" and that their desks were nearer to the other students than to each other. She welcomed them warmly when they started and then tried not to treat them any differently than she treated her other students.

However, it was clear almost immediately that the three students, particularly Donald, were very different. All of them seemed to need more attention than the typical fourth-grader. None of them was very outgoing in the class, and they were hesitant about their work, asking many questions and regularly seeking reassurance that they had the correct answers or were doing the right task. Donald took much longer than the other two to complete any in-class assignment, and he never volunteered to read in class.

When Joan gave her first surprise quiz, something she did regularly to keep the students on their toes and actively involved in the daily assignments, Donald was unable to answer any of the questions. While Barry and Michael did poorly on the quiz (as Joan had anticipated), they tried to answer the questions and showed some evidence of preparation. Joan was so startled by Donald's blank paper that she went to see Marilyn Coe to discuss his quiz.

Marilyn explained, "Donald probably couldn't read your test. You know that he reads on the first-grade level."

Joan reacted immediately. "He shouldn't be in fourth grade if he can't read the work! I just can't imagine how a child that poor in reading can stay in my class."

It was clear to Joan that her reaction troubled Marilyn, who responded to Joan in a very soft voice. "Yes, Donald can't read very well. But he's a very nice little boy who has been isolated from his peers for a long time. If he doesn't have an opportunity soon to get to know kids his age, he'll start middle school isolated and probably acting inappropriately. And you must be making some progress with him. He actually has begun doing some things with other kids that he didn't do before he went into your class. I saw him on the playground with a bunch of your students, and he talks about your class and his new friends a lot when he's in my room."

Joan quickly retreated from her hard-line position. She nodded at Marilyn and said, "OK. I'll try to help him with the content. And I won't give any surprise quizzes without warning you."

For the next few weeks Joan observed Donald closely in her class. He contributed in class discussions if she called on him, and he participated in small-group activities. (In the first marking period the students were creating murals depicting the growth of the American colonies.) However, she also noticed that he did none of the reading or writing activities, nor did the other students ever ask him to contribute to the academic aspects of his group's project. When it came time to reorganize work groups, no group actively chose Donald, and Joan had to ask one of the students to include him. The student did so willingly, mentioning that Donald was a nice kid but not too smart. The only appropriate work he turned in was done with Marilyn Coe's help. He continued to fail Joan's tests.

Joan often described her teaching by saying that she believed that her students' reach should exceed their grasp and that she continually asked more and more from her students. They knew and expected that from her and were even disappointed if one of her assignments turned out to be "easy." But Donald was unable to achieve even her simplest goals. To ask more from him would mean increasing his frustration level. Yet she couldn't decrease her expectations for the class as a whole or for the small groups. And if she created individual assignments for him, she would be defeating the purposes of mainstreaming by setting him up as different and less able. As the days passed, she came to believe that Donald did not belong in her class. She felt strongly that mainstreaming was not good for students if they ended up hating the class and school or if they felt "dumb" as a result of the mainstreaming. Though he did not seem to be unhappy in the class, Joan suspected that Donald was feeling that way. Given her classroom requirements, it was clear that Donald was failing social studies and that Joan would have no choice but to give him an F for the marking period. It wasn't that Joan thought Donald was a failure; he just could not meet the reading and writing demands of her class.

Feeling frustrated and angry that she had brought this on herself, Joan met with Warren Groves for some advice. Warren had been her principal for nine years, and they liked and respected each other. His response was straightforward: He told Joan that if Donald could not do the work, he did not belong in her class. Warren volunteered to make that position clear to Marilyn and the CSE, but Joan felt that was her responsibility. She arranged to meet the next day with Marilyn to discuss returning Donald to the LD classroom. Although she had been meeting with Marilyn regularly and knew this would come as no surprise, Joan was feeling terrible about making this request. She understood why Marilyn felt Donald needed to be mainstreamed and she appreciated that Marilyn had chosen her as the teacher to accomplish this. She also knew that Marilyn had a lot riding on Donald's success and that this would be a blow to her mainstreaming efforts in the school.

Joan sighed and got up from Donald's seat. She returned to her desk and packed her briefcase with work to take home. She knew that even though there were no papers in her bag to indicate it, most of her thoughts that evening would center on Donald and her meeting with Marilyn the following day.

* * *

Marilyn Coe sat in her classroom thinking about tomorrow morning's meeting with Joan Martin. She realized that she might have blundered when she decided to mainstream Donald Garcia into Joan Martin's fourth-grade social studies class this fall. Marilyn knew that Joan was upset by Donald's poor reading skills and that, despite his efforts, Joan was going to give him a failing grade. At the moment, however, Marilyn felt that it was she who had failed, and now she was wondering if there was anything she could do to remedy the situation. She didn't have much time to figure out a solution: She and Joan were meeting in the morning, and it looked like the only option Joan would offer would be for Marilyn to remove Donald from her class. Otherwise, Joan would have to give him a failing grade in social studies for the first marking period.

Marilyn understood many of Joan's reactions because she had spent nine years as an elementary school teacher before beginning a new career in special education. Now 39, she had "retired" from teaching for several years to raise her children and had spent three years tutoring remedial students before returning to a local university to complete a master's degree and become certified in special education.

She was remembering just now the excitement she felt last January as she approached her return to full-time teaching after accepting a midyear position in a self-contained LD classroom in the Littleton school district. With some trepidation, but also with lots of excitement, Marilyn started her new assignment.

Marilyn found herself in a medium-size elementary school supervised by Warren Groves, a very professional principal, and staffed by conscientious, hardworking teachers. Marilyn's class was one of two self-contained learning disabilities classes in the building. There was also an LD resource room in the school. Because there were two types of LD classes in the building, many teachers thought the children in the two self-contained classes were too difficult to mainstream.

Marilyn tried to set up a classroom that was visually appealing and educationally interesting and stimulating. She was determined to find success in her new position. By March, Marilyn felt that the class was doing well and that things were going smoothly. The students, all boys ranging in age from 6 to 9, settled into a consistent routine and seemed happy in the structured classroom environment Marilyn had created.

When Marilyn took over the class, she was surprised to learn that none of the boys was mainstreamed into any regular education classes. In May, as Marilyn prepared to meet with the CSE to make recommendations for the following school year for her students, she wanted to suggest that several of her students be mainstreamed into some academic subjects. However, Marilyn found herself hesitating, since she had so little experience with this type of decision. The CSE was available to guide her but felt the final decision to mainstream should be left to her. As she tried to make up her mind, Marilyn was feeling the double handicap of her inexperience in special education and her brief time in the school.

When she turned to the principal for guidance, Warren Groves offered his views on mainstreaming but avoided the actual decision. He told Marilyn that he did not know enough to make appropriate recommendations; he felt that was her job, in cooperation with the CSE. However, he did tell her that he believed that students should be mainstreamed primarily for reading and math and only when success could almost be guaranteed so that the children would not have to deal with more failure. The CSE's attitude was that more mainstreaming should be attempted in all areas; it felt that too many children were placed in self-contained classes in the district. When Marilyn asked why so little mainstreaming had occurred with her students, the CSE explained that it didn't want to take a position that the principal might not support unless it had a strong special education teacher behind the mainstreaming effort.

After spending a lot of time going over student records and talking with anyone who might help her, Marilyn decided to mainstream two of her students for math. Both boys had developed enough competence in the subject area to be successful in the regular class, particularly if she provided a little additional help in her classroom.

Marilyn also decided to mainstream the three oldest boys in the class, Barry, Michael, and Donald, into the fourth-grade social studies class even though one of them, Donald, was very weak in reading skills. Her rationale was based on three premises. First, in three years these students would start middle school, and it seemed that the present time was not too soon to begin preparing them for the demands they would face there. Second, Marilyn felt that she "cheated" her students in the areas of science and social studies, since reading, math, and language arts took up the largest part of each school day in her class. Third, all three boys were shy children who had spent most of their school years apart from their same-age peers. Marilyn felt they needed more time with other 9-year-olds, who could serve as models.

All her recommendations were agreed to by the CSE and the principal. They suggested that she closely monitor the students mainstreamed into social studies. Warren paid particular attention to Donald's case when she presented her ideas to him. That reinforced for Marilyn that the principal was "tuned in," since Donald had been her greatest concern.

Donald, a 9-year-old, had spent two years in the self-contained LD class. He was an only child, living with his mother and father. Donald's original psychological report confirmed his academic deficits and described him as "immature, with a short attention span." There were no reported health, financial, marital, interpersonal, housing, or community problems; nor were any significant birth, medical, or developmental difficulties reported.

The CSE report noted that Donald's mother, whose native language was Spanish, spoke English with some difficulty. Donald understood but did not speak Spanish. Donald's father reported that he had experienced difficulty reading when he was in school. The parents had always been supportive of the CSE decisions and welcomed help for Donald.

The main drawbacks for mainstreaming Donald were his primer reading level and his shyness and low self-esteem. However, Marilyn knew that despite his reading difficulties, Donald was able to understand concepts presented at his age and grade level and had very good listening comprehension skills. He was aware of current events, and he would bring a wide range of educational and cultural experiences to the class. He had traveled to South America with his parents several times and could relate those trips to other experiences. Yet Marilyn knew that Donald did not fit Warren's "model" for mainstreaming.

Joan Martin, the fourth-grade teacher whose class Donald would join for social studies, had a reputation for creativity and flexibility, but she was known for teaching to the upper levels of her class and holding high expectations for all her students. She was selected on the basis of Warren's recommendation and a meeting with the CSE at which the committee recognized that she was willing to accept all three of Marilyn's fourth-grade students.

In September, Joan welcomed the three self-contained LD students warmly, giving each his own desk and materials. The students were so enthusiastic about attending the fourth-grade class that Marilyn began to relax about her decision.

Her sense of comfort was short-lived, however. At the end of the third week of school, Joan came to see Marilyn to discuss Donald. She showed Marilyn the results of the first social studies quiz, given as a surprise to make sure all the students were keeping up with the reading. Donald had not responded to any of the questions. When Marilyn reminded Joan of

Donald's reading level and explained that he probably could not read the test questions, Joan reacted strongly. "He shouldn't be in fourth grade if he can't read the work. I just can't imagine how a child that poor in reading can stay in my class."

Marilyn was shocked by the strength of Joan's response. She decided to try to focus on Donald's needs, not his weaknesses, as she answered Joan. "Yes, Donald can't read very well. But he's a very nice little boy who has been isolated from his peers for a long time."

Marilyn went on to explain Donald's social needs for being in the class, and she discussed how important it was to prepare classified students for their next educational level. She also told Joan that she had noticed that Donald was now involved with other fourth-grade students on the playground. Marilyn concluded, "He talks about your class and his new friends a lot when he's in my room."

Marilyn realized her explanation had made an impact when Joan responded by agreeing to keep Donald in her class and to try to help him with the content. Joan observed that his contributions to class discussions were very appropriate and said she would watch him in class to see if he made any progress.

After the meeting with Joan, Marilyn began to work with Donald in her class on his social studies assignments. She knew that the best solution would be for Donald to learn to read the social studies material, but Marilyn also knew that she would not be able to bring him to grade-level reading. She continued to meet with Joan to talk about Donald's progress and to see if Joan would consider changing her grading procedures to accommodate Donald's needs. Marilyn knew that she had to go slowly, since she was an untenured teacher and it was not her role to tell other, more experienced teachers how to handle their classes. She did not feel that she was making much progress with Joan, since Joan kept talking about Donald's failing grades.

Marilyn decided to talk with the principal and the CSE to see if they could help her find a solution to the problem. It was clear to Marilyn that Joan was not comfortable making an exception to her strict grading policies for Donald.

When Marilyn met with Warren, she felt she was receiving mixed messages. On the one hand, the principal told her that she, not he, was the expert in special education and mainstreaming. Yet he reminded her that he believed that students who could not be successful in meeting the teacher's demands should not be mainstreamed.

On the other hand, the CSE supported Marilyn's decision to keep Donald in fourth-grade social studies, since the committee had also noticed the difference in his social interactions. The CSE was willing to meet with Joan to support Marilyn's position.

Marilyn appreciated the support of the CSE but did not think that it would affect Joan's position on her grading policy. As long as Donald had to meet Joan's standards, he was bound to fail, and Marilyn felt she would appear stubborn if she insisted that he remain in the class even though he would fail. It seemed to her that Joan's grading system was the key to solving the problem. However, Marilyn did not know how to convince Joan to alter the system.

* * *

Warren Groves watched Joan Martin leave his office; as the door closed behind her, he sat down heavily in his chair and sighed aloud. In the past week two of his strongest teachers had come to him to discuss the same child, Donald Garcia. It was clear to him that these two caring, sensitive teachers were on a collision course over the best setting for Donald. Warren knew that one of his responsibilities as the principal would be to mediate if they could not reach an amicable, appropriate solution.

Warren tended to trust his teachers and preferred to let them make their own decisions. He typically offered an opinion that would not tie a teacher's hands and then suggested that the teacher was the front-line expert. He only took a firm stand when he saw that a teacher's decision would lead to a real problem or when there was a conflict that the parties were unable to resolve without his intervention. The problem with Donald seemed to be leading him to the latter situation.

As Warren retraced the events that led to his meeting with Joan today, he reminded himself that he could have prevented this entire situation last May if he had told Marilyn Coe then that Donald was not an appropriate candidate for mainstreaming. When Marilyn and the CSE met with him to discuss mainstreaming some of the students from Marilyn's self-contained LD classroom, it was obvious that Donald did not have the reading skills necessary to deal successfully with a fourth-grade social studies text. But Marilyn made a strong case for social mainstreaming for this student, a case that Warren knew made sense as a long-term solution to Donald's problems. As long as Donald remained in the self-contained setting, he would not have the opportunity to make friends with the nonclassified students, nor would he have those students as models for the behaviors that preadolescents needed to learn.

Warren went along with Marilyn for a second reason. In addition to believing that her social mainstreaming argument was a good one, Warren wanted Marilyn to know that she could have the opportunity to implement her policies without having to fight for each one. Although she was a new teacher, she had the potential to be one of the strongest teachers in his building. Warren knew that if he encouraged and supported her, she would gain the confidence needed to emerge as a leader within the school. Since he believed that strong teachers were an asset to a school, he wanted to help Marilyn try to implement her ideas.

He suggested that Joan Martin be the teacher who mainstreamed the three fourth-grade students because he wanted Joan to have a new challenge.

Joan was one of those teachers whose classroom could make any principal look good, and Warren appreciated her skills. He knew, however, that she was easily bored and that he did not have another opening in his school for her. He feared that Joan would leave his school for a more interesting classroom if he could not provide one for her. He hoped that she would rise to the challenge of these hard-to-teach students and, in doing so, find sufficient reason for remaining in his school.

But now Warren had the feeling that his plans had backfired. Although he had warned Marilyn that mainstreaming Donald could prove to be a difficult undertaking, Marilyn had not taken that warning seriously enough. She should have better prepared both Donald and Joan for their mainstreaming roles. Was it too late to help her save her plan and keep Donald in a regular fourth-grade social studies class?

Additionally, he should have given Joan more incentive to guarantee that the mainstreaming of these students would be successful. He wondered if it was too late to do that now. Would Joan be willing to rethink her position about grading just days before the report period ended?

Warren knew that the two teachers were meeting the following day. He called to his secretary and asked her to find out when their meeting was scheduled. He realized he was about to spend the remainder of the day trying to come up with an idea that would help them resolve their conflict over Donald. His plan would have to meet two goals: It would have to be in Donald's best interest, and it would have to allow both Joan and Marilyn to save face and leave the meeting feeling that their professional beliefs had not been compromised. Warren was not sure he could accomplish that. He sighed again. It was days like this that made Warren wonder why he had not gone into his father's insurance business.

PART FIVE

EVALUATION

SARAH HANOVER

*A first-year high school math teacher is confronted by angry
parents when she gives their son, an outstanding math student,
a lower grade than expected because he never turned in his
homework.*

The secretary's voice on the faculty lounge intercom was difficult to hear
because of the static. "Mrs. Hanover, there's a call for you on line seven,"
Sarah heard dimly.

She called toward the speaker, "I'm on my way," and headed down the
hall to the math office, wondering who was trying to reach her at 7:40 on a
Monday morning.

The caller identified himself as James Kilson's father.

"Good morning, Mr. Kilson. Is James OK?" Sarah asked.

"Well, he's OK except for his math grade," Mr. Kilson responded. "I'm
unclear as to why James got a B in your class."

"Did you ask James? I'm pretty sure he knows why he got a B." Sarah
softened her voice so that her comment would not seem hostile.

Mr. Kilson responded. "He told us that he got a B because he didn't do
the homework."

Sarah said, "That's exactly right. Homework is one of the class requirements."

Mr. Kilson's voice sounded angry. "But he gets perfect scores on the
tests without doing homework. Why would you have such a requirement?"

"Not all the students understand new concepts in math as quickly as
James. In fact, most students need all the practice they can get. If I didn't
require homework and base part of the grade on its being completed, most
students wouldn't do it and they'd learn less."

Mr. Kilson sounded puzzled. "I understand that. But why should James
have to do the homework when he doesn't need it?"

"All students need to do homework. It's part of learning some discipline."

"Forget that. James is not a discipline problem." His tone moderated as he went on: "You must know how important grades are to high school students, particularly students like James, who plan to apply to highly competitive colleges. This is not a contest between your will and James's. He *needs* high grades for college. All his test scores show that he's doing A work. His math grade should reflect what he knows."

Sarah forced herself not to sound angry or defensive as she responded to Mr. Kilson. "I think you're missing the point here. Homework was one of the course requirements. James got a B because he chose not to do the homework."

"I'm assuming from this conversation that you're not going to change James's grade." Sarah thought that Mr. Kilson sounded frustrated.

"I don't think that he earned a higher grade. When he meets all the class requirements, he'll get an A."

"My wife and I would like to talk to you in person about this. I would ask you to think about what I said so that there might be room for some more discussion between us. When would be a convenient time?" Mr. Kilson did not sound like the type of person who would take no for an answer.

Sarah quickly brought her schedule to mind. "I have a preparation period from 11:06 to 11:48, or we could meet after school. The students leave at 2:50 and I'd be willing to meet you at 3, if that would be more convenient."

Mr. Kilson responded, "We'll see you at three o'clock this afternoon, if today is convenient. Where shall we meet?"

Sarah replied, "This afternoon is fine. I'm in room 336 at that time; that's on the third floor of the math wing. When you come in the front door, walk past the office and take the first stairs to your left."

"We'll find it. Thank you for making yourself available."

Sarah said, "You're welcome, Mr. Kilson. Have a nice day." Once the words were out of her mouth, she could have kicked herself. She hated that expression, but in her nervousness she had used it to end her conversation with James Kilson's father.

Sarah replaced the receiver and left the math department office, her heart pounding. She was a new teacher, and Mr. Kilson was the first parent to call her with a complaint. In the two months since school started, her only parent contacts were ones she initiated, and they were made to ask for the parents' help with a problem student.

As she walked to her classroom, she thought about James Kilson. It occurred to her that this call should *not* have come as a surprise. After all, James was the best math student in her third-period honors precalculus class.

James was a pleasant boy, easy to have in the class (although he informed her on the first day of class that he did not like to be called Jim, or Jimmy, or Jimbo, and offered about half a dozen nicknames or variations on his name that he would not answer to). He had a 98 average on the tests and quizzes Sarah had given during the marking period. He was also her best peer tutor and a willing participant in class discussions. James was obviously an A student, except for one flaw: He never turned in homework. And that was why Sarah gave him a B for the grading period.

In September, Sarah was overly prepared to begin the school year—intense preparation was her typical response to anxiety. Although becoming a math teacher was something she had been working toward for the past two years, actually being offered a job had caused her as much anxiety as pleasure.

Sarah described herself as a "traditional rebel"—an oxymoron she took delight in. When she graduated from college in the early 1970s, she was one of only a few women in her class with a degree in business. She married immediately after college graduation (her traditional side) and went to work for a Fortune 500 company as a management trainee. Within a few years she was earning as much as her husband, a computer engineer. After ten years with the company, she took a leave of absence to have a child. She returned to work when her son was 6 months old. A year later she was pregnant with a second child, and she and her husband agreed that raising young children was going to be very difficult with both parents pursuing corporate careers; so after her daughter was born, she resigned from the company. As her children grew, Sarah started to think about another career.

Teaching seemed a natural choice. Sarah had done some training on her job and had enjoyed helping others gain new skills. She investigated options and discovered that she could be certified in math with two years of part-time study. By the time her daughter was ready for kindergarten, Sarah was a certified math teacher. She was offered a full-time position at Littleton High School early in June, giving her nearly three months to prepare for her new position.

Her preparation included establishing overt grading standards, which she shared with her students on the first day of class. She even put her requirements on the topic schedule she handed out to each class, believing that she should identify class requirements explicitly so that the students would know exactly what she expected. She didn't want them to be surprised by their grades, as she often had been as a student, and as were so many students she had observed as a student teacher.

One of her requirements was homework, and she made it clear that she took homework seriously. As she explained to her students: "I'm assigning you homework every night but Friday because you will need to practice what we are learning in class, and there won't be enough time in class for you to get that practice. By doing homework every night, you'll get a better handle on the material, and I'll have a better idea of what you know."

In each of her classes, several students asked if she would grade the homework. The first time she was asked the question, Sarah paused before answering. "Let me put it like this. I will go over all your homework as a way of finding out how you are doing with the material. Your homework will let me know who needs extra practice and what I'll need to reteach if lots of you didn't understand something. It will also tell me that we can move ahead faster than I had planned if I see that everyone in the class is doing very well. But I won't put a grade on each homework assignment. You need to have the freedom to use the homework as a means of indicating that you don't understand something. So the only grade will be a check or minus. If you try to do the homework each night, even if you get stuff wrong, you'll get a check. If you don't turn it in, or if you turn in only part of it, you'll get a minus. With a few minuses, your grade will be affected. I expect all of you to do each of the homework assignments.''

Sarah thought about that conversation and realized that she was on firm ground with the grade she had given to James. She tried to put her upcoming encounter with the Kilsons out of her mind as she went through her day. Nevertheless, her thoughts kept returning to the afternoon's meeting, particularly during third period. Sarah did not say anything to James about his parents' upcoming visit, and he did not mention the early morning call to her. She wondered if he knew about it.

By the end of the day, the meeting with the Kilsons was all Sarah could think about. When the door of room 336 swung closed behind the last student at 2:50, Sarah stood to erase the board as she nervously awaited Mr. and Mrs. Kilson's arrival. As she mentally went over their position and tried to imagine the additional arguments they might make, she began to wonder, for the first time since she had established her grading requirements, if they were correct. A nagging doubt began to grow that her focus on the explicitness of the grading system had obscured her attention to its content. Were the requirements themselves wrong? Since the conversation with Mr. Kilson hadn't been a lengthy one, she hadn't really had the opportunity to expand on her position or to hear theirs in detail. Was she really clear about the arguments on both sides of this issue?

Sarah heard a sound at the classroom door and quickly set down the eraser and dusted off her hands. She took a deep breath as she walked toward the opening door.

DIANE NEWS

*In a school district beginning a gifted and talented program, a
first-year elementary school teacher must choose four students to
recommend for the program, but she has five potential candidates.*

Diane News sat at her desk watching the first gold and orange leaves falling
onto the Talner Elementary School playground. "It's time to take down the
'Welcome Back to School' display," she thought. As she pulled a pad of
paper toward her to begin sketching ideas for a new social studies bulletin
board, she glanced around her room with pride. Diane had been teaching
part-time for two years; this fifth-grade class was her first full-time position.
Her room reflected her love of the arts and her understanding of enrichment
materials. A science table invited exploration. Books and magazines in a
well-stocked library in the back could be checked out by her students. A
bulletin board labeled "Where in the World?" contained a map and
photographs. Originally, Diane brought in the photos for the display, but
now her students were bringing in pictures, putting them up, and connecting
them with yarn to places on the map. The room was bright and colorful. It
looked like the kind of place where students could be active and involved
learners.

Diane, 27 years old, was married and had recently completed a master's
program in arts and education. Prior to her current position, she taught at
an alternative school in the district, where she helped to develop after-
school enrichment programs for gifted and talented students. She had
become interested in gifted education when she took a course on creativity,
and she had taken several more courses in the area as part of her master's
program.

As Diane sketched ideas, she began to think about a more immediate
problem. She was faced with an issue that she did not know how to
resolve. On the surface, the situation appeared straightforward: She had to
recommend no more than four students from her classroom for a new gifted
and talented program (called "G&T" by everyone) for students in the

second through sixth grades. Students were being chosen from each grade level since the program was in a start-up year. The students would be taken from classes to another school twice a week for half a day. Each grade-level teacher was asked to recommend no more than four students because class size would be limited. The G&T coordinator was urging each teacher to pick the maximum number of students, but no one was allowed to exceed four. Of her twenty-seven students, three were obvious choices, but her selection of the fourth was complicated by other factors. However, this decision was only part of Diane's dilemma.

Diane had to choose the four students using criteria that she considered unacceptable. The district required a score at the 90th percentile or above on the Iowa Test of Basic Skills (ITBS) as the primary consideration for admission to the program. Class grades and group-administered IQ scores also had to be high. There was room for a brief personal evaluation of each student recommended by the teacher, but the form stated that this opinion was of less consequence than IQ and achievement-test scores and class grades.

Diane's standards for choosing students had little in common with those of the district. She felt that individual creativity in a variety of areas had to be evaluated when assessing children for placement in a gifted and talented program. For example, creativity in problem solving, choices of imagery in writing, and analytic thinking skills in a variety of subjects all needed to be considered. Diane also thought that some students who did not fit a standard profile and who met only some of the criteria often flourished in the challenge of such a program. She was troubled that she had to ignore these factors as she made decisions about her students.

In addition to having doubts about whether she would be able to make her recommendations according to the district's standards, Diane had other concerns about her decision. While in graduate school, she had taken a number of courses in women's studies. She had read enough in the field to know that girls scored lower than boys on standardized tests and that they were underrepresented in programs for the gifted and in other advanced courses, especially in math and science. Diane was aware that young girls were not sufficiently encouraged to participate in these programs. Yet she was considering recommending four boys.

The dissonance that this created in her was not helped by another recent event. The father of one of the students in her class had called to pressure Diane into including his daughter in the gifted program. Even now, Diane was furious as she recalled the conversation.

George James, a high school teacher and football coach in the district, had called the previous evening. James, who was black, had a reputation for being critical of other staff. Diane knew from other teachers that he was quick to call whenever he thought that they were not providing sufficient challenges for his daughter. When James called Diane, the conversation began calmly enough but escalated quickly to an unpleasant pitch.

"Hello, Mrs. News, this is George James, Margie's father. I've heard about the start-up of the G&T program, and I wanted to make sure that Margie will be included in it."

"Mr. James, I'm glad that you're so interested in Margie's progress, and. . ."

"Progress? I'm not calling about her progress. My daughter is smart enough to be in the program, and I intend to see that she gets there."

"Go on."

James was only too happy to continue. "I know she's gifted, and she deserves a lot more than she's been getting in your class. If she's having any school problems, *you* have got to be the cause. How can you let her get away with such sloppy writing and careless spelling on her papers? Don't you ever take time to look at the assignments these kids turn in? I have to go over every single thing she's written in class—everything she's done in there! What kind of teacher lets kids do such work? It's not my job to be on her case every night, correcting her, seeing that she does her work neatly and properly. You should be setting those standards, and I'm warning you now, I'm giving you notice that I'm going to be watching your teaching very carefully. You have an obligation to teach my daughter well and to recommend her for G&T. If Margie isn't in it, you better have some good reasons why a bright black girl was excluded."

Diane hardly knew how to respond to George James's tirade. She muttered something about the doorbell ringing and hung up. Diane was both upset and angry as she replaced the receiver. She felt that James had practically threatened her. And she was angry that he hadn't given her a chance to tell him about the creative writing assignments she gave. They allowed for inventing spelling and sloppiness in early drafts so that students could concentrate first on the creative process of writing stories and poems.

But Diane recognized that she could not discuss certain aspects of Margie's classroom performance with her father. How could she tell him that although Margie's test scores were at the 91st percentile, the girl was what the literature called a "concrete thinker"? When class discussions veered away from straight recall of text material, Margie would not participate; slouching low in her seat, she would rest her head on her desk as if exhausted. Diane tried to encourage Margie to think more analytically, but her responses always remained at the level of concrete thought. She never brought new insights to the group. She did not seem to be a prime candidate for the G&T program.

The obvious choices were Mark Sullivan, Seth Cohen, and Josh Arnold, all of whom scored in the 99th percentile on the ITBS; they were the only three in the class to do so. Their daily homework and quiz grades were equally high, their classwork was consistently excellent, and they were lively participants in class projects and discussions. But all three were white and male.

Diane thought about the other student she wanted to recommend. Stuart

Johnson's offbeat humor and easygoing manner had won him many friends in the class. He was genuinely funny and could easily have become the class clown, but he never called out jokes or disrupted the class. Diane believed that he was truly gifted. She smiled as she remembered her original impressions of him.

Stuart was a 10-year-old slob. His lank, black hair was rarely combed. His clothes looked as if he dressed in the dark; everything was clean but rumpled and mismatched. Diane often had trouble reading Stuart's scrawled handwriting, but once she could decipher it, she found that his work was consistently accurate. His creative writing seemed beyond his years, and he always completed the bonus critical-thinking questions she included on worksheets.

When Diane began a new topic, Stuart was the student who made insightful connections to related material. Last week Diane introduced the topic of Eskimos in Canada. Stuart was the one to notice the closeness of Alaska to Siberia and to speculate about the existence of an ice bridge between the two regions. Students enjoyed having Stuart in their group for class projects because he often provided a creative edge.

Stuart was new to the area, but he quickly became friends with Seth, Mark, and Josh. Diane would hear them cheerfully arguing with each other at lunch time, with Stuart often defending his more unusual views. His friends also loved challenging Stuart's math ability. Diane once overheard a problem the boys had given Stuart.

"C'mon, Stuart," said Josh. "You'll never get this one. What's 32 times 67—and no paper!"

Stuart paused for only a moment. "2144," he replied.

His friends quickly took out paper and pencils to check him.

"Tell us your trick," said Mark. "There's no way I can do that stuff in my head. Are you a pen pal of Blackstone or something?"

Stuart grinned and shook his head. "I don't know how I do it. I can just see the answers." The boys were then off arguing about some new topic, and Diane walked away, amazed.

While Stuart's skills were outstanding, his test scores didn't reflect his ability. Diane had checked Stuart's records from his former school. His grades were just above average, and he scored in the 88th percentile on the standardized achievement test. Even so, there was no question in Diane's mind that Stuart was gifted.

Diane decided to ask Bob Garrett, the principal, for advice. Garrett was in his first year as principal of Talner Elementary School. He had been a teacher in the district for several years and then an assistant principal. Diane was the first teacher he hired, and she knew that he liked her teaching style so far. He seemed to be the appropriate person to talk to about her concerns.

"Mr. Garrett, I'm in a bind. I received the district memo about the gifted and talented program, and the limits on four students per classroom sound absolute. But I have five possible candidates and several questions about two of them.''

"Who are the five?'' he asked.

"Well, Mark Sullivan, Seth Cohen, and Josh Arnold are clear choices because of their scores and class performance. The other two are Margie James and Stuart Johnson. Their scores are fairly close, but there are some other issues that concern me.''

Mr. Garrett said, "If those two seem about equal, I'd say that you really need to consider the issue of racial balance. All our programs, and especially this one, need to reflect the diversity of our student population.''

"I realize that,'' said Diane. "But they are both black.''

Mr. Garrett looked puzzled. "Stuart? Really?''

Diane nodded. "I know. I met Stuart's dad when he came to a parent conference. He's black.''

Garrett shook his head. "Look, Diane, you've got a tough problem. You're a good teacher, and I certainly trust your judgment. I'll back you up on your decision, but at this point I can't tell you whom to pick. You know the kids, so it's your call.''

Diane appreciated the vote of confidence, but her meeting with the principal hadn't been much help. While her background and experience should have made the decision process an easy one, she was faced with a set of unfair criteria, an angry parent, and two students who were competing for one slot. Diane again turned her thoughts to Margie. Using district criteria only, Margie should be her choice. But Margie did not show the brilliance and thinking skills that Stuart displayed, skills that flourish in a gifted and talented program. However, Margie was a girl. Perhaps in a more intimate setting, Margie's skills might develop. So much of Diane's energy had gone into the study of women's issues. How could she choose four boys from her class? And it would look as if she had chosen four white students, since no one seemed to know that Stuart Johnson was black. George James would be furious. Diane had picked up his implication that she was a racist, but she was so angry at his demands that it was just one more unreasonable piece of her conversation with him.

"Why can't the district's standards be more flexible?'' Diane thought. "Why must I choose only four students?'' Diane stared at the five names on her list, wondering what to tell Mr. Garrett tomorrow.

MELINDA GRANT

*A first-year elementary school teacher with many innovative ideas
is uncertain about her classroom activities because the teacher in
the next classroom continually warns her that she will be held
responsible for the students' end-of-year standardized test scores.*

Melinda Grant sat down at Andrea's kitchen table and accepted the cup of
coffee gratefully. It was a cold, wet day, and the warm kitchen and sharp
aroma of coffee made Melinda feel good. She had been looking forward to
this Thanksgiving break as a chance for professional reflection and for
catching up with her friend and neighbor, Andrea Samson. Melinda had
been teaching full-time at Conway Elementary School in Littleton since
September, and the time demands of her new job prevented her from
enjoying a long visit with Andrea until now.

"Mel, it's been so long! I feel like I never see you anymore." Andrea's
welcoming smile erased the weeks since the friends had last spoken. "How
many people did you have for dinner yesterday?"

"Ten!" replied Melinda. "And I didn't even start—I mean not even the
shopping—until school was out on Wednesday afternoon. I can't believe
how much time teaching takes." Melinda's smile belied the complaint in
her words. "How about you? Did you feed a small army?"

"Just my family and my sister and her kids," answered Andrea. "But
let's not talk about cooking. I want to hear all about your new career. Is it
working out the way you expected?" Andrea passed Melinda the sugar and
leaned forward expectantly. Melinda doctored her coffee and settled into
her chair, pondering where to begin.

Melinda had entered her third-grade classroom sure of her methods and
convinced about the kind of teacher she intended to be, but ten weeks of
exposure to the way other teachers did things had made Melinda pause to
reflect. She remained committed to her beliefs but had been looking forward
to this discussion with her friend. As a parent, Andrea was familiar with
the school district; Melinda had a family of her own, and she knew that

Andrea shared most of her ideas about children, learning, and the role of schools. They had spent many Saturday mornings commiserating at this same table about their children's education, and now that her role had changed, Melinda needed some of Andrea's reassurance.

This change in her life began two years ago when Melinda, who had worked for twelve years as a part-time computer software designer, became dissatisfied with her position. Her company was acquired by a larger computer firm, and her job description was altered dramatically. She decided to change careers and returned to graduate school to become certified in elementary education. Melinda enjoyed being a student again and dealing with the theoretical problems of education, but after a year attending full-time she was eager to put the theory into practice. She was delighted when Littleton offered her a teaching position. Melinda, her husband, and their daughter had lived in the community for the past nine years, and Melinda was familiar with many of the school district's personalities and philosophies, though the school in which she would be teaching was not the one her daughter attended.

Melinda spent most of August eagerly preparing for her first class. Knowing she wanted her classroom to be an interesting and exciting learning environment, she started to collect items she knew she would use: books, a fish tank, cushions, all kinds of art materials, even an old sand table rescued from a closing nursery school—"garage-sale material," her husband complained, only half kidding. Melinda justified the trouble she went to by asking herself, "How could I explain on the one line on Littleton's requisition form what a sand table would be used for?" She emptied her garage and brought everything to her classroom in the last week of August, and she and Shawna, her 11-year-old daughter, spent the week preparing the room for the beginning of school. At the end of the week, both agreed that the room looked great. Melinda valued Shawna's opinion and her input. After all, Shawna had experienced third grade more recently than Melinda had.

Her class was a normal one for Littleton: twenty-five students. Of the thirteen boys and twelve girls, ten were white students, eight black, five Hispanic, and two oriental. She found them an eager, active group of children, some intellectually more mature, some physically more mature, some emotionally more mature, and all with potential for success in school. That was Melinda's attitude toward education, formulated on her own but reinforced by her year of studying educational theory. She truly believed that every child could learn if motivated, challenged, and helped to develop his or her potential.

Melinda settled into her new position more easily than she ever imagined she would have. As it turned out, the children were more nervous and unsure of themselves than she was, and all her hard work in preparation, combined with her good sense and easy manner, made the job a pleasure. Melinda had strong ideas about how to approach her class. She wanted to focus on critical-thinking skills and to use an interdisciplinary approach to all the content subjects. She wanted to use lots of group work, especially cooperative learning groups, to channel the natural bent of 8-year-olds toward positive social activity. She also hoped to integrate artistic projects into the standard subject areas as much as she could. In her week of preparation she had arranged the room to accommodate her teaching strategy, with the desks forming groups of five students each, with tables for science and reading centers located at the periphery of the room, and with the sand table ready for a class project she was planning that would last for at least half the year. Melinda envisioned a classroom full of activity and movement, fun and learning.

On the first day of class, Melinda met Barbara Stratton, the third-grade teacher from the room next door, and quickly saw how differently two people could approach the same job. A friendly woman in her forties, Barbara had been teaching at Conway for almost twenty years, working mostly with the third grade. She was quick to offer her help and invited Melinda into her classroom at the end of the day. Barbara Stratton had arranged the desks in her room in four rows of six, with two desks placed several feet away from the others. "For the troublemakers," Barbara explained. "And, as usual, I have several of those," she chuckled. "I find this seating arrangement keeps them somewhat controlled." Melinda nodded, preferring not to get into a discussion of behavior management with a twenty-year veteran on her first day on the job. In that first meeting, Barbara seemed a curious mixture of tough and tender as she alternated between complaining about the bad behavior and low intelligence of her students and offering insightful ideas about who needed help and how to provide it. "All this in only six hours of observation," marveled Melinda to herself.

As the school year progressed, Melinda found that Barbara was always willing to extend help and advice; Barbara was happy to play the role of mentor as long as Melinda accepted the role of eager novice. She offered worksheets she used for basic math and language arts skills, suggested ideas for seatwork, and shared birds' eggs, hornets' nests, and other nature finds. Melinda appreciated Barbara's attention despite the fact that she and Barbara were as far apart as two teachers could be in regard to educational strategy. Shawna noticed it when she visited her mother's classroom in October. "You both teach third grade, but your rooms look so different. She has all those posters that kids hate, about good foods and good punctuation, and she hangs up those boring math tests, and only the ones with '100 percent' on them. Almost everything on your walls was made by your students, and your room is full of class projects. I love your room, especially the city of the future in the sand table. If I were in third grade, I'd want to be in your room. It looks like it would be more fun!"

Melinda accepted the praise even though she wasn't sure an 11-year-old's definition of fun would stand as an evaluation of teaching performance. Besides, she valued much of the advice Barbara Stratton so regularly dispensed. The day after Shawna had registered her performance appraisal, Barbara came into Melinda's room to share lunch with her. Between bites of tuna salad, Barbara asked, "Have you begun organizing your practice work for the Iowa test yet? I know it seems a long way off, but you need to get your kids ready. So much depends on their scores. You get measured right along with the children. I have some great workbooks you can borrow to begin making copies for practice for the class."

"Barbara, the test is months away. We're doing so many things in class right now. I'm starting a writing workshop, and the students will begin making animal habitats next week. I think I'll dampen their enthusiasm if I introduce workbook drills. They'll get the skills some other way. I'm sure my class will do OK on the test."

"I hate to keep reminding you that you're new at this, Melinda, but there are parents out there who will measure *your* ability, not their children's, by how well the students score on standardized tests. Your job is to teach these children how to get the best scores they can. It will make them look good, and it will certainly help your position."

"But the kids need so much more, and school can give them so much more. The parents must know that the kind of work their kids bring home now is as important as standardized test scores."

Barbara smiled and patted Melinda's hand. "I'm only telling you this for your own good. Children need to master basic skills before they deserve special projects. Every year they give me the dullest students. The district claims it doesn't track at this age, but every year I get the worst kids. I spend all my time on skills with them—drill, drill, drill. Sometimes I get depressed because it's not much fun, for me or for them, but my students always have the highest scores in the entire district. If I let them spend their time building projects and drawing pictures and writing stories, they will score poorly on the Iowas. And I know my success as a teacher here depends on my students' scores on that test."

Melinda nodded her agreement and changed the subject. Later that week she began to do some checking. Barbara had not boasted idly. Her classes were, in fact, consistently among the highest in the district on the Iowa tests. And Barbara's class of third-graders this year did seem to have an overabundance of students with problems, at least in comparison to Melinda's class. Barbara regularly told her stories of the children's problems, both academic and behavioral, which Melinda was sure she wouldn't know how to handle. "A value-added comparison of teachers would make Barbara Stratton a candidate for 'Teacher of the Year,'" thought Melinda.

As she finished telling Andrea about her classroom and about the concerns that Barbara raised, Melinda leaned back in her chair and concluded, "So I can't argue with the results she gets, but I just can't bring myself to teach that way." It had taken Melinda an hour to summarize her situation for her friend, sharing her doubts about the efficacy of Barbara Stratton's approach and her own disdain for standardized tests. "I know my class learns basic skills through children's literature, creative writing, math projects, even activities like drawing pictures, creating masks, and building futuristic cities. Since I'm not drilling the students directly, as Barbara does, they probably won't show dramatic test scores, but the learning will last.''

Melinda leaned forward again and spoke emphatically, confident that Andrea would be sympathetic to her position. "They'll be more critical and more creative thinkers; they'll be able to use their whole brains; they'll be able to see more around them; they'll be better citizens; they'll know how to work cooperatively. Surely district administrators and parents must know that knowledge can't be measured just by standardized tests.''

Melinda ended her speech with her hands open and extended, both to emphasize her point and to welcome Andrea's support. In spite of her confident delivery, Melinda was anxious for moral support from her friend.

But Andrea let a moment pass before replying, and while her tone was kind, her response was devastating. "Don't be naive about this school district, Mel. Littleton is a small city with some urban problems and a middle class that's worrying about becoming the minority. If we want to keep a strong middle class here and encourage other families like us to move in, we've got to maintain high test scores at all levels. You read the local paper. The test scores of each district in the county and of each school in each district are published every year. The school board receives tremendous pressure from local citizens to keep those scores high. People who own their own homes are particularly strident on this issue. You know that. All anyone talks about is property values in Littleton. And even though the papers don't publish individual class scores, everyone in the school knows which teachers' classes score the highest and which the lowest. Even parents know! I think your classroom sounds terrific, Mel, but you better cover all the bases. I hate to say this to you, but I think Barbara Stratton is right.''

LEIGH SCOTT

A high school social studies teacher gives a higher-than-earned report-card grade to a mainstreamed student, on the basis of the boy's effort, and is confronted by another student with identical test grades who received a lower report-card grade.

Leigh Scott felt the flush slowly leave her face as she watched Aaron Washington leave the classroom, slamming the door behind him. It was the end of the second grading cycle; students had received their report cards the day before. Leigh had just taken off her coat and was on her way to the teachers' room to get a cup of coffee before the bell rang when Aaron came into the room.

He began, "We got to talk about my American government grade." It was clear that he was angry.

Leigh moved to her desk and responded, "Hi, Aaron. What's up? You're upset about your grade?"

"You gave me a D."

"You did D work."

"So did Dale, and he got a C." Aaron was leaning over the desk toward Leigh.

"Aaron, this is not a good time to talk about this. The bell is going to ring in a few minutes. Why don't you see me after school this afternoon."

Aaron shook his head at her suggestion. "I have practice after school. We have to talk now."

Now it was Leigh's turn to shake her head. "This is not a good time; I have to get ready for homeroom. Besides, there's not really anything to talk about."

Aaron straightened up, took a couple of steps back from the desk, and said, "You gave a white kid who got the same grades I did a C, and you gave me a D. I even did more homework than Dale. I say we *do* have something to talk about."

Leigh capitulated. "Come in tomorrow morning at 7:30, and we'll talk before homeroom period."

Aaron nodded, strode out of the room without another word, and let the door slam as he left.

Leigh had been teaching social studies at Littleton High School for eleven years, and this was the first time a student accused her of racial bias. Students sometimes complained about their grades, and Leigh was always willing to reconsider a grade. But she never had a student suggest she was biased. Leigh had spent her entire teaching career at Littleton, so she had been teaching classes that were mixed racially and ethnically for a long time. She considered herself color blind when it came to assigning grades.

At Littleton High School, students were placed into one of four academic tracks: honors, above average, average, and remedial. Teachers were responsible for five classes a day, with the honors classes typically assigned to senior faculty. Newer faculty taught mostly average and remedial sections. Leigh taught a senior-level honors American history course, two freshman above-average sections of world history, and two sophomore average-level sections of American government.

Leigh graded her two sophomore American government sections on the following requirements each cycle:

- Tests (usually three or four, depending on the material)
- Homework (collected three times a week)
- A project
- Participation in class discussions based on the textbook readings

The textbook was written on an eighth-grade reading level. Leigh's tests were a combination of vocabulary, multiple-choice, and short-answer items. Leigh didn't require that students in the average sections answer essay questions. Students selected projects from among several choices: writing papers, constructing something appropriate to the topic, making a presentation to the class, or writing book reports on pertinent readings.

During homeroom period, Leigh consulted her grade book and confirmed that Aaron's information was accurate. Neither he nor Dale had done particularly well this grading cycle. Both had received mostly D grades, with an occasional C. Neither participated in class discussions unless called on. However, she knew that she had given Dale the higher grade because of his effort, not because of his color. Dale was a learning-disabled student mainstreamed into Leigh's class.

Typically, a mainstreamed student would be placed in a remedial section, but Dale's case was an exception. He was in an average-level class because his resource room teacher, Meg Dament, requested the placement, feeling that Dale needed a more academic environment and a higher-achieving peer group than he would have had in a remedial section. Meg and Leigh had known each other since Leigh came to Littleton. Leigh admired Meg's dedication and her tenacity on behalf of her students. It was clear that Meg cared deeply about the students she served and wanted them to have whatever educational normality she could engineer for them. Meg was able to mainstream her "best" students into average-level, not remedial, classes. She actively sought teachers who would be responsive to her students' needs and to their efforts. It was not easy to convince high school teachers to work with classified students, but of the four resource room teachers in the high school, it was Meg who made the most regular class placements.

When Meg requested Leigh as Dale's teacher, Leigh understood that Dale was not a very good reader and that he would not volunteer in class. Leigh and Meg spoke regularly about Dale's progress, as well as the classroom requirements. Meg helped Dale prepare for Leigh's class, and he was showing real improvement since the first cycle, when his grade had been a low D.

Additionally, Dale's attitude in class was positive. He had learned to exhibit "teacher-pleasing behaviors": He looked attentive, he tried to take notes, he almost always carried his textbook and notebook and a pencil, and he never disrupted the class. Aaron had a different style: He would put his head on his desk during class discussions, he seldom brought materials to class, and he often talked to friends while Leigh was lecturing.

Nevertheless, their grades during the cycle were nearly identical, and Aaron was demanding an explanation. Leigh drove home that day wondering what she would tell Aaron during their appointment the following morning. Aaron's anger, coupled with his charge of racism, exacerbated her anxiety about their meeting. She also knew that she would have to figure out what she might do to prevent this from happening in the future, since she anticipated that she would continue to have mainstreamed students in her classes and she believed they should be rewarded for effort and improvement.

JANE VINCENT

A high school math teacher is asked by her principal to consider giving a higher grade to a student whose numerical average for the marking period is just below the math department's cutoff score for that grade.

Jane Vincent ran her fingers through her hair, wrapped her left leg around the chair rung, and hunched over her dining-room table. In front of her was her open grade book, resting on a pile of folders of various colors, one for each of the students in her tenth-grade above-average algebra II class. Moaning aloud and then giggling at the sound she had just made, Jane pushed the grade book off to one side and searched for the folder marked "William Lawrence." Using a calculator, she figured Willie's average for the first marking period, and again it came out to 89.3.

She wanted to scream. Actually, she wanted to yell at Willie. 89.3! Two-tenths of a point more and he'd have an A for the marking period. Sighing as she wrote a B beside his name in her grade book, Jane uncurled her leg, pushed back from the table, and walked barefoot into her kitchen to refill her coffee cup. Shivering a little from the cold tile beneath her feet, she thought about the grading system of the Littleton High School math department and about Willie Lawrence.

Math seemed to be the perfect subject for absolute grading standards based on numerical averages. The math faculty had agreed at the end of the previous school year, after several unpleasant grade challenges by unhappy students three years in a row, to institute a departmentwide system based strictly on test scores and homework grades, leaving no room for the subjective variables that typically influence a borderline grade. The system was familiar: 90 to 100 was an A; 80 to 89 a B, and so on. (The Littleton grading system did not allow for plus or minus grades.) It was agreed that with a borderline score (for example, 89.2 or 69.7), a .5 or higher would yield the higher grade. And it was this ruling that affected Willie Lawrence.

If his average were 89.5 instead of 89.3, he would automatically have an A for the marking period, and Jane would not be feeling so troubled.

"Interesting that it should be Willie," she thought as she walked back to the dining room. This was the second year that Willie was a student in one of Jane's math sections, and last year he had also been on the borderline. In fact, it was students like Willie who caused Jane to finally support the new grading system. In the past, whenever the issue of a departmentwide grading system was raised, Jane always opposed it; she felt that teachers had to retain the right to award grades that were based on more than just numerical scores. But this past June when the issue came up again, Jane supported the more rigid system, to the surprise of her colleagues in the math department.

She responded to her colleagues' reactions by telling them about Willie.

"Last year his grades were always on the edge; he would be just shy of the points needed for a B or an A. But I knew his history, so I gave him the benefit of the doubt. He always got the higher grade from me."

"What's his history?" two of her colleagues asked at once.

"He'd never gotten good grades in math—felt like he couldn't do it. His standardized test scores were pretty high—percentiles in the seventies, but his grades were C's and D's."

"So what happened?"

"Well," Jane continued, nodding at Ralph Jones, the math department coordinator, "Ralph told me about Willie and sort of challenged me to reach him."

Ralph started to laugh. "That's Jane's polite way of saying I begged her to work with him. When I was at the middle school, I had Willie for sixth-grade math, and he was one of the bigger frustrations of my teaching career. The kid's so bright—straight A's in all his other subjects—but it was as if he had a block about math."

Jane continued: "So something happened; for some reason geometry made sense to him, and he and I got along pretty well. He began to see himself as someone who could do OK in math, who could understand it. So I gave him the benefit of the doubt each grading period. He got a B for the first two marking periods and an A for the last two. Each marking period he was right on the line—79, 88.7, you know."

"And that's why you want a more rigid system?" the teacher sitting beside Jane asked.

"Actually, yes. After the first marking period, I felt funny each time I gave Willie the higher grade. I began to wonder if Willie engaged in this kind of brinksmanship on purpose. And I wondered if it was fair to the other kids. Would I have been as generous to a student that Ralph hadn't talked to me about, or one who wasn't quite as engaging as Willie? There's something to be said for agreed-upon standards; I wouldn't have to make a decision each time."

Now Jane was remembering that conversation as she wrote Willie's grade in her book. She did not have to put herself through her typical end-of-the-marking-period ritual of deciding if someone should be "pushed up" to the higher grade. The answer was in the numbers.

Jane thought back to the way she had introduced the new grading system when school started in the fall, and she recalled how naive her responses to the students' questions had been. She had gone into school the first day excited, as always, about meeting new students and getting them to be enthusiastic about learning more math. While her colleagues teased her about her enthusiasm, reminding her that high school kids were not terribly likely to get excited about math, Jane felt that her excitement had the potential to be contagious. Jane also thought the new grading system would be a help, and she wanted her students to see it that way.

Jane began by putting the numbers 90-100, 80-89, 70-79, 60-69, <60 on the board and then writing "A, B, C, D, F" next to the numbers.

"This is how your math grades will be figured this year. For every test and homework assignment, you will get a number grade. The tests will be worth twice the homework. The grades will be averaged at the end of each marking period, and your report-card grade will be based on your nine-week average. That way you'll know exactly where you are as the marking period progresses, and grades won't be a surprise."

The students were waiting for her to go on. "Any questions?"

One of the students raised his hand. "Say you're between a cutoff. Say you have a 79 point something. What would your grade be?"

Jane smiled. "If the 'point something' is point 5 or more, you get the higher grade. If it's less than point 5, you get the lower grade."

The student then asked, "So a 79.4 is a C, and a 79.5 is a B?"

Jane nodded. "Any other questions?"

"Do you think that's fair?" Another student asked this question.

Jane was surprised. "What do you think? Anyone else have an opinion on this?"

Several students raised their hands.

"Sure it's fair; you can't argue with the numbers," one of the boys in the back of the room responded.

Another student, a girl sitting near the front, said, "I don't think it's fair at all. Why should a few tenths of a point make the difference between one grade and another? It would make sense maybe if we had pluses and minuses, but you know how much grades count in your class rank."

As other students started to join the argument, Jane raised her hand and called for quiet. "You know, none of this may matter. Given what I know and what I hope you'll learn this year about probability, it's unlikely that we'll have to face this problem. But if we do, I promise that I'll try to be fair."

Now, as Jane recorded Willie's grade, she wondered if anyone knew how to define *fair*. She sighed one more time, looked at the next name in her grade book, and began to average the student's grades.

In class the next day, interested students came up to Jane's desk during seatwork to check their calculations for the marking period against hers. When Willie came up, Jane agreed that his average was 89.3. "That's going to be a B, Willie."

Willie seemed surprised. "Why, Miss Vincent? You going to zap me for two-tenths of a point?"

"You know the department's rules, Willie. An 89.3 is a B. You're going to have to push two-tenths more next cycle." Jane smiled at Willie to soften her comment. Willie shrugged and went back to his desk.

The next day, Jane found a note in her mailbox from David King, the high school principal, asking her to stop in to see him when she had a chance. King was a pleasant, thoughtful principal, interested in the students and supportive of his teachers. His relationship with Jane was based on a teasing camaraderie. They liked each other and got along well. Jane walked into King's office during her preparation period, and he welcomed her with a smile as he motioned for her to take a seat.

"How's it going, Janey?" King was the only person in Jane's life except for her father who called her by her childhood nickname, and she responded the way she had always replied since the first time he had done it.

"Just fine, Davey. How about you?"

"I could be better. What I'm concerned about is William Lawrence. I took a look at his grades; they are in the office ready to be distributed. He's down to a B in math. What happened?"

"You're not going to believe this, but he did it again. An 89.3 average. I had to give him a B. You know our department's new policy."

David King frowned.

Jane responded to the frown. "You think I should change it?"

"I'm not going to tell you what to do, you know that. I'm just concerned that a B for an average of 89.3 will kill what little motivation that kid's got for working in your class. You know that his best math class ever was geometry with you last year. What kind of effect will a B have on him?"

"I thought about it a lot last night, Dave. I should have called you instead of pacing the floor." Jane grinned ruefully at her principal. "I just don't think I can go against the department guidelines. I was in on the decision to grade like this; I supported it. I don't know what I would tell the other teachers."

King smiled back, came around his desk, and said, "You know that I won't challenge your final decision. But maybe you should think about this a little bit more before the grades become official. That's not too much to do for a man my age and weight, is it?"

Jane left his office smiling and thought, "What a nice style he has. He just challenged my decision, and I still feel good. But now I've got to figure out what to do about Willie Lawrence's grade. And what do I tell the other math teachers if I don't stick to our plan?"

PART SIX

CONTEMPORARY TEACHING ISSUES

DAVID BURTON

A high school computer teacher whose principal brooks no
challenges to his authority discovers that two students are being
given unequal punishments by the principal for the same infraction.

David Burton, a computer teacher at Cromwell Junior High in Newtown, carefully hung up the phone and pondered the call he had just received from Walt Jordan, his counterpart at Blair Junior High School. The computer crash that occurred three days ago, causing serious problems for the three junior high schools that were linked into a central mainframe located at Blair, had been traced to Cromwell. A technician at Blair was able to pinpoint the exact time and place of the crash: the computer room at Cromwell during David's lunch hour. "Damn it," muttered David. He was not looking forward to trying to find out who, among all the students at Cromwell, was responsible. But he had to do it. The crash had caused too much trouble. It was just the kind of event that would encourage school administrators to limit access to the computer system for all students.

David Burton had been a computer teacher at Cromwell for ten years, and he was also the site manager of the computer room at the school. He got along well with his colleagues and the students at Cromwell, and he described his situation as "the best job in the best location." He had taught at the other two junior high schools in Newtown before coming to Cromwell, but Cromwell was where he had made a home for himself.

Cromwell Junior High School, located on a well-maintained campus, served 800 students in grades 7 to 9. Of the three junior high schools in Newtown, Cromwell was the most progressive in using computers across the curriculum. Unlike the situation at the other two schools, where only math teachers saw a use for computers in their classrooms, there were teachers in each of the disciplines at Cromwell who were excited about computer applications in their classes. David attributed this interest, at least in part, to the population of students at Cromwell. The school drew the majority of its students from the wealthier sections of Newtown. Most of these students came to school eager to learn and presented few behavior problems. In addition, many of them had access to computers at home and were avid computer students.

Because of the interest of the faculty and the students, David was able to introduce several new computer courses into the junior high school curriculum at Cromwell. Among his accomplishments was an increased student enrollment in the computer courses. Moreover, students were demonstrating interest in the use of computers in general. Students could be found in the computer lab at any time. Even when a computer class was not scheduled, the lab was filled with students; when a class was going on, it was not unusual to see one or two students looking for an empty terminal to complete a school or personal project. David was proud of the interest the students showed in computers and always encouraged students to use the equipment as much as possible, feeling that the only way they could really learn was by experimenting on their own. But he allowed access only when he was in the room to supervise. When he was not there, students could use the room only with his written permission.

David thought back to the day of the crash. He had taken a rather long lunch with Sue Hanson, the new librarian, who was interested in computerizing the library holdings. No one had asked permission to use the room. He decided to consult Fred Collins, who taught a course at that time in another classroom that was separated by a glass partition from the computer classroom.

David caught up with Fred Collins as he was on his way out of school that afternoon and explained the situation to him. "Now that you mention it, I did see Paul Arnold and Mike Miller in there that day," Fred said. "But I never thought anything about it. They're always in there at lunchtime."

"Thanks," said David. "Paul and Mike," he thought to himself. "That makes sense; they could have easily gotten the password while they were watching me log on."

Paul Arnold and Mike Miller, ninth-graders, were close friends, though from very different backgrounds. Paul, an honor student and a computer whiz, came from a wealthy home. His father was a local businessman who was well known in the community, and his parents often came to school functions. Paul had a computer at home and ran a computer bulletin board from there. Mike, on the other hand, came from a more modest background. His family's income was not exceptional, and his parents rarely took an interest in school matters. Mike was an average student whose skills with computers did not match Paul's. However, he seemed very interested in computers and was doing well in David's course this semester.

David reasoned that Paul might well have considered breaking into the computer system a challenge to his rapidly developing skills. He doubted that either of the boys wanted to crash the system and guessed that the crash was an accident. Clearly, he needed to confront them with what he knew and what he guessed and find out from them what really happened.

A full confession and an apology would be enough for David, who would then mete out a minimal punishment for the two boys.

David found Paul and Mike together the next day in the computer lab. He got right to the point, telling them what he had learned the previous day. "I can't figure out why you would want to do it, but I know that you were responsible for breaking into the mainframe system and crashing it. Want to tell me what possessed you guys to do that?"

Mike stirred in his seat, but Paul responded before Mike had a chance to say anything. "What are you talking about? What crash?"

"Come on, Paul. Mr. Collins saw you here, in the computer room, at the exact time of the crash. I know that you were working on the computer then, and I know that you're one of the few kids in the school who could have figured out how to get access to the system. What I don't understand is why you would want to."

"Mr. Burton, I have no idea what you're talking about. Mike and I always ask you before we come into the computer room. Isn't that right, Mike?"

Mike nodded, but he didn't say a word. It was clear to David that Paul was going to handle this by trying to bluff his way out of it, if he could. David felt himself get angry. "Don't play dumb, Paul. Mr. Collins saw you here, in this room."

Paul looked directly at David. "I can't believe that, Mr. Burton. How could he have seen us if we weren't here? Mike and I always ask you before we use the lab. If you didn't give us permission to be in here that day, we weren't here."

David sighed and told them to get out of the computer room. There was no question in his mind that the boys were guilty. However, if he couldn't get them to tell him the truth, he had no choice but to bring the matter to the attention of John Carter, principal of Cromwell. That was a task he did not relish. Carter had been principal for four years, and Cromwell was his first principalship. A former English teacher, Carter spent most of the school day in his office. Always pleasant to the faculty, he had made it clear early in his tenure that he preferred not to be presented with problems and not to have his authority challenged. Since principals in the Newtown school district were very powerful—they could transfer teachers, change assignments, and modify individual teaching schedules—most teachers tried to please him.

"Carter's going to love this," thought David. "But best to get unpleasant tasks over with. They can only get worse." David smiled ruefully to himself as he remembered his mother saying this to him more than once.

Later that day, Carter listened patiently to David's story. He agreed that he and the assistant principal would question the boys. Two days later, he called David to report that the boys had stuck to their story and insisted that they had not been in the computer room at the time of the crash. Carter was convinced that they were lying.

"What do you suggest for punishment?" Carter asked.

"Well, I would have been inclined to be lenient if they had admitted they were responsible," said David, "but now I think we've got to be pretty tough."

"I agree," answered Carter. "Jim Morris over at Blair is really fuming. He claims he lost all the payroll records for the last month. What about barring them from using the computer room for the rest of the school year?"

"Yes, I guess so. But they're both in my computer course. Since they can't use the computer room, they've got to be dropped and failed. That seems appropriate."

"OK, if you say so." Carter sounded less than enthusiastic. "Boy, Ken Arnold is not going to like this. He's already got MIT in mind for his son. But justice is justice. Draft letters for the parents, will you, Burton? Try to have them for me before you go home today."

A week later, Paul Arnold walked into David's office. "Hi. I came to talk to you about my independent study assignment."

"What independent study assignment?" snapped David. He still had not forgiven Paul.

"Didn't Carter tell you? My dad went to see him when he got the letter in the mail. My dad was really mad about the punishment you handed out—failing the computer course. He threatened to sue the school district. Carter agreed to let me complete the course at home as an independent study project, since he was sure you would never let me in the computer room."

David wanted to say, "Why wasn't I informed about all this?" but thought better of it. Paul, after all, bore no responsibility for Carter's behavior or for his father's. After a moment David said quietly, "OK, if that's how Mr. Carter wants it. Go see if you can find Mike while I work out an assignment. I don't want to go over it twice."

Paul shifted his feet. "Uh, Mike isn't completing the course."

"What do you mean? Why not?"

"Well, Carter didn't say anything about him. He made the arrangement for me."

"Didn't you tell Mike?"

"Yeah, we talked. But he knows his mom or dad wouldn't come in to see Carter, and he's afraid to talk to him."

"How do you feel about that?"

Paul shrugged and looked uncomfortable. "I don't know. I really don't. The whole thing is weird. Can't we just get this over with?"

David pushed deeper into his chair. "Yeah, let's get this over with. Come back tomorrow at this time, and I'll have some assignments for you." As he watched Paul walk out of his office, he was really angry. He felt like calling Carter and giving him an earful. "But," reasoned David, "if I let him know how angry I am, he'll probably transfer me to the custodial staff tomorrow."

AMANDA JACKSON

*A first-year elementary school art teacher wrestles with her
response to a principal, whose drinking problem is well known but
who has never been confronted about it or acknowledged it herself.*

Amanda Jackson rounded the corner of the front hall of Twin Pines School
and tried to hide behind the box of ceramics she was carrying. Too late.
Mrs. Stewart spotted her and strolled over, grinning.

"Goofing off again, Ms. Jackson?"

Feeling foolish, Amanda smiled and said, "Sure, Mrs. Stewart, I've got
nothing at all to do."

"Well, don't stand here taking up my time. Get busy!" Joanna Stewart,
principal of Twin Pines School, gave Amanda a mock serious look and
continued down the hall.

Amanda practically ran to the open display case at the front entrance,
where she was arranging work done by her third-grade art classes. "Why
do I give her such stupid answers?" she asked herself for the hundredth
time. "I smile and try to joke but never understand what I'm really supposed
to say. The rest of the teachers seem to find her genuinely amusing. Why
can't I just relax about her kidding?" Amanda thought she knew why, but
it seemed so preposterous to her that she stopped thinking about it and
concentrated on arranging the clay pieces.

Twin Pines Elementary School was one of two K–5 schools in Glendale,
a small district in a neighboring community to Chicago. Glendale had a
population that was quite heterogeneous, but because it was small, there
were few services to both children and teachers. Nevertheless, the district
was known for its innovative programs, and Amanda thought it was a small
miracle that she had found a job as an art teacher immediately after she
completed her teacher preparation program.

Amanda had worked as a medical illustrator in San Francisco for ten
years. Two years ago, her husband was transferred to Chicago, near the

area where they both had grown up and gone to college. Amanda was unable to find work there as an illustrator and decided to try the career her family and friends had discouraged her from pursuing when she first started college, teaching. She was able to enter a program near her new home that offered the courses she would need for certification as an art teacher, and she completed the course requirements and student teaching in two semesters.

Since this was Amanda's first teaching assignment, it took her about three months to settle into the routine of teaching six art classes a day, arranging student work on the big front-hall bulletin boards and in the display cases, and helping the music teacher with scenery for concerts and plays. She loved it all, but she was looking forward to Christmas vacation so that she could relax. Sometimes, she wondered how much of her tension came from her interactions with Mrs. Stewart.

Amanda thought back to her first meeting with Joanna Stewart. The principal had an imposing presence. She was large-boned, with short, steel-gray hair, a florid complexion, and intense hazel eyes. Mrs. Stewart had been principal of Twin Pines for twenty-five years, and she was fiercely proud of her school. When Amanda interviewed for the position at Twin Pines, Mrs. Stewart took her on a tour of the building and spoke fondly of her loyal staff, of the popularity of the school as a showcase for visitors to the district, and of the high academic standards that the school maintained.

When Amanda received notification of her appointment to the school, she felt excited about being on the Twin Pines staff. She was sure that Mrs. Stewart would set high expectations but would be fair in her evaluations. Now she was confused. The woman's sarcasm and odd humor had not been evident during the interview, and Amanda still did not know how to react.

As she returned to working on the display case, Amanda watched Anne Turner's first-grade class returning from the music room. The children were trying hard to stay in two straight lines, walking behind their teacher like small ducklings. Mrs. Stewart came out of her office and fell into line with the children. "Mrs. Turner, this can't be your class. Look how big these children are. Aren't first-graders supposed to be little? Why these children are practically giants!" The children started to giggle, and the two nearest the principal reached up to hold hands with her. Mrs. Turner smiled and said, "Good morning, Mrs. Stewart."

The children called greetings to her also, and she pinched a few and tousled the hair of some others before turning back to Amanda. "You're still out here? What are we paying you for, anyway?"

Amanda gave her a weak smile, hoping the principal would find another target for her sarcasm. But she was not finished with Amanda yet.

She stood with her hands on her ample hips and in her mock stern voice said, "You better be finished loafing by the time I get back from Bartlett Street." Everyone in the district referred to the administrative offices by their location. She sighed. "I hate these meetings, all these damn meetings."

Before Amanda could respond, Mrs. Stewart was out the door. Amanda quickly finished arranging the case and stopped by the faculty room to grab a soda before her next class.

"I hope that's not your lunch," said Sandy Atherton, one of Amanda's first friends at the school. Sandy had been the music teacher at Twin Pines for six years. She had welcomed Amanda in September and readily included her in lunchtime conversations with the other teachers. Amanda found her easy to talk to and as relaxed about teaching as Amanda was edgy.

"Lunch? I think I'll be eating lunch after school. Some kids are coming down at lunchtime to finish the gifts they've been making for the holidays."

As Sandy started to respond, the school nurse came to the doorway. "Have you seen Joanna? I've got a sick kid and a disconnected phone number for the parent. Maybe she knows something that's not on the emergency card."

Amanda shook her head. "She left a couple of minutes ago for a meeting at Bartlett Street."

The nurse looked concerned and left.

"I'm not sure I'd want to be a principal," Amanda said. "Aside from the responsibility, Mrs. Stewart seems to have to sit through an endless number of meetings."

Sandy looked at her friend and said nothing. Amanda was surprised at the slightly awkward silence and wondered what was wrong today. "I'm definitely in need of a vacation," she thought. "I'm overreacting to all sorts of things."

At 3:30, Amanda headed for the office to drop off a supply list. She hoped that Mrs. Stewart would not be around and felt guilty for the thought. But as she turned into the office, Joanna Stewart greeted her. She was practically purring now, displaying a completely different attitude from her morning interaction with Amanda.

"Heading home, Amanda? You've put in a full day. You know, the bulletin board looks great. Several parents were in and said some very nice things about the display."

Amanda took a step back. She could smell the alcohol and knew she had not been imagining the same odor on other occasions. She mumbled a few words of thanks and quickly left the office.

That evening, Amanda called Eric Harris. Eric was an artist and an art teacher at the middle school. He and Amanda knew each other from college, and Amanda was delighted when she found her old friend teaching in the Glendale school district.

"Eric, how well do you know Joanna Stewart? I know you've never worked for her, but you must know something about her."

"Why are you asking? Is everything OK with your job? It's a little early for evaluations."

"My job is fine. I love it. The kids are great; the other teachers are easy to be with. I'm happy. . . . I'm happy. It's just that there's something funny about Joanna. I thought maybe there was something I should know that no one is telling me. Everyone at school gets a little weird when I talk about her.''

''I really don't know much. I know that she likes things her way and that Twin Pines is definitely Joanna Stewart's school. But you must know that by now.''

Amanda began to get exasperated. ''See? You're doing it now—being evasive when her name comes up, only talking about what a strong personality she has or all the positive things she's done for teachers or how good she is at getting what the school needs from Bartlett Street. And you're right: I do know all that. But no one talks about her drinking.''

Eric was silent. Amanda was thinking about what she could possibly say next when he spoke. ''It didn't take you long, Amanda. Some people, especially parents at Twin Pines who are friends of mine, never mentioned it to me until after their kids were out of the school.''

''But why? If a new teacher like me can pick up on Joanna's drinking after a couple of months, why won't anyone else acknowledge it? Eric, no one ever mentions it; no one makes a joke or a snide remark. . . .''

''I don't know why they're silent, Amanda. I guess people think that it couldn't be too bad because the school runs so well. A couple of my friends said that as long as their kids were with good teachers, they weren't going to make waves. As for the teachers—maybe she leaves them alone.''

Amanda knew that part to be true. Joanna took care of the teachers she liked and got the ones she didn't like transferred to other buildings. While she wasn't the only principal to do this, she seemed to have the most success keeping the teachers that she wanted in her building and getting rid of the others. And most of the teachers seemed content with their jobs. Amanda had not been there long enough to judge how creative the classroom programs were, but in her wanderings through the rambling, single-story building, she saw and heard few disturbances. She knew that most of the teachers used basal curriculum texts, because she often asked what the students were working on so that she could relate art projects to the curriculum. Only one teacher had taken her up on her offer, and Amanda was working with her on a joint project for second-grade science. Amanda hoped to do more projects as she got to know the teachers better.

Eric brought Amanda back to the present. ''Amanda, you're new and treading dangerous waters. I'm sure folks at Bartlett Street know about Joanna, but if no one else is talking, then you shouldn't say anything either.''

''This must be the best-kept open secret around. I can't talk about it to anybody at school.''

''Maybe you should just let it go. Get through the year, and stay on Joanna's good side. She seems to have a lot of pull. You're right, though. It's not a new problem. But you won't get anyone other than me to talk about it.''

Amanda hung up the phone feeling worse now that she had confirmed Joanna's drinking problem. She knew that not even Sandy would discuss it with her. Everyone covered Joanna's absences and ignored her erratic comments and behavior. Amanda sighed and thought, "Why should I care if parents and older staff don't? If I can just get through until Christmas vacation, I'll get a chance to relax and maybe I'll figure out how to deal with it."

* * *

It was late in the afternoon in early February. Snow had started falling heavily, and Amanda was anxious to leave for home. Most of the staff had already gone, and Amanda was hurrying to finish the front bulletin boards before she left.

"Well, Amanda, you are a real eager beaver. You're supposed to go home when it snows." Joanna Stewart stood right behind Amanda, and the smell of alcohol was strong. "Why don't you finish the display tomorrow? The snow is getting worse."

Amanda straightened up, concerned. This was the first time she detected some slurring in the principal's speech. Between the alcohol and the weather, she wondered how Mrs. Stewart was going to get home. They both turned at the sound of a child crying. The buses had left nearly an hour ago. A first-grade boy had opened the front door and stood there, sobbing.

"Clifford, what happened?" Amanda knelt down to comfort the child.

Clifford sniffled. "I had a note that said my mommy was coming to pick me up, and I waited and waited and then I went outside and she didn't come." He began to sob again.

Mrs. Stewart had gone into the office when Clifford started talking. She came out now shaking her head.

"I just tried to call his home. There was no answer. I'll check his emergency card in the nurse's office." She walked only slightly unsteadily into the room adjoining hers.

Amanda continued talking to Clifford, calming him. She looked up and saw Mrs. Stewart smiling and giving a thumbs-up sign. "Good news, Clifford. Your Aunt Glenda is home, and I'll take you there. You mom is fine, and she'll pick you up at your aunt's house later."

Clifford immediately stopped crying, but Amanda was alarmed at the prospect of the principal driving Clifford anywhere. "Oh, Mrs. Stewart, I'm finished here. Let me take Clifford home. It won't be any trouble at all."

"Don't be silly, Amanda. You finish putting your children's work away, and then take off. I'm ready to leave right now, and his aunt's house isn't too far out of my way."

Amanda became more upset. The principal's slurred speech was becoming more pronounced. Amanda wondered how drunk the woman really was. "Please, Mrs. Stewart, I can be ready in just a minute. The road seems pretty bad out front. Look! A car is skidding on the hill. Let me take Clifford.''

Joanna Stewart's eyes narrowed, and she stood directly in front of Amanda. "I *said* that I was on my way out right now. I'll take Clifford home. You be careful, Amanda, when you go home.'' With that, she turned toward her office to get her coat.

ELLEN NORTON

*A high school teacher whose concern for a shy, underachieving
student has caused the student to become her "shadow," learns
that another student is being abused at home, and the teacher
does not know if she should become involved.*

"Hi, Miss Norton. Is this a good time?"

"Sure, Abby. Come on in. Just let me get these things cleared away."
Ellen Norton smiled at the slight, dark-haired student who stood at the
threshold of the classroom doorway. She stacked the papers she had been
grading in order to clear a work space on her desk and made a waving
gesture to indicate that Abby should come in.

"Pull up a chair, Abby. How did you do on the problems I gave you
yesterday? Did you understand them?"

Rather nondescript in appearance and in behavior, Abby Maxwell impressed Ellen as an average high school sophomore. Abby's family had
moved to Littleton recently, and Abby had not made many friends in her
new school. She was withdrawn and shy—pleasant enough but always alone.

A few weeks ago, just after the Christmas break, Abby hesitantly
approached Ellen for extra help in math. Ellen was touched that the child
sought her out for help and tried to make her feel comfortable during their
tutoring sessions. She attributed the child's shyness to the typical adolescent
hesitancy about interacting with adults and sensed that Abby needed a more
mature friend with whom to converse.

"Well, sure, I think I did all right. Here." Abby smiled tentatively as
she slid her paper toward Ellen and sat down in the chair she had brought
to the front of the room. She sat on its edge and leaned forward toward
Ellen to look at the paper with her.

"OK, you had the right idea on the first problem, but you forgot to divide.
Remember, to find the area of a triangle, you take half the base times the
height. Do you remember why?"

"Oh, sure, I forgot. I guess I was going pretty fast on these," Abby replied. She hesitated and then abruptly changed subjects. "Miss Norton, did you decide to go into teaching when you were in high school?"

Ellen smiled at the question and leaned back in her chair. Abby's increasing tendency to want to discuss subjects other than math and her interest in Ellen's own life were the clues that made Ellen believe that Abby needed an older friend or role model. She knew little of Abby's family life, but she was young enough to remember that universal teenage need to identify with someone older than oneself but less "ancient" than one's parents.

"As a matter of fact, I did, Abby. I had a camp counselor the summer between ninth and tenth grades who taught English during the school year. She sort of befriended me, I guess, and I decided I'd like to make my living the same way."

"Do you like teaching?" Abby seemed encouraged by Ellen's response and began to let down her reserve.

"Very much, Abby. I like working with young people, and I like math. Which reminds me that we should get back to work." As Ellen steered the conversation back on track, she reflected that it was a good thing she liked her job, since she spent so much time at it. Besides teaching math at Littleton High School, Ellen coached the cheerleading squad, chaperoned dances, and volunteered for most extracurricular "duties," particularly those surrounding school sporting or social events. Ellen grew up in a community near Littleton and now lived at home with her widowed mother. She was a bright, attractive 25-year-old, and Littleton High School and her teaching responsibilities consumed a major portion of Ellen's time and energy.

This was Ellen's tenure year. In the Littleton school district, teachers were evaluated throughout their first three years of teaching, and at the end of the third year were either granted tenure or dismissed. Ellen's evaluations since beginning her career had been positive, and she had always been careful to adopt the suggestions her principal did make, so she had little concern about the administration's decision in the spring. Even so, she knew it didn't hurt to make herself as useful outside the classroom as she could. Besides, Ellen had few personal obligations that would compete with her career, since her fiancé, a law student, worked even longer hours than she did.

Ellen and Abby finished their review of Abby's work, and Ellen felt fairly confident that Abby understood the material. "Tomorrow in class we will be starting areas of geometric solids, so it's important that you feel comfortable with this chapter, Abby. Was this helpful?"

"Oh, yes, Miss Norton," replied Abby. "Thanks a lot!" Abby rose and pushed the chair back toward the front row. Ellen also stood and began to fill her briefcase with the papers she had not finished grading. "Are you going home, now, Miss Norton?" asked Abby as she observed Ellen's activity.

"No, I'm headed for the gym," said Ellen as she locked the desk. "Cheerleading practice at 3:30." She smiled ruefully as if to minimize the importance of this responsibility. Ellen was always sensitive to the reaction cheerleading evoked in others. Some girls who were not on the squad desperately wished they were, while others thought cheerleading was a ridiculous throwback that mocked every advance feminism had achieved in two decades.

"Oh, can I walk with you? I left my English book in the gym before, and I have to go get it anyway."

"Well, I have to stop by the math department office and do a few other things first. I'll see you tomorrow in class, Abby." Ellen smiled again, and Abby, looking a little disappointed, took her cue and ducked out the door.

Ellen smiled to herself as she headed for the gym. She had felt slightly "crowded" by Abby's interest in accompanying her, but now she thought of Jane Caldwell—the camp counselor—and chuckled aloud. "I used to be poor Jane's shadow," Ellen thought as she took the stairs two at a time. She was a little late.

"Hi, Miss Norton!"

"Hi. Hello." Various greetings echoed through the cavernous gymnasium as Ellen entered through the locker-room door and met her squad. The girls were attired in gym clothes and ready to go.

"Hi, girls, thanks for starting without me. Sorry I'm late. Becky, have you received the schedule yet?"

Becky Kaplan handed Ellen a clipboard and nodded affirmatively. Becky was the captain of the cheerleading squad this year, and Ellen couldn't have asked for a more responsible leader. Becky, a senior, had been on the squad since enrolling at Littleton. Her dependability and her popularity with the other girls made her invaluable to Ellen. She had already covered the schedule of upcoming games with the squad, noting which members couldn't perform and jotting notes about routines in the margins.

As Ellen started the girls on their warm-up exercises, she watched Becky bend and stretch and felt the ache of sympathy swell again. Rumor had it that Becky had been physically abused by both parents since childhood. Her parents were now divorced or separated—Ellen wasn't sure which— and apparently the mother's new boyfriend was no improvement. Sometimes Ellen wondered if she should try to find out more about Becky's status at home; her knowledge was based only on hearsay.

The situation was the basis for gossip among the teaching staff, and Ellen and some of her colleagues had spoken about whether or not they should help or intervene. But Becky never displayed a specific need that would justify district action. She was tardy and absent more than other students, but her schoolwork was not adversely affected. Becky often lingered after practice as though hesitant to go home, but Ellen wasn't sure whether or not she was imagining that.

Last spring, Ellen discovered from another girl on the team that Becky wanted to go to the prom but that, because Becky's parents didn't allow her to date, she had no escort. Ellen enlisted the support of a young male teacher on the staff, and they arranged a date for Becky. Ellen called Becky's mother and explained that the "cheerleading captain-elect" really should be at the prom and that Ellen would be chaperoning. Mrs. Kaplan's reaction was supportive. But beyond this brief interaction, Ellen had no personal knowledge about Becky's home life.

Suddenly Ellen's heart skipped a beat, and she stared at Becky again. "Ten more windmills," she directed. The girls groaned and resumed the exercise they had just finished. As Becky bent at the waist to touch her opposite toe, the shadow Ellen thought she had seen before was clearly visible. Becky's motion bared the skin between her gym shorts and blouse, revealing a dark purple and yellow bruise spread across her waist from hip to rib cage.

Ellen could hardly breathe. "Five laps," she said as the girls finished the exercise. She desperately needed time to collect her thoughts.

"You're kidding!"

"What is this—September?"

"Is she mad at us?"

The girls griped loudly as they raggedly fell into a trot around the gym. Ellen hadn't asked them to do laps since the early days of the school year when conditioning was most important, but she needed the time to think. Suddenly the innuendo and rumor surrounding Becky's situation had become painful reality, and Ellen didn't know what to do.

As the girls ran, Ellen took several deep breaths and forced herself to calm down. "I cannot ignore this," she thought, and with that realization Ellen felt the courage of conviction. She led the girls through the practice she had planned, vowing to draw Becky aside later.

An hour later, as the girls headed toward the locker-room door, Ellen called to Becky, motioning with the clipboard as if she needed her help on a scheduling matter. "Becky, can you help me here?"

Becky turned back from her conversation with another cheerleader and retraced her steps to Ellen. "Come into the office with me a minute, will you, Becky?" asked Ellen.

"Sure." Becky looked puzzled but followed Ellen.

Ellen had developed a comfortable relationship with Becky and the rest of the team in the two years she had been coaching cheerleading. She was a competent coach and physically capable in her own right, and she felt she had earned the girls' respect. Besides, Ellen knew from her own experience that cheerleading was fun, and her youth and attitude were assets when the squad traveled to games on the bus or decorated the boys' locker room on game night. Several of the girls had even tried calling Ellen by her first name. She had resisted the urge to encourage them, but Ellen sometimes did feel as though she had more in common with her students than with her colleagues.

Becky had always seemed slightly aloof from the more raucous team activities, but her relationship with her peers was friendly. Now Ellen wished she knew Becky better personally in order to predict her reaction to the topic at hand. Her courage began to evaporate as she searched for a way to introduce the subject. "Becky, I hope you feel comfortable about coming to me if you need to talk about anything. You're a great asset to me, and I want to help if I can."

Becky looked apprehensive. "Well, thanks, Miss Norton, but I'm OK."

Ellen decided to come to the point. "Becky, during warm-ups I couldn't help noticing the bruise on your left side. If you are in danger at home, I think someone should intervene."

Becky gazed at Ellen a moment, as if evaluating alternative responses. Finally she said quietly, "Miss Norton, everything is all right. I fell off my bike on my way home from practice last week."

Ellen was surprised by the matter-of-fact way in which Becky reacted. She had been concerned that her question would embarrass the child, but Becky's expression and tone of voice were calm and emotionless. Suddenly Ellen was the one who was embarrassed, concerned that she had made an improper assumption and reacted to innuendo rather than facts.

"Oh! I'm sorry. I thought . . ." Ellen knew she was compounding the error. "Never mind, Becky. Please just know that I am here if you need to talk, OK?"

Becky smiled—a little sadly, Ellen thought—and turned to go.

* * *

Ellen looked out her classroom window at the drizzly March afternoon. Her mind wandered back to those first tutoring sessions with Abby Maxwell in early January, and she wondered where she had gone wrong. For in spite of all the extra time she had spent with Abby this semester, the child's performance in math was deteriorating. Abby was making obvious errors on homework assignments and seemed to make deliberate mistakes on tests. In fact, her grades were so bad that Ellen was worried that Abby would fail. Ellen guessed that she would be assigned to teach this class again next year, assuming the tenure decision was positive, and she frankly did not want to have Abby in class again.

Abby's demands on Ellen's time had gradually escalated. For a while, Ellen enjoyed their after-school conversations about teaching, growing up in the area, and math. Abby expressed an interest in cheerleading, and Ellen suggested some summer activities she might pursue to make herself more competitive at the tryouts next fall. Abby seemed so lonely and so buoyed by Ellen's attention that Ellen at first relished the opportunity to help the child adjust to her new community and school. But eventually Abby's constant presence became oppressive. It seemed to Ellen that Abby was everywhere she turned; it was uncanny how the girl could surface at Ellen's every move. She attended dances Ellen chaperoned and games Ellen coached. Abby always came alone to these events and hovered somewhere in Ellen's vicinity. Some of the other teachers began to joke about "Ellen's sidekick'' or ''the leech.'' Ellen knew she had a serious problem when Abby began leaving notes on her desk and driving by her house.

''What is it this child wants from me?'' Ellen wondered as she watched the rain. Ellcn was very worried that in befriending Abby she had encouraged an unhealthy emotional dependency, which she did not know how to sever. Ellen did not want to cause Abby pain, but she desperately wanted to be rid of her. Furthermore, Ellen was sure that Abby's poor performance in math was purposeful, staged in order to justify more tutoring sessions and even a repetition of the class with Ellen next year.

Ellen sighed and packed up for practice. She was anxious for the basketball season to end so that she could close down cheerleading for this year.

As Ellen walked toward the gym, half expecting Abby to appear at every hallway intersection, her thoughts shifted to Becky. Neither Ellen nor Becky had broached the subject of Becky's personal life since their conversation two months ago. Ellen had decided to respect Becky's apparent desire that she mind her own business, and Ellen's worsening situation with Abby made her wary of personal involvement with her students, anyway. Ellen had, however, helped Becky apply to colleges that granted cheerleading scholarships and had written letters of recommendation for her. She knew that Becky had been accepted at a good school in the midwest. ''In two months she will graduate and be far from home,'' thought Ellen, ''and I can stop worrying.''

As Ellen approached the gym, she was surprised to see Becky standing in the hall outside the locker-room doors.

''Hi, Becky. How's it goin'? Let's get inside. You should be suited up by now,'' said Ellen. As she got closer to Becky, it seemed to her that the girl was hiding in the shadows created by the locker-room entranceway—*cowering* was the word that came to Ellen's mind.

''Miss Norton, can I ask you a big favor?'' Becky whispered in spite of the fact that they were the only two people in the hall.

''Of course, Becky. What is it?''

''Can I go home with you tonight?''

The request caught Ellen totally off guard. She had become so comfortable with the idea that Becky was going to graduate and leave home that she had easily been able to deny the possibility of further danger for the girl. Now she didn't even know what to say. ''What's happened, Becky?'' Ellen blurted.

''I found out when I went home for lunch that my stepfather lost his job this morning. I think he'll be drinking, and I'm afraid to go home.'' Having asked her question, Becky was regaining her straightforward manner in spite of the horrible situation she was describing.

''Oh, Becky. I don't think it would be a good idea for me to take you to my home. Let me call the school social worker. She'll know what to do.''

''No! Please don't do that, Miss Norton. She'll call the police or someone, and my stepfather will really go nuts. No, I just need to keep out of his way tonight.''